The

NYSTROM

CANADIAN DESK ATLAS

NYSTROM

DIVISION OF HERFF JONES, INC.

CREDITS

Educational Consultants

Angelo Bolotta, Coordinator of Social Studies
Metropolitan Separate School Board, Toronto, Ontario

John R. Chalk, Principal
Templeton Secondary School, Vancouver, British Columbia

Walter Donovan, Professor, Faculty of Education
University of Toronto, Toronto, Ontario

John Lohrenz, Social Studies and Sustainable Development Consultant, K–12
Manitoba Education, Winnipeg, Manitoba

Photo credits by page **21** *from left:* Dept. of Interior/National Archives of Canada/C-19935 (detail); Alan Marsh/First Light **32** *clockwise from top left:* Joan Pederson; Willard Clay/FPG International; Willard Clay/Tony Stone Images; S.J. Krasemann/Peter Arnold, Inc.; David Matherly/Visuals Unlimited; William J. Weber/Visuals Unlimited; Paul Osman **38** *from top:* Ron Thomas/FPG International; Stan Osolinski/Tony Stone Images **39** Dave Gleiter/FPG International **45** *from top:* Juergen Vogt/The Image Bank; Philip & Karen Smith/Tony Stone Images **47** George Hunter/Tony Stone Images **49** *from left:* Vic Cox/Peter Arnold, Inc.; Thomas Kitchin/First Light **51** *from top:* Greg Stott/Masterfile; J.A. Kraulis/Masterfile **53** *from top:* Kjell B. Sandved/Visuals Unlimited; Ken Straiton/First Light **55** *from left:* George Hunter/Tony Stone Images; George Hunter/Tony Stone Images **56** Stephen Homer/First Light **57** Mike Dobel/Masterfile **62** Larry Fisher/Masterfile **65** *from top:* Fred Bruemmer/Peter Arnold, Inc.; Phil Degginger/Tony Stone Images **71** Jim Pickerell/FPG International **73** Richard Laird/FPG International **79** Doug Armand/Tony Stone Images **83** Salomon Cytrynowicz/D. Donne Bryant Stock **84** Haroldo & Flavia de Faria Castro/FPG International **85** David Levy/Tony Stone Images **92** AP/Wide World Photos **94** *from left:* Bruce Berg/Visuals Unlimited; Vladimir Pcholkin/FPG International **101** Freeman Patterson/Masterfile **103** *clockwise from upper left:* Guido Alberto Rossi/The Image Bank; Telegraph Colour Library/FPG International; Jeffrey L. Rotman/Peter Arnold, Inc.; Telegraph Colour Library/FPG International **104** Travelpix/FPG International **114** David Sutherland/Tony Stone Images **115** Travelpix/FPG International **116** Paolo Negri/Tony Stone Images **117** David Bartruff/FPG International **118** Adrian Master/Tony Stone Images **124** *from top:* Buddy Mays/FPG International; Mitch Reardon/Tony Stone Images **128** Larry Williams/Masterfile **130** David Hiser/Tony Stone Images **131** AP/Wide World Photos

2000 Edition
Copyright © 1995 **NYSTROM**
Division of Herff Jones, Inc.
3333 Elston Avenue
Chicago, Illinois 60618
**For information about ordering this atlas,
call toll-free 800-621-8086.**

10 9 8 7 6 5   01 00
ISBN: 0-7825-0587-2   Printed in Canada   9A94C

CONTENTS

THEMATIC MAPS AND GRAPHS

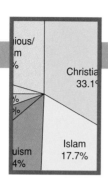

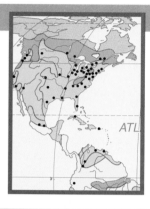

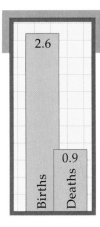

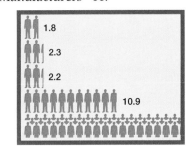

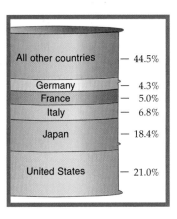

INTRODUCTION

The Nystrom Canadian Desk Atlas includes physical and political maps of large areas, regional maps of smaller areas, thematic maps, graphic presentations of data, and illustrative photographs. Each map, graph, and photo is best suited to providing specific kinds of information.

Physical Maps

Physical maps in this atlas are designed so that the names and relative locations of natural features can be seen at a glance. Colours represent water depths and land elevations. Although the emphasis is on natural features, countries and key cities also are named.

Political Maps

Political maps are coloured by state, province, or country, making it as easy as possible to tell where one ends and another begins. The names of capitals and other major cities are quickly found because the maps are carefully edited to keep them uncluttered.

Thematic Maps

Thematic maps focus on single topics or themes, and the subject can be anything that is mappable. Among the thematic maps in this atlas are maps of rainfall, land use, and population. Often the patterns on one thematic map become more meaningful when compared to the patterns on another.

Regional Maps

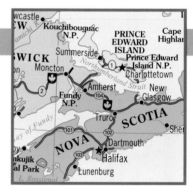

Regional maps in this atlas offer close-up views of areas on the political maps. Because regional maps enlarge the areas shown, they can name more cities while remaining highly readable. Other details also are added, such as the names of landforms, including some not given on the physical maps.

Legends

Legends are provided for all maps. For most of the thematic maps, the legends are simple keys showing what the map colours stand for. The legends for the physical, political, and regional maps are lengthier. To save space, the complete legend for these maps is given only once, on the facing page.

Graphs

Graphs summarize facts in a visual way, making it easier to see trends and make comparisons. Many different topics are presented in a variety of graphic styles. Some topics are graphed only once, while others form strands that run through the whole book.

Photographs

Photographs can portray the characteristics of a place like nothing else can. The photos in this atlas were carefully chosen to illustrate the natural setting and cultural aspects of places around the world. Photographic realism is the perfect complement to the abstract symbolism of maps.

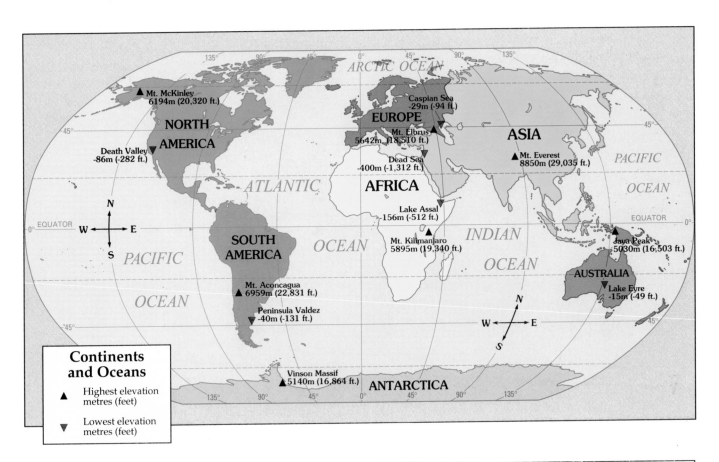

Continents and Oceans

▲ Highest elevation metres (feet)

▼ Lowest elevation metres (feet)

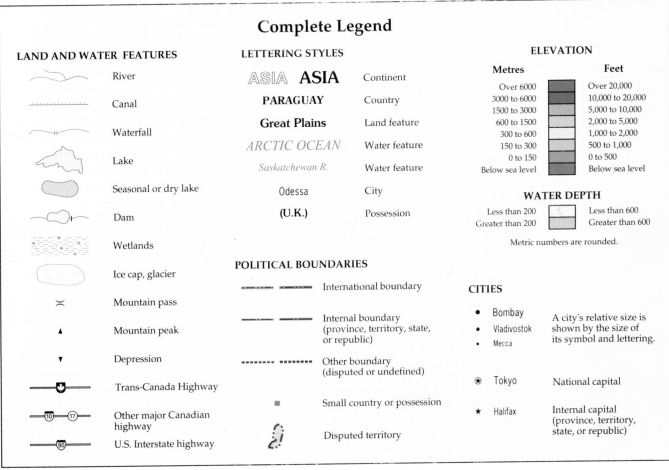

Complete Legend

LAND AND WATER FEATURES

River

Canal

Waterfall

Lake

Seasonal or dry lake

Dam

Wetlands

Ice cap, glacier

✕ Mountain pass

▲ Mountain peak

▼ Depression

Trans-Canada Highway

Other major Canadian highway

U.S. Interstate highway

LETTERING STYLES

ASIA **ASIA** Continent

PARAGUAY Country

Great Plains Land feature

ARCTIC OCEAN Water feature

Saskatchewan R. Water feature

Odessa City

(U.K.) Possession

POLITICAL BOUNDARIES

International boundary

Internal boundary (province, territory, state, or republic)

Other boundary (disputed or undefined)

Small country or possession

Disputed territory

ELEVATION

Metres	Feet
Over 6000	Over 20,000
3000 to 6000	10,000 to 20,000
1500 to 3000	5,000 to 10,000
600 to 1500	2,000 to 5,000
300 to 600	1,000 to 2,000
150 to 300	500 to 1,000
0 to 150	0 to 500
Below sea level	Below sea level

WATER DEPTH

Less than 200	Less than 600
Greater than 200	Greater than 600

Metric numbers are rounded.

CITIES

• Bombay
• Vladivostok
• Mecca

A city's relative size is shown by the size of its symbol and lettering.

⊛ Tokyo National capital

★ Halifax Internal capital (province, territory, state, or republic)

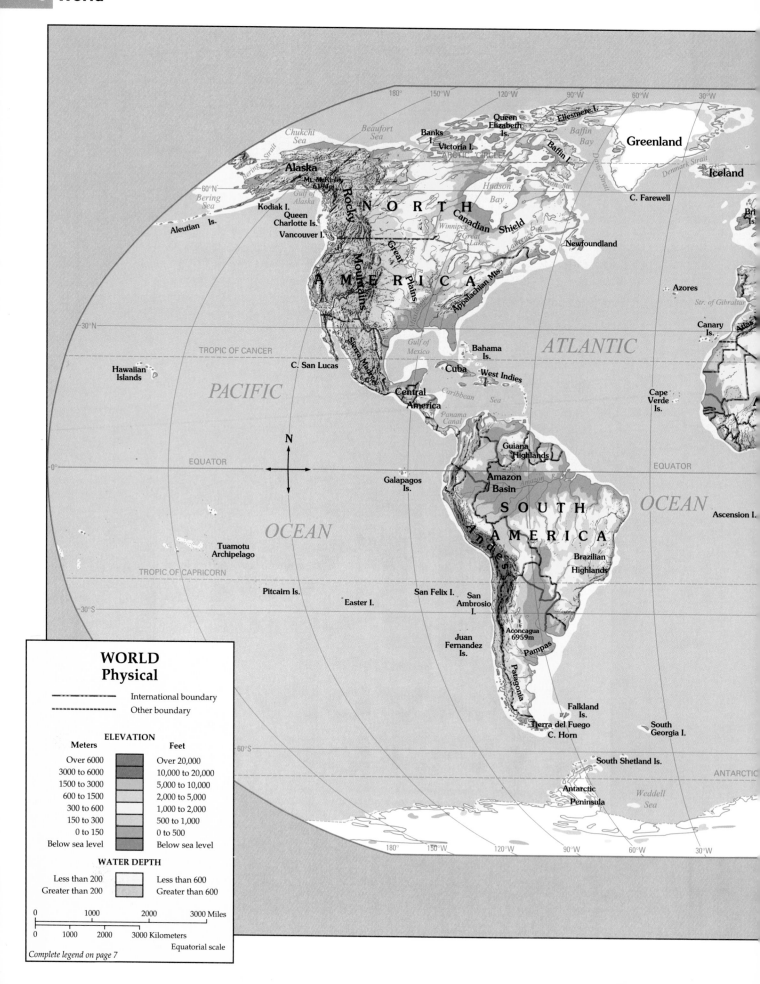

WORLD
Physical

——————	International boundary
- - - - - -	Other boundary

ELEVATION

Meters		Feet
Over 6000		Over 20,000
3000 to 6000		10,000 to 20,000
1500 to 3000		5,000 to 10,000
600 to 1500		2,000 to 5,000
300 to 600		1,000 to 2,000
150 to 300		500 to 1,000
0 to 150		0 to 500
Below sea level		Below sea level

WATER DEPTH

Meters		Feet
Less than 200		Less than 600
Greater than 200		Greater than 600

0 ___ 1000 ___ 2000 ___ 3000 Miles
0 ___ 1000 ___ 2000 ___ 3000 Kilometers

Equatorial scale

Complete legend on page 7

Chukchi Sea
Beaufort Sea
Banks I.
Queen Elizabeth Is.
Ellesmere I.
Baffin Bay
Greenland
Victoria I.
Baffin I.
Iceland
Alaska
Mt. McKinley 6194m
Gulf of Alaska
Hudson Bay
Denmark Strait
Davis Strait
C. Farewell
Bering Sea
Bering Strait
Rocky
NORTH
Canadian Shield
Hudson Str.
Aleutian Is.
Kodiak I.
Queen Charlotte Is.
Vancouver I.
Mountains
Winnipeg
Great Lakes
St. Lawrence R.
Newfoundland
Br. Is.
AMERICA
Great Plains
Appalachian Mts.
Azores
Str. of Gibraltar
TROPIC OF CANCER
Sierra Madre
Mississippi
Gulf of Mexico
Bahama Is.
ATLANTIC
Canary Is.
Atlas
Hawaiian Islands
C. San Lucas
Cuba
West Indies
Cape Verde Is.
PACIFIC
Central America
Caribbean Sea
Panama Canal
N
EQUATOR
Galapagos Is.
Guiana Highlands
Amazon Basin
Amazon R.
SOUTH
OCEAN
EQUATOR
Ascension I.
OCEAN
Tuamotu Archipelago
AMERICA
Brazilian Highlands
TROPIC OF CAPRICORN
Pitcairn Is.
Easter I.
San Felix I.
San Ambrosio I.
Andes
Aconcagua 6959m
Juan Fernandez Is.
Pampas
Patagonia
Falkland Is.
South Georgia I.
Tierra del Fuego
C. Horn
South Shetland Is.
ANTARCTIC
Antarctic Peninsula
Weddell Sea

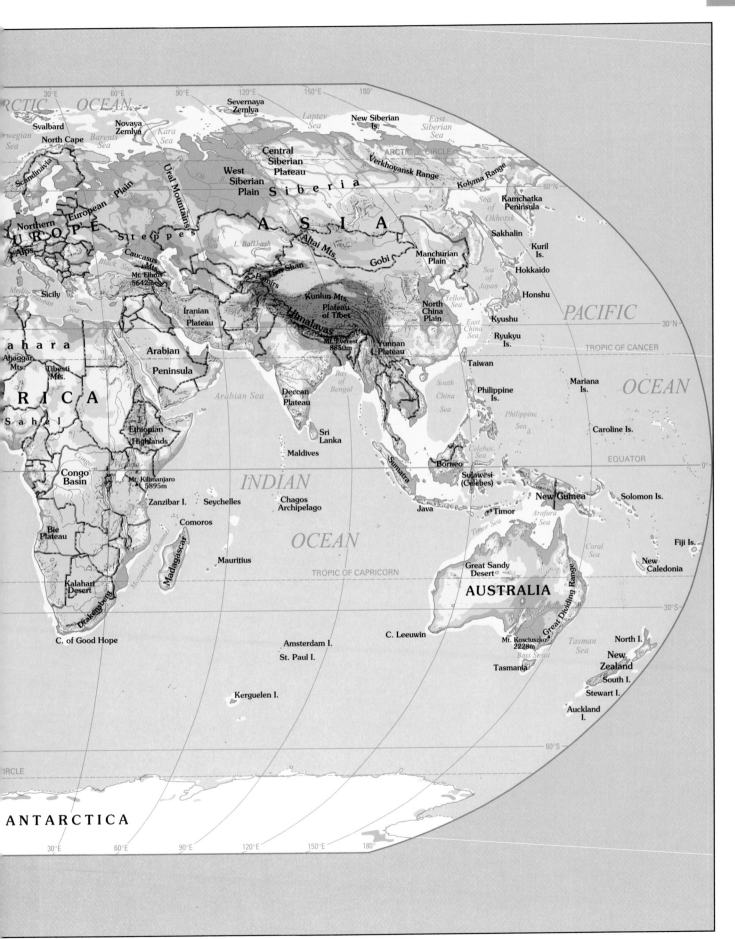

ARCTIC OCEAN

Svalbard
North Cape
Novaya Zemlya
Kara Sea
Barents Sea
Severnaya Zemlya
New Siberian Is.
Laptev Sea
East Siberian Sea

Scandinavia
Northern European Plain
Ural Mountains
Central Siberian Plateau
West Siberian Plain
S i b e r i a
ARCTIC CIRCLE
Verkhoyansk Range
Kolyma Range
60°N

EUROPE
Alps
Steppes
Volga R.
Ob R.
A S I A
Kamchatka Peninsula
Sea of Okhotsk
Sakhalin
Kuril Is.

Black Sea
Caucasus Mts.
Mt. Elbrus 5642m
Caspian Sea
Aral Sea
L. Balkhash
Altai Mts.
Tien Shan
Gobi
Manchurian Plain
Sea of Japan
Hokkaido
Honshu

Mediterranean Sea
Sicily
Pamirs
Kunlun Mts.
Plateau of Tibet
North China Plain
Yellow Sea
Kyushu
PACIFIC

Iranian Plateau
Himalayas
Amur R.
East China Sea
Ryukyu Is.
30°N

ahara
Ahaggar Mts.
Tibesti Mts.
Arabian Peninsula
Mt. Everest 8850m
Yunnan Plateau
Taiwan
TROPIC OF CANCER

RICA
Sahel
Arabian Sea
Deccan Plateau
Bay of Bengal
Philippine Is.
Mariana Is.
OCEAN

Ethiopian Highlands
Sri Lanka
South China Sea
Philippine Sea
Caroline Is.

Maldives
Congo Basin
Mt. Kilimanjaro 5895m
L. Victoria
Congo R.
Zanzibar I.
Seychelles
Chagos Archipelago
Sumatra
Borneo
Celebes Sea
EQUATOR
0°

INDIAN
Sulawesi (Celebes)
New Guinea
Solomon Is.

Java
Timor
Arafura Sea

Bie Plateau
Comoros
Madagascar
Mozambique Channel
Mauritius
OCEAN
Timor Sea
Coral Sea
Fiji Is.
New Caledonia

Kalahari Desert
Great Sandy Desert
TROPIC OF CAPRICORN

C. of Good Hope
Drakensberg
Amsterdam I.
St. Paul I.
C. Leeuwin
AUSTRALIA
Great Dividing Range
Darling R.
Mt. Kosciuszko 2228m
Tasman Sea
Bass Strait
North I.
New Zealand
30°S

Kerguelen I.
Tasmania
South I.
Stewart I.
Auckland I.

60°S

CIRCLE

ANTARCTICA

30°E 60°E 90°E 120°E 150°E 180°

RUSSIA
Chukchi Sea
Beaufort Sea
Baffin Bay
GREENLAND (KALAALLIT NUNAAT) (Denmark)
Jan Maye (Nor.)
ARCTIC CIRCLE
Inuvik
Bering Strait
ALASKA (U.S.)
Anchorage
Yukon
60°N
Bering Sea
Gulf of Alaska
Hudson Str.
Denmark Strait
ICELAND
Reykjavik
Faero (D
Hudson Bay
L. Winnipeg
Davis Strait
Aleutian Is.
CANADA
Great Lakes
IRELAND
UNI KING
Vancouver
St. Lawrence R.
Missouri
BELG
Toronto
Montreal
Chicago
Madrid
UNITED STATES
New York
PORTUGAL SPA
Washington, D.C.
Colorado R.
Los Angeles
Azores (Port.)
30°N
MOROCCO
TROPIC OF CANCER
Gulf of Mexico
Miami
BAHAMAS
ATLANTIC
Canary Is. (Sp.)
WESTERN SAHARA (adm. Morocco)
MEXICO
Mississippi
CUBA
HAITI
DOMINICAN REPUBLIC
MAURITANIA
Mexico City
JAMAICA
Puerto Rico (U.S.)
ANTIGUA AND BARBUDA
M
BELIZE
CAPE VERDE
SENEGAL
PACIFIC
GUATEMALA
HONDURAS
DOMINICA
GAMBIA
BURK FAS
Hawaii (U.S.)
EL SALVADOR
NICARAGUA
BARBADOS
GUINEA-BISSAU
GUINE
COSTA RICA
TRINIDAD AND TOBAGO
SIERRA LEONE
CÔTE D'IVOIRE (IVORY COAST)
PANAMA
GUYANA
LIBERIA
N
VENEZUELA
SURINAME
FRENCH GUIANA (Fr.)
EQUATOR
COLOMBIA
EQUATOR
Galapagos Is. (Ecuador)
ECUADOR
Amazon R.
OCEAN
Ascension (U.K.)
SAMOA
PERU
BRAZIL
Am. Samoa (U.S.)
Society Is. (Fr.)
Lima
TONGA
Tahiti (Fr.)
OCEAN
BOLIVIA
TROPIC OF CAPRICORN
Rio de Janeiro
PARAGUAY
Sao Paulo
Pitcairn Is. (U.K.)
Easter I. (Chile)
San Felix (Chile)
San Ambrosio (Chile)
30°S
Juan Fernandez Is. (Chile)
URUGUAY
CHILE
Buenos Aires
ARGENTINA

Falkland Is. (U.K.)
South Georgia (U.K.)
60°S
South Orkney Is. (U.K.)
ANTARCTIC
Weddell Sea

WORLD
Political

BOUNDARIES

———————— International boundary

- - - - - - - - Other boundary (disputed or undefined)

CITIES

● Shanghai
• Vancouver   A city's relative size is shown by the size of its symbol and lettering.
· Darwin

⊛ Cairo   National capital

0	1000	2000	3000 Miles
0	1000	2000	3000 Kilometers

Equatorial scale

Complete legend on page 7

ARCTIC OCEAN

Svalbard (Nor.)

Franz Josef Land

Novaya Zemlya

New Siberian Is.

Laptev Sea

East Siberian Sea

Norwegian Sea

Barents Sea

Kara Sea

ARCTIC CIRCLE

NORWAY

SWEDEN

FINLAND

Yenisey

Ob R.

60°N

DENMARK

NETHERLANDS

ESTONIA

LATVIA

LITHUANIA

BELARUS

Moscow

RUSSIA

Lena R.

Sea of Okhotsk

GERMANY

POLAND

CZ.

SL.

AUS.

LIECH.

SWITZ.

HUNGARY

SLOV.

CRO. BOS.

UKRAINE

MOLDOVA

KAZAKHSTAN

Aral Sea

L. Balkhash

MONGOLIA

Amur R.

Vladivostok

FRANCE

ITALY

YUGO.

ROMANIA

MAC.

BULGARIA

GEORGIA

Black Sea

Caspian Sea

UZBEKISTAN

KYRGYZSTAN

Hwang He

NORTH KOREA

JAPAN

ANDORRA

ALBANIA

GREECE

TURKEY

ARMENIA

AZERBAIJAN

TURKMENISTAN

TAJIKISTAN

CHINA

SOUTH KOREA

Tokyo

PACIFIC

Mediterranean Sea

CYPRUS

LEBANON

SYRIA

Tehran

AFGHANISTAN

Shanghai

Yellow Sea

East China Sea

30°N

TUNISIA

ISRAEL

JORDAN

IRAQ

IRAN

Ganges R.

NEPAL

BHUTAN

Taipei

TROPIC OF CANCER

ALGERIA

Cairo

KUWAIT

PAKISTAN

BANGLADESH

TAIWAN

OCEAN

LIBYA

EGYPT

SAUDI ARABIA

BAHRAIN

QATAR

U.A.E.

INDIA

Bay of Bengal

MYANMAR (BURMA)

LAOS

Hong Kong

INTERNATIONAL DATE

NIGER

CHAD

Nile

Red Sea

OMAN

YEMEN

Bombay (Mumbai)

Arabian Sea

THAILAND

VIETNAM

CAMBODIA

PHILIPPINES

Manila

Philippine Sea

Northern Mariana Islands (U.S.)

NIGERIA

SUDAN

ERITREA

DJIBOUTI

SRI LANKA

PALAU

FEDERATED STATES OF MICRONESIA

GUINEA

CAMEROON

C. AFR. REP.

ETHIOPIA

SOMALIA

MALDIVES

BRUNEI

MALAYSIA

Celebes Sea

EQUATOR

0°

GABON

CONGO REP.

Congo

UGANDA

KENYA

SINGAPORE

INDONESIA

PAPUA NEW GUINEA

SOLOMON IS.

SAO TOME & PRINCIPE

RWANDA

BURUNDI

L. Victoria

SEYCHELLES

INDIAN

Chagos Archipelago (U.K.)

Jakarta

EAST TIMOR (adm. UN)

CABINDA (Ang.)

CONGO (ZAIRE)

TANZANIA

Arafura Sea

ANGOLA

MALAWI

COMOROS

Timor Sea

Darwin

Coral Sea

VANUATU

FIJI

ZAMBIA

MOZAMBIQUE

OCEAN

NAMIBIA

ZIMBABWE

MADAGASCAR

MAURITIUS

TROPIC OF CAPRICORN

New Caledonia (Fr.)

30°S

BOTSWANA

Mozambique Channel

Reunion (Fr.)

AUSTRALIA

SWAZILAND

SOUTH AFRICA

LESOTHO

Amsterdam I. (Fr.)

Perth

Darling R.

Sydney

Auckland

Cape Town

St. Paul I. (Fr.)

Tasman Sea

NEW ZEALAND

Prince Edward Is. (S. Afr.)

Crozet Is. (Fr.)

Bass Strait

Tasmania

Stewart I.

Kerguelen I. (Fr.)

60°S

CIRCLE

A N T A R C T I C A

30°E   60°E   90°E   120°E   150°E   180°

30°E   60°E   90°E   120°E   150°E   180°

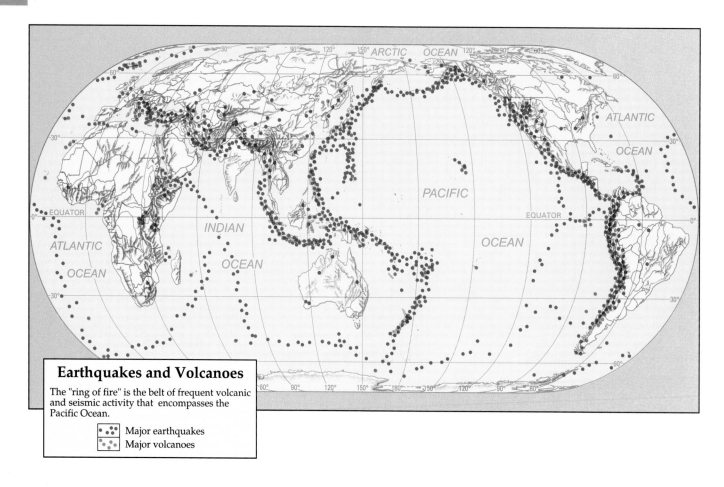

Earthquakes and Volcanoes

The "ring of fire" is the belt of frequent volcanic and seismic activity that encompasses the Pacific Ocean.

- • Major earthquakes
- • Major volcanoes

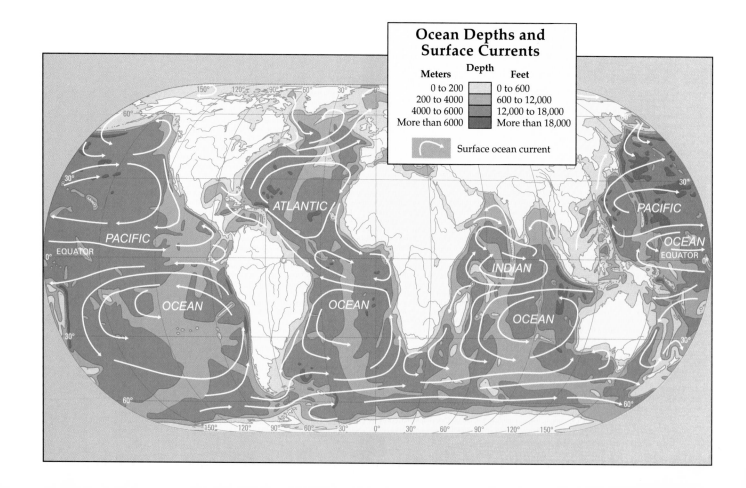

Ocean Depths and Surface Currents

Meters	Depth	Feet
0 to 200		0 to 600
200 to 4000		600 to 12,000
4000 to 6000		12,000 to 18,000
More than 6000		More than 18,000

Surface ocean current

Notable Earthquakes

Earthquake	Date	Magnitude (Richter Scale)	Deaths
Central India	Sept. 30, 1993	6.4	22,000
Northwestern Iran	June 21, 1990	7.7	40,000+
Loma Prieta, CA, U.S.	October 17, 1989	6.9	62
Northwestern Armenia	December 7, 1988	6.8	55,000+
Mexico City, Mexico	Sept. 19-21, 1985	8.1	4,200+
Tangshan, China	July 28, 1976	7.6	242,000
Guatemala	February 4, 1976	7.5	22,778
San Fernando, CA, U.S.	February 9, 1971	6.5	65
Northern Peru	May 31, 1970	7.8	66,794
Kenai Pen., AK, U.S.	March 28, 1964	8.6	131
Nan-Shan, China	May 22, 1927	8.3	200,000
Yokohama, Japan	September 1, 1923	8.3	143,000
Gansu, China	December 16, 1920	8.6	100,000
Messina, Italy	December 28, 1908	7.5	83,000
San Francisco, CA, U.S.	April 18, 1906	8.3	700
New Madrid, MO, U.S.	December 16, 1811-February 7, 1812	8.7	unknown
Calcutta, India	October 11, 1737	---	300,000
Shemaka, Azerbaijan	November 1667	---	80,000
Shaanxi, China	January 24, 1556	---	830,000
Antioch, Syria	May 20, 526	---	250,000

Notable Volcanic Eruptions

Volcano	Place	Year	Deaths
Kilauea	Hawaii, U.S.	1983-present	1
Pinatubo	Philippines	1992	200+
Redoubt	Alaska, U.S.	1989-1990	0
Nevada del Ruiz	Colombia	1985	22,940
Mauna Loa	Hawaii, U.S.	1984	0
El Chicon	Mexico	1982	100+
St. Helens	Washington, U.S.	1980	57
Erebus	Ross I., Antarctica	1970-1980	0
Surtsey	N. Atlantic Ocean	1963-1967	0
Paricutin	Mexico	1943-1952	1,000
Kelud	Java, Indonesia	1919	5,000
Pelee	Martinique	1902	26,000
Krakatoa	Sumatra, Indonesia	1883	36,000
Tambora	Sumbawa, Indonesia	1815	56,000
Unzen	Japan	1792	10,400
Etna	Sicily, Italy	1669	20,000
Kelud	Java, Indonesia	1586	10,000
Etna	Sicily, Italy	1169	15,000
Vesuvius	Italy	79	16,000
Thera (Santorini)	Aegean Sea	1645 B.C.	thousands

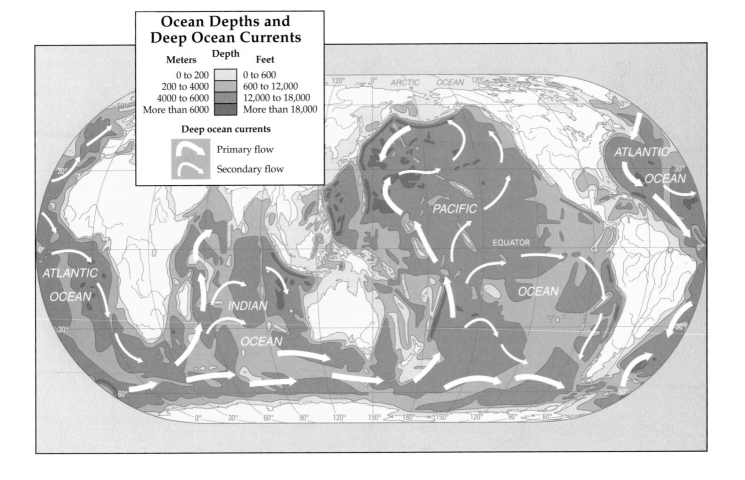

Ocean Depths and Deep Ocean Currents

Meters	Depth Feet
0 to 200	0 to 600
200 to 4000	600 to 12,000
4000 to 6000	12,000 to 18,000
More than 6000	More than 18,000

Deep ocean currents

Primary flow

Secondary flow

World Climates

Tropical Climates
- Tropical rain forest
- Savanna

Dry Climates
- Steppe (semi-desert)
- Desert

Mild Climates
- Mediterranean
- Humid subtropical
- Marine

Continental Climates
- Hot summer
- Cool summer
- Subarctic

Polar Climates
- Tundra
- Ice cap

Highland Climate
- (Varies greatly with elevation and latitude.)

Climographs

Letters refer to locations on the map.
Colors correspond to climate regions.
Curved lines show temperatures in Celsius and Fahrenheit degrees.
Bars show rainfall in inches and millimeters.

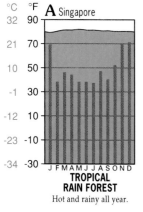

A Singapore

TROPICAL RAIN FOREST
Hot and rainy all year.

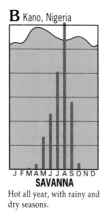

B Kano, Nigeria

SAVANNA
Hot all year, with rainy and dry seasons.

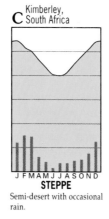

C Kimberley, South Africa

STEPPE
Semi-desert with occasional rain.

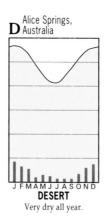

D Alice Springs, Australia

DESERT
Very dry all year.

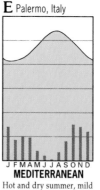

E Palermo, Italy

MEDITERRANEAN
Hot and dry summer, mild and rainy winter.

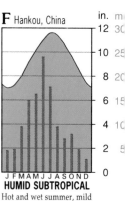

F Hankou, China

HUMID SUBTROPICAL
Hot and wet summer, mild and damp winter.

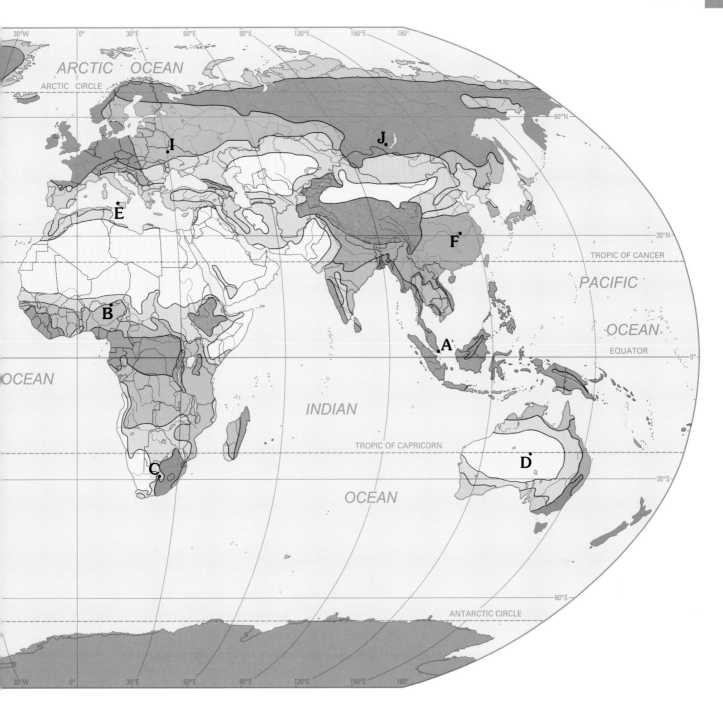

ARCTIC OCEAN
ARCTIC CIRCLE

I

J

E

F

PACIFIC

B

A

OCEAN

OCEAN

INDIAN

EQUATOR

TROPIC OF CANCER

TROPIC OF CAPRICORN

D

C

OCEAN

ANTARCTIC CIRCLE

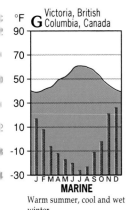

G Victoria, British Columbia, Canada

MARINE
Warm summer, cool and wet winter.

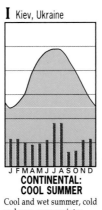

H Omaha, Nebraska, United States

CONTINENTAL: HOT SUMMER
Hot and wet summer, cold and snowy winter.

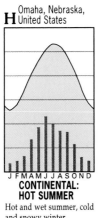

I Kiev, Ukraine

CONTINENTAL: COOL SUMMER
Cool and wet summer, cold and very snowy winter.

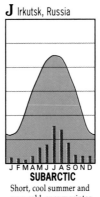

J Irkutsk, Russia

SUBARCTIC
Short, cool summer and very cold, snowy winter.

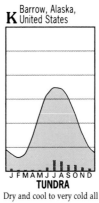

K Barrow, Alaska, United States

TUNDRA
Dry and cool to very cold all year.

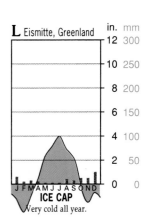

L Eismitte, Greenland

ICE CAP
Very cold all year.

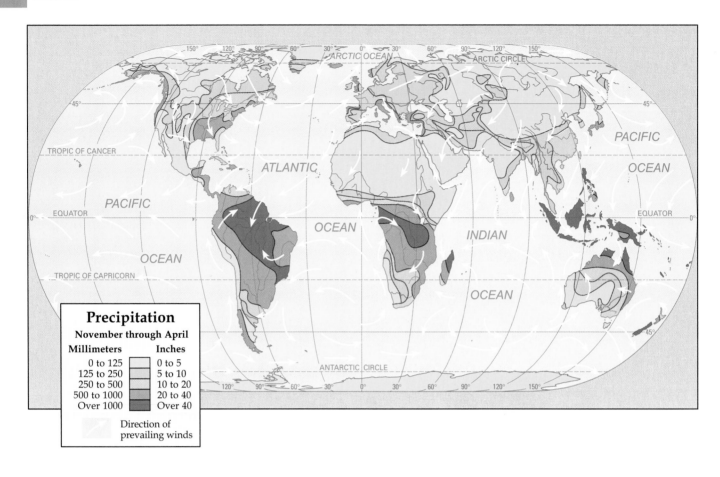

Precipitation

November through April

Millimeters		Inches
0 to 125		0 to 5
125 to 250		5 to 10
250 to 500		10 to 20
500 to 1000		20 to 40
Over 1000		Over 40

Direction of prevailing winds

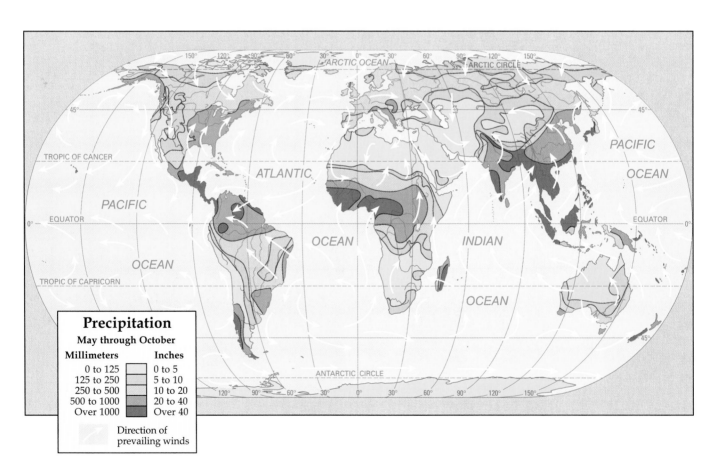

Precipitation

May through October

Millimeters		Inches
0 to 125		0 to 5
125 to 250		5 to 10
250 to 500		10 to 20
500 to 1000		20 to 40
Over 1000		Over 40

Direction of prevailing winds

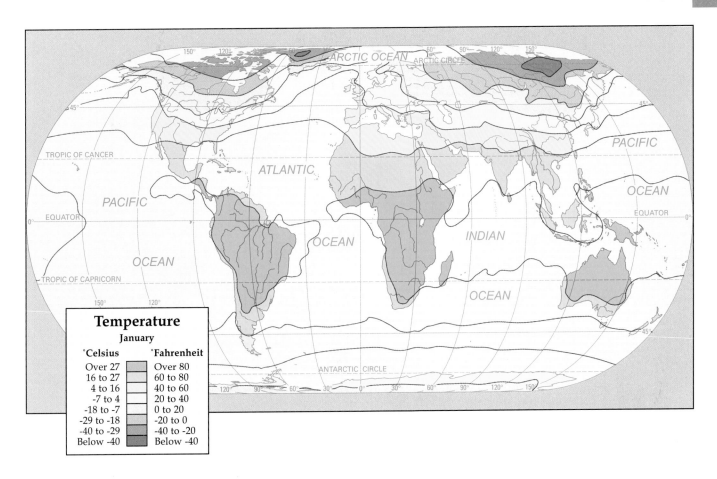

Temperature
January

°Celsius		°Fahrenheit
Over 27		Over 80
16 to 27		60 to 80
4 to 16		40 to 60
-7 to 4		20 to 40
-18 to -7		0 to 20
-29 to -18		-20 to 0
-40 to -29		-40 to -20
Below -40		Below -40

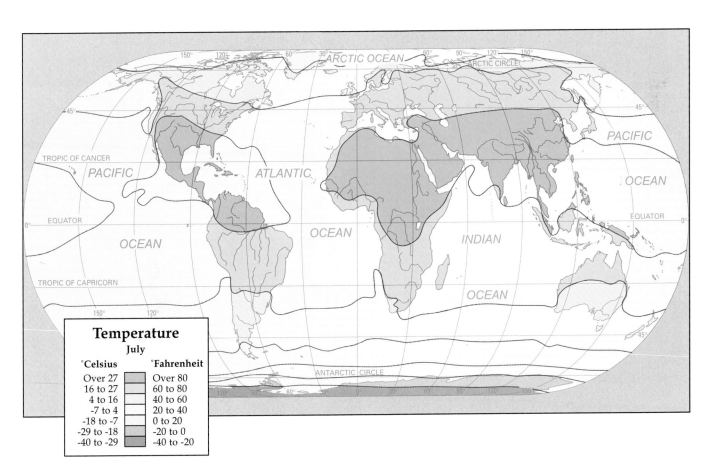

Temperature
July

°Celsius		°Fahrenheit
Over 27		Over 80
16 to 27		60 to 80
4 to 16		40 to 60
-7 to 4		20 to 40
-18 to -7		0 to 20
-29 to -18		-20 to 0
-40 to -29		-40 to -20

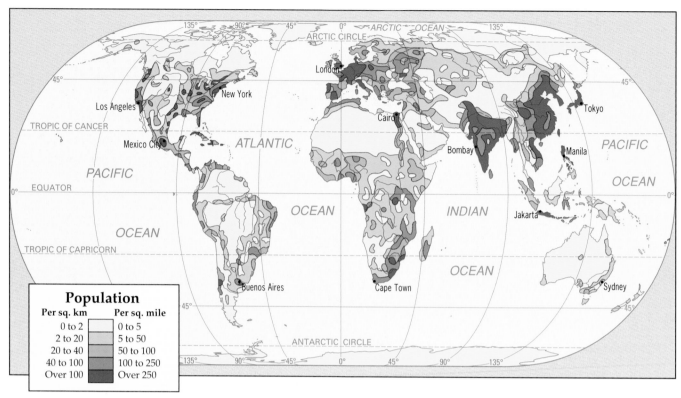

Population

Per sq. km	Per sq. mile
0 to 2	0 to 5
2 to 20	5 to 50
20 to 40	50 to 100
40 to 100	100 to 250
Over 100	Over 250

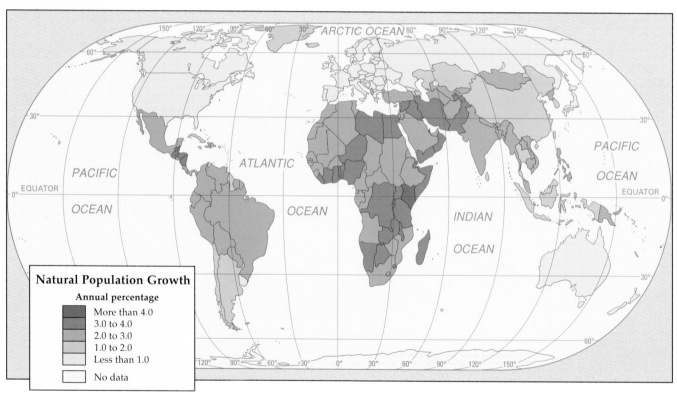

Natural Population Growth

Annual percentage

	More than 4.0
	3.0 to 4.0
	2.0 to 3.0
	1.0 to 2.0
	Less than 1.0
	No data

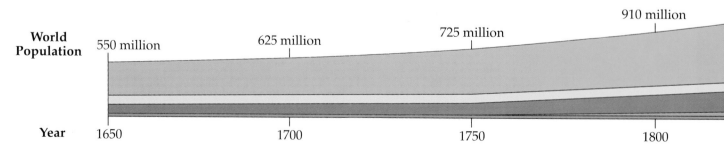

World Population

550 million   625 million   725 million   910 million

Year 1650   1700   1750   1800

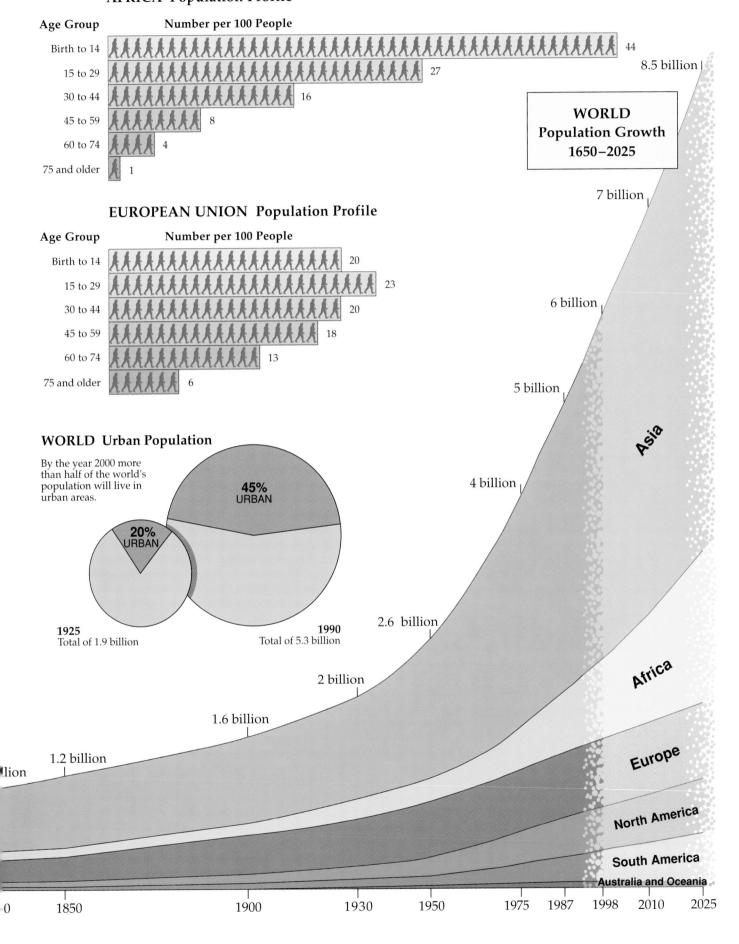

AFRICA Population Profile

Age Group	Number per 100 People
Birth to 14	44
15 to 29	27
30 to 44	16
45 to 59	8
60 to 74	4
75 and older	1

EUROPEAN UNION Population Profile

Age Group	Number per 100 People
Birth to 14	20
15 to 29	23
30 to 44	20
45 to 59	18
60 to 74	13
75 and older	6

WORLD Urban Population

By the year 2000 more than half of the world's population will live in urban areas.

20% URBAN

45% URBAN

1925
Total of 1.9 billion

1990
Total of 5.3 billion

WORLD Population Growth 1650–2025

8.5 billion

7 billion

6 billion

5 billion

4 billion

Asia

2.6 billion

2 billion

1.6 billion

1.2 billion

...lion

Africa

Europe

North America

South America

Australia and Oceania

1850 1900 1930 1950 1975 1987 1998 2010 2025

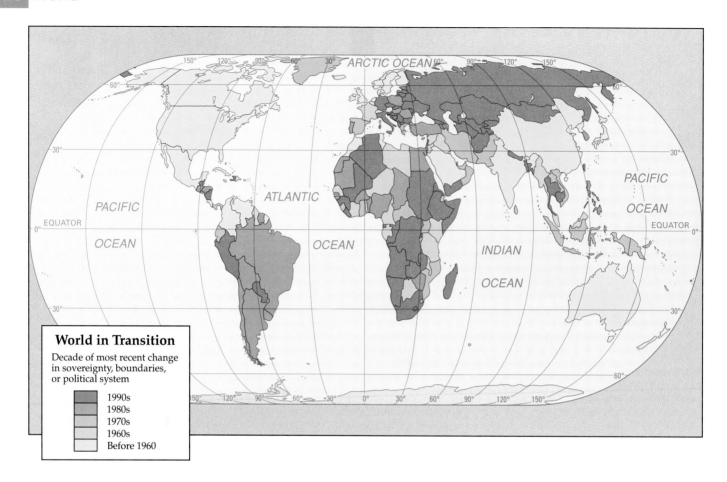

World in Transition

Decade of most recent change in sovereignty, boundaries, or political system

- 1990s
- 1980s
- 1970s
- 1960s
- Before 1960

Worldwide Immigration to Canada

Primary migration in 1991

Place of origin

- Australia and Oceania
- Asia
- Europe
- Africa
- Americas (except United States)
- Other countries*
- United States

* "Other countries" refers to countries of the former U.S.S.R.; also includes Africa and Latin America through 1981.

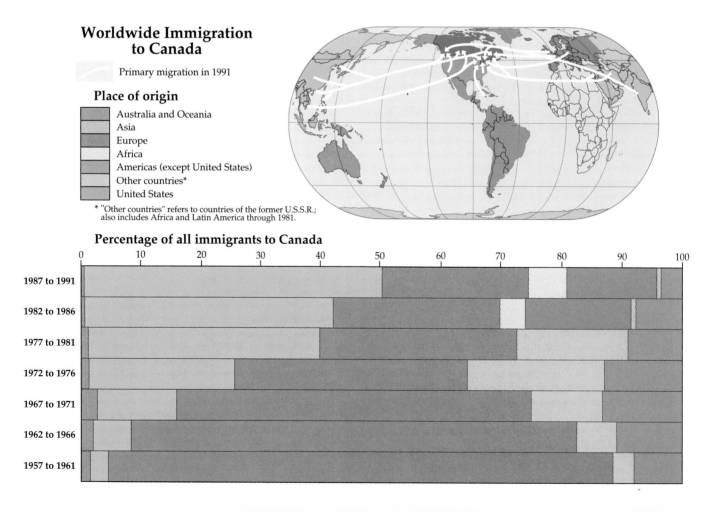

Percentage of all immigrants to Canada

	0	10	20	30	40	50	60	70	80	90	100

- 1987 to 1991
- 1982 to 1986
- 1977 to 1981
- 1972 to 1976
- 1967 to 1971
- 1962 to 1966
- 1957 to 1961

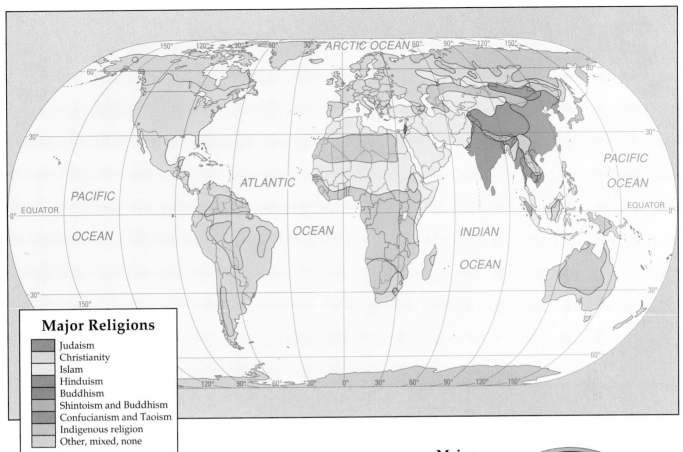

Major Religions

- Judaism
- Christianity
- Islam
- Hinduism
- Buddhism
- Shintoism and Buddhism
- Confucianism and Taoism
- Indigenous religion
- Other, mixed, none

World Migration

Countries with highest net annual immigration		Countries with highest net annual emigration	
United States	+ 880,000	Malawi	− 371,000
Mozambique	+ 522,000	Mexico	− 285,000
Germany	+ 323,000	Sudan	− 184,000
Canada	+ 158,000	Pakistan	− 160,000
Ethiopia	+ 157,000	Vietnam	− 112,000

Major Religions

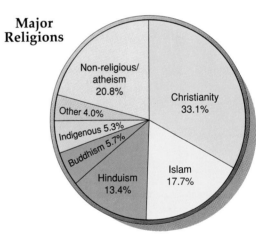

- Christianity 33.1%
- Non-religious/atheism 20.8%
- Islam 17.7%
- Hinduism 13.4%
- Buddhism 5.7%
- Indigenous 5.3%
- Other 4.0%

Until recently Quebec was the principal port of entry for immigration into Canada. In every year until 1971, most immigrants came from Europe.

Today most Canadian cities have growing communities of immigrants from Latin America and Asia. In recent years nearly as many people have emigrated from Hong Kong alone as from all of Europe.

World's Fastest Growing Urban Areas

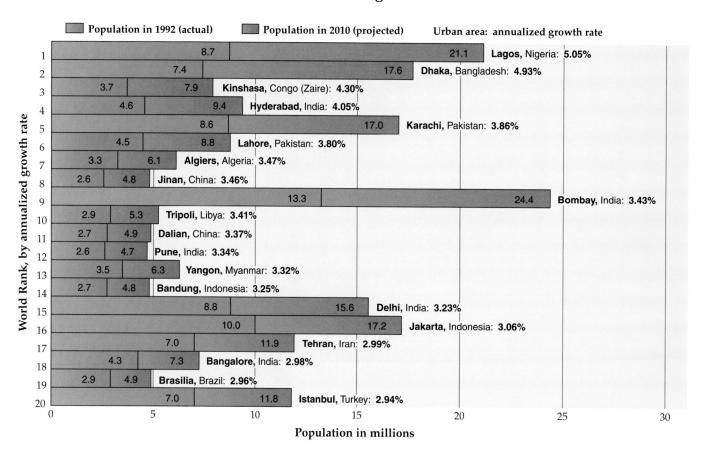

■ Population in 1992 (actual) ■ Population in 2010 (projected) Urban area: annualized growth rate

World Rank, by annualized growth rate

1. 8.7 — 21.1 — **Lagos,** Nigeria: **5.05%**
2. 7.4 — 17.6 — **Dhaka,** Bangladesh: **4.93%**
3. 3.7 — 7.9 — **Kinshasa,** Congo (Zaire): **4.30%**
4. 4.6 — 9.4 — **Hyderabad,** India: **4.05%**
5. 8.6 — 17.0 — **Karachi,** Pakistan: **3.86%**
6. 4.5 — 8.8 — **Lahore,** Pakistan: **3.80%**
7. 3.3 — 6.1 — **Algiers,** Algeria: **3.47%**
8. 2.6 — 4.8 — **Jinan,** China: **3.46%**
9. 13.3 — 24.4 — **Bombay,** India: **3.43%**
10. 2.9 — 5.3 — **Tripoli,** Libya: **3.41%**
11. 2.7 — 4.9 — **Dalian,** China: **3.37%**
12. 2.6 — 4.7 — **Pune,** India: **3.34%**
13. 3.5 — 6.3 — **Yangon,** Myanmar: **3.32%**
14. 2.7 — 4.8 — **Bandung,** Indonesia: **3.25%**
15. 8.8 — 15.6 — **Delhi,** India: **3.23%**
16. 10.0 — 17.2 — **Jakarta,** Indonesia: **3.06%**
17. 7.0 — 11.9 — **Tehran,** Iran: **2.99%**
18. 4.3 — 7.3 — **Bangalore,** India: **2.98%**
19. 2.9 — 4.9 — **Brasilia,** Brazil: **2.96%**
20. 7.0 — 11.8 — **Istanbul,** Turkey: **2.94%**

Population in millions

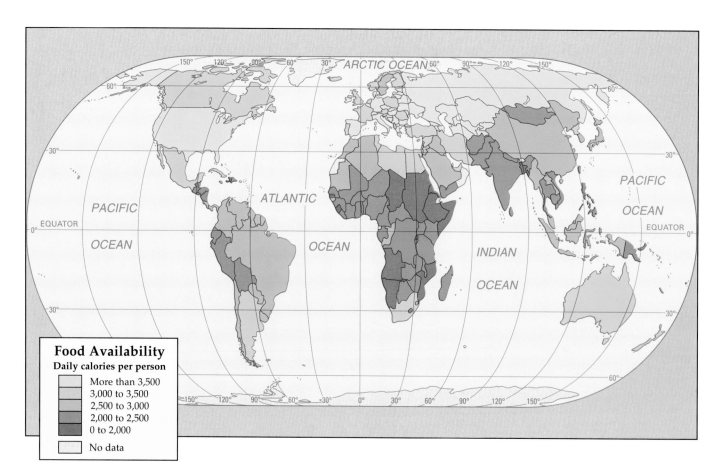

Food Availability
Daily calories per person

- More than 3,500
- 3,000 to 3,500
- 2,500 to 3,000
- 2,000 to 2,500
- 0 to 2,000
- No data

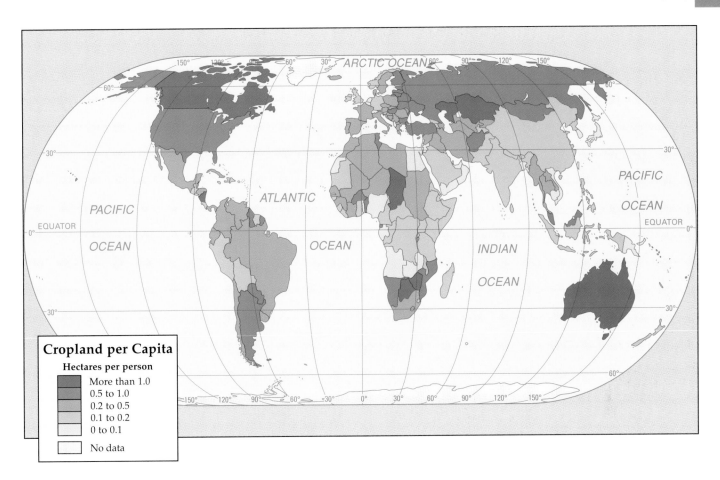

Cropland per Capita

Hectares per person

- More than 1.0
- 0.5 to 1.0
- 0.2 to 0.5
- 0.1 to 0.2
- 0 to 0.1
- No data

Staple Food Production

Grains are the main source of food for most of the world's population. Many grains are also used in processed foods and livestock feed. Grain producers range from large commercial farms that export their harvest to small farms that grow grains for regional consumption.

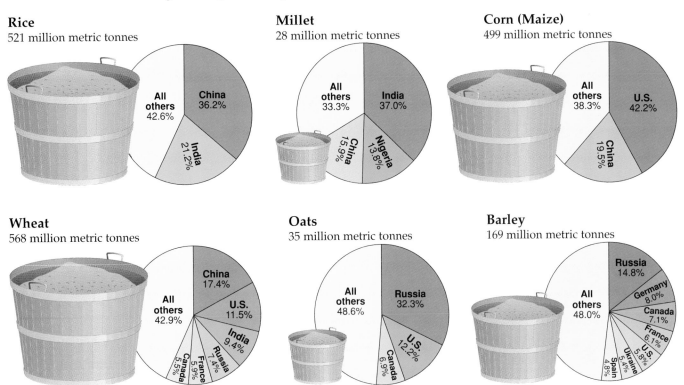

Rice
521 million metric tonnes

- China 36.2%
- India 21.2%
- All others 42.6%

Millet
28 million metric tonnes

- India 37.0%
- China 15.9%
- Nigeria 13.8%
- All others 33.3%

Corn (Maize)
499 million metric tonnes

- U.S. 42.2%
- China 19.5%
- All others 38.3%

Wheat
568 million metric tonnes

- China 17.4%
- U.S. 11.5%
- India 9.4%
- Russia 7.4%
- France 5.9%
- Canada 5.5%
- All others 42.9%

Oats
35 million metric tonnes

- Russia 32.3%
- U.S. 12.2%
- Canada 6.9%
- All others 48.6%

Barley
169 million metric tonnes

- Russia 14.8%
- Germany 8.0%
- Canada 7.1%
- France 6.1%
- Ukraine 5.8%
- U.S. 5.4%
- Spain 4.8%
- All others 48.0%

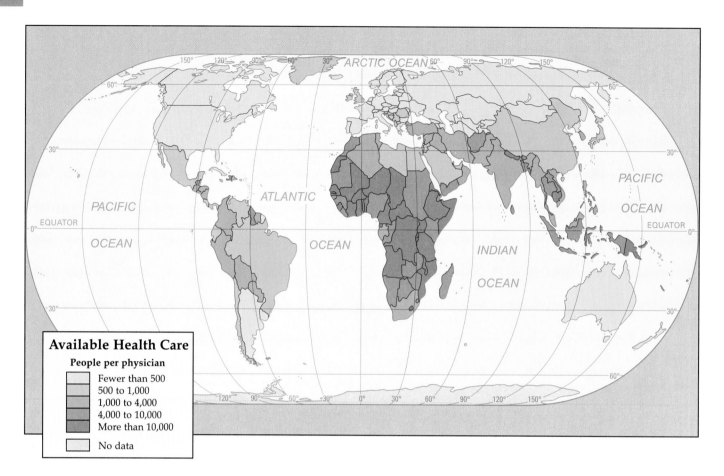

Available Health Care

People per physician

- Fewer than 500
- 500 to 1,000
- 1,000 to 4,000
- 4,000 to 10,000
- More than 10,000

- No data

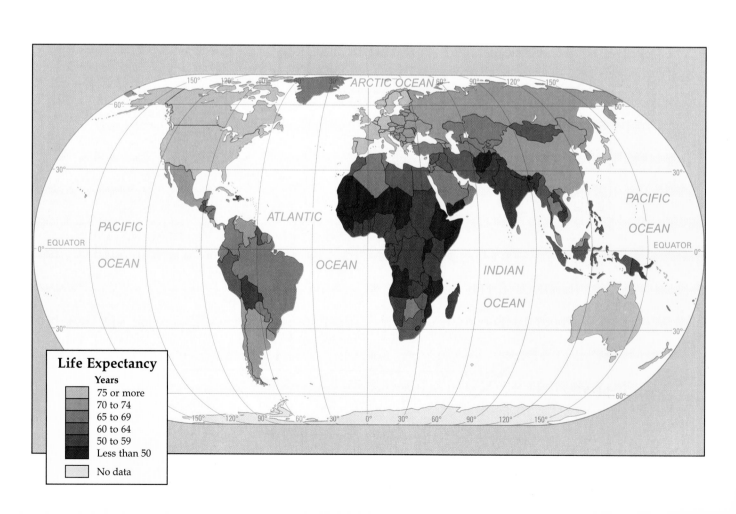

Life Expectancy

Years

- 75 or more
- 70 to 74
- 65 to 69
- 60 to 64
- 50 to 59
- Less than 50

- No data

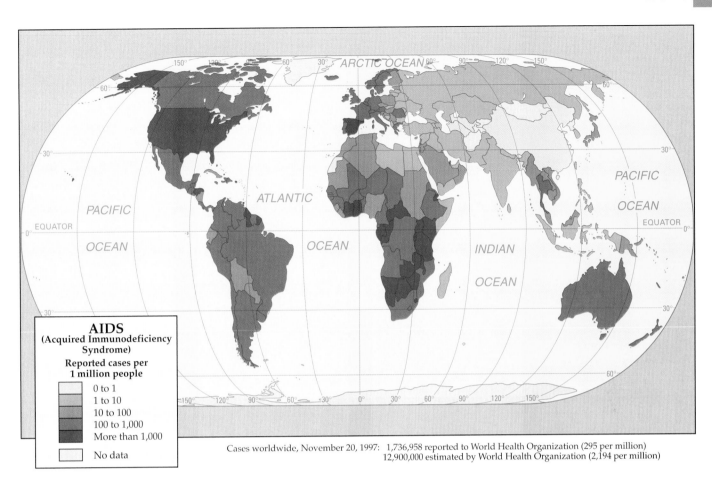

AIDS
(Acquired Immunodeficiency Syndrome)
Reported cases per 1 million people

- 0 to 1
- 1 to 10
- 10 to 100
- 100 to 1,000
- More than 1,000
- No data

Cases worldwide, November 20, 1997: 1,736,958 reported to World Health Organization (295 per million)
12,900,000 estimated by World Health Organization (2,194 per million)

Causes of Death

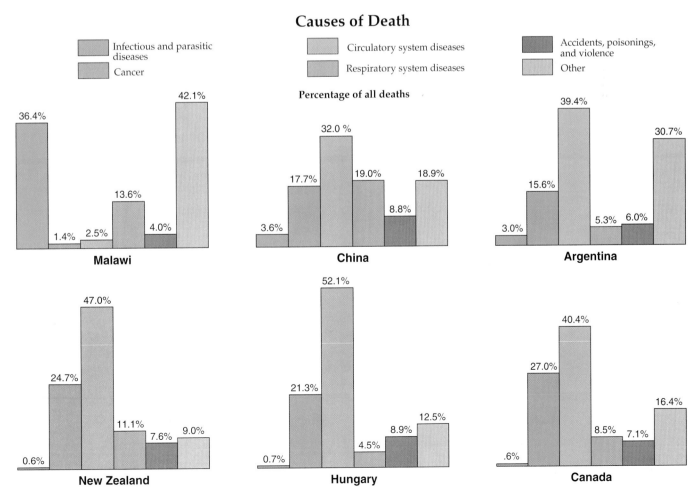

- Infectious and parasitic diseases
- Cancer
- Circulatory system diseases
- Respiratory system diseases
- Accidents, poisonings, and violence
- Other

Percentage of all deaths

Malawi
36.4% 1.4% 2.5% 13.6% 4.0% 42.1%

China
3.6% 17.7% 32.0% 19.0% 8.8% 18.9%

Argentina
3.0% 15.6% 39.4% 5.3% 6.0% 30.7%

New Zealand
0.6% 24.7% 47.0% 11.1% 7.6% 9.0%

Hungary
0.7% 21.3% 52.1% 4.5% 8.9% 12.5%

Canada
.6% 27.0% 40.4% 8.5% 7.1% 16.4%

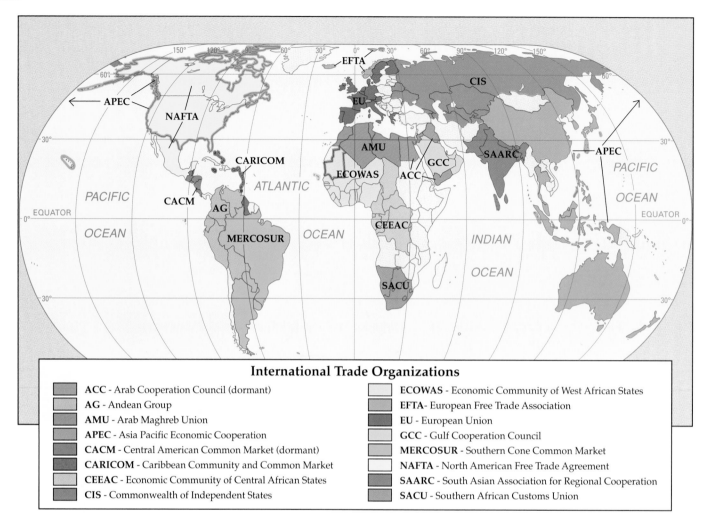

International Trade Organizations

ACC - Arab Cooperation Council (dormant)	**ECOWAS** - Economic Community of West African States
AG - Andean Group	**EFTA** - European Free Trade Association
AMU - Arab Maghreb Union	**EU** - European Union
APEC - Asia Pacific Economic Cooperation	**GCC** - Gulf Cooperation Council
CACM - Central American Common Market (dormant)	**MERCOSUR** - Southern Cone Common Market
CARICOM - Caribbean Community and Common Market	**NAFTA** - North American Free Trade Agreement
CEEAC - Economic Community of Central African States	**SAARC** - South Asian Association for Regional Cooperation
CIS - Commonwealth of Independent States	**SACU** - Southern African Customs Union

Single-Commodity Economies

Many countries rely on only one natural resource to support 75% or more of their export economies.

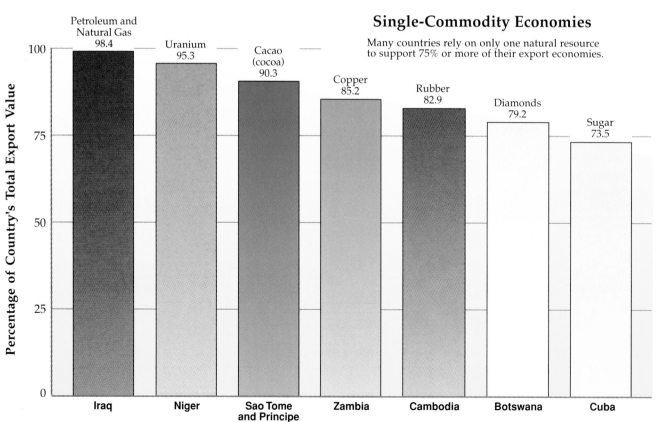

Percentage of Country's Total Export Value

Commodity	Country	Percentage
Petroleum and Natural Gas	Iraq	98.4
Uranium	Niger	95.3
Cacao (cocoa)	Sao Tome and Principe	90.3
Copper	Zambia	85.2
Rubber	Cambodia	82.9
Diamonds	Botswana	79.2
Sugar	Cuba	73.5

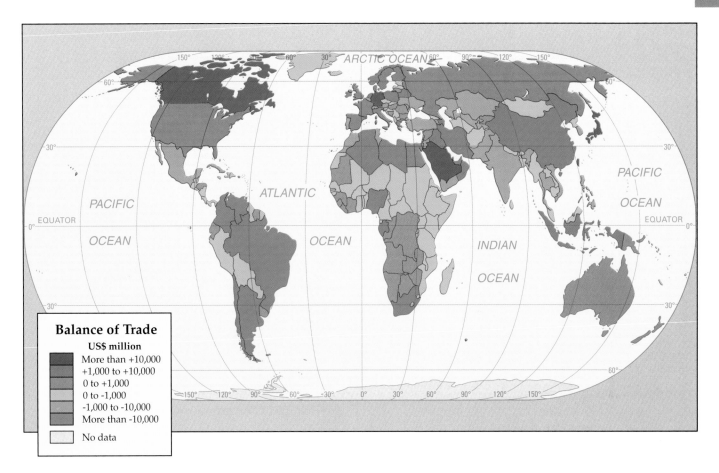

Balance of Trade

US$ million

- More than +10,000
- +1,000 to +10,000
- 0 to +1,000
- 0 to -1,000
- -1,000 to -10,000
- More than -10,000
- No data

Disparity of Income

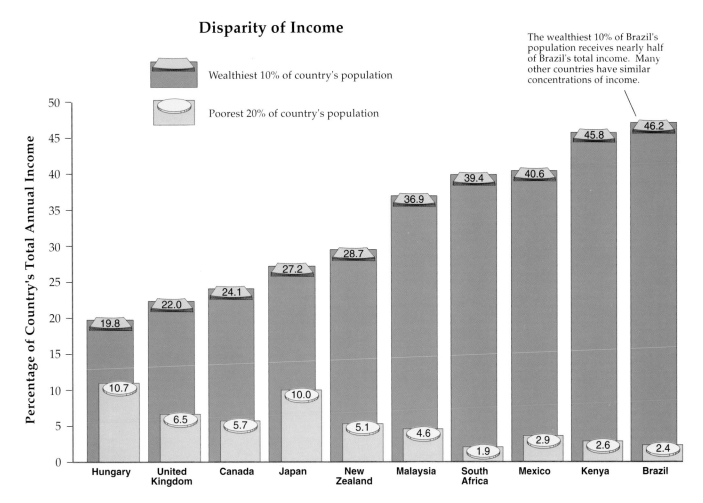

Wealthiest 10% of country's population

Poorest 20% of country's population

The wealthiest 10% of Brazil's population receives nearly half of Brazil's total income. Many other countries have similar concentrations of income.

Percentage of Country's Total Annual Income

Country	Wealthiest 10%	Poorest 20%
Hungary	19.8	10.7
United Kingdom	22.0	6.5
Canada	24.1	5.7
Japan	27.2	10.0
New Zealand	28.7	5.1
Malaysia	36.9	4.6
South Africa	39.4	1.9
Mexico	40.6	2.9
Kenya	45.8	2.6
Brazil	46.2	2.4

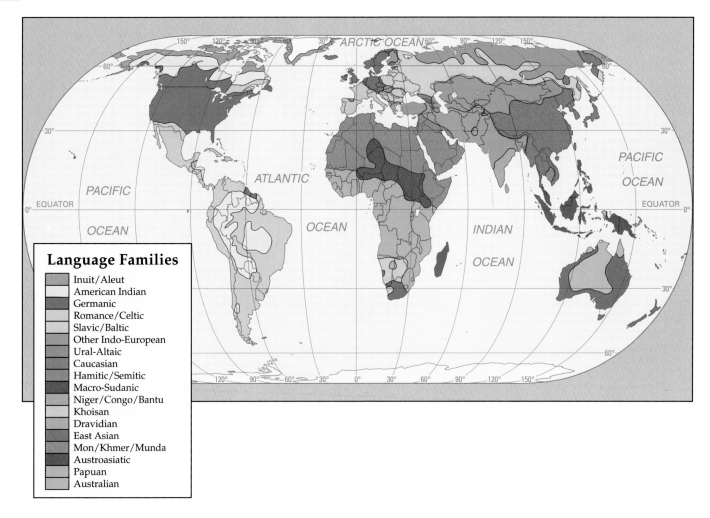

Language Families

- Inuit/Aleut
- American Indian
- Germanic
- Romance/Celtic
- Slavic/Baltic
- Other Indo-European
- Ural-Altaic
- Caucasian
- Hamitic/Semitic
- Macro-Sudanic
- Niger/Congo/Bantu
- Khoisan
- Dravidian
- East Asian
- Mon/Khmer/Munda
- Austroasiatic
- Papuan
- Australian

GREENWICH MEAN TIME
(GMT)

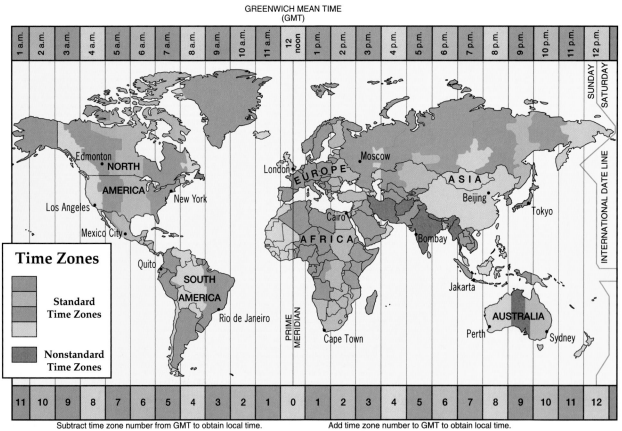

Time Zones

- Standard Time Zones
- Nonstandard Time Zones

11	10	9	8	7	6	5	4	3	2	1	0	1	2	3	4	5	6	7	8	9	10	11	12

Subtract time zone number from GMT to obtain local time.   Add time zone number to GMT to obtain local time.

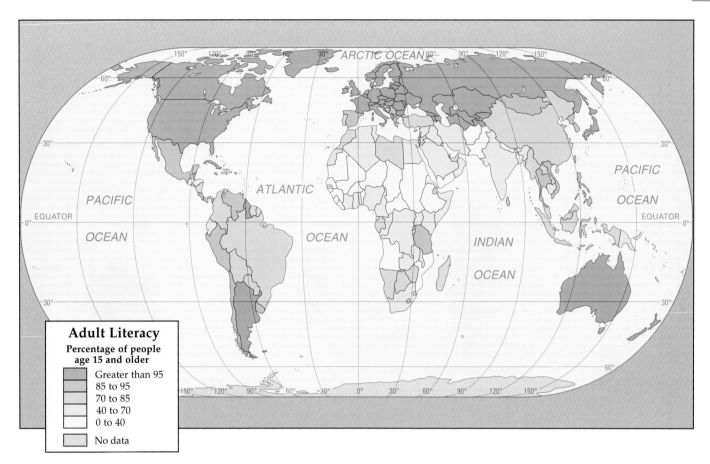

Adult Literacy

Percentage of people
age 15 and older

- Greater than 95
- 85 to 95
- 70 to 85
- 40 to 70
- 0 to 40
- No data

Daily circulation		Persons per Newspaper	
2,340,000	**Norway**		1.8
5,570,000	**Canada**		4.8
11,300,000	**Mexico**		7.3
17,000,000	**India**		47.6

Telephones owned		Persons per Telephone	
20,000,000	**Canada**		1.3
14,000,000	**Brazil**		10
576,000	**Nigeria**		210
233,000	**Bangladesh**		476

Radios owned		Persons per Radio	
520,000,000	**United States**		0.5
22,600,000	**Canada**		1.2
7,000,000	**Vietnam**		10
200,000	**Burkina Faso**		46

Televisions owned		Persons per Television	
83,000,000	**Japan**		1.5
16,500,000	**Canada**		1.7
540,000	**Bolivia**		14
31,000	**Congo (Zaire)**		1,776

Speed of Travel

Route	Year	Means of travel	Length of time
North America to Europe via air	1978	Concorde SST — supersonic jet	3.5 hours
	1950	Intercontinental jet — twin engine jet	10 hours
	1927	*Spirit of St. Louis* — single engine aircraft	33.5 hours
North America to Europe via ocean	1898	*Lucania* — ocean liner	5.5 days
	1838	*Sirius* — steamship	18 days
	1497	John Cabot — sailing vessel	35 days

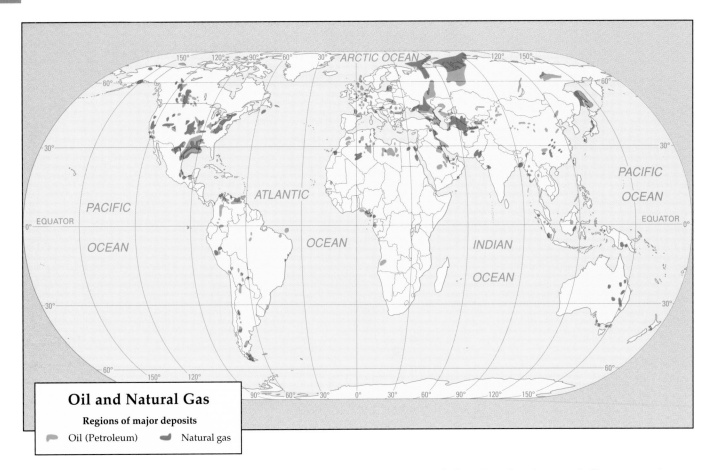

Oil and Natural Gas

Regions of major deposits

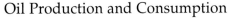 Oil (Petroleum)   Natural gas

Oil Production and Consumption

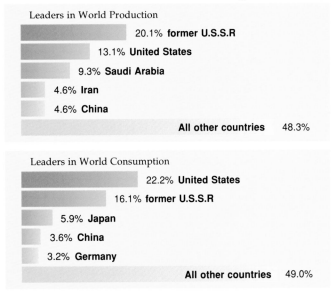

Leaders in World Production

20.1% **former U.S.S.R**
13.1% **United States**
9.3% **Saudi Arabia**
4.6% **Iran**
4.6% **China**
All other countries 48.3%

Leaders in World Consumption

22.2% **United States**
16.1% **former U.S.S.R**
5.9% **Japan**
3.6% **China**
3.2% **Germany**
All other countries 49.0%

Natural Gas Production and Consumption

Leaders in World Production

38.0% **former U.S.S.R**
24.4% **United States**
5.5% **Canada**
3.2% **Netherlands**
2.5% **United Kingdom**
26.4% **All other countries**

Leaders in World Consumption

33.1% **former U.S.S.R.**
26.4% **United States**
3.5% **Canada**
3.3% **Germany**
3.1% **United Kingdom**
30.6% **All other countries**

Automobiles Owned		Persons per Automobile	
143,039,503	United States	1.8	
35,025,155	Germany	2.3	
12,811,318	Canada	2.2	
14,039,745	Brazil	10.9	
1,660,235	China	701.7	

One 🚗 represents 15 million automobiles

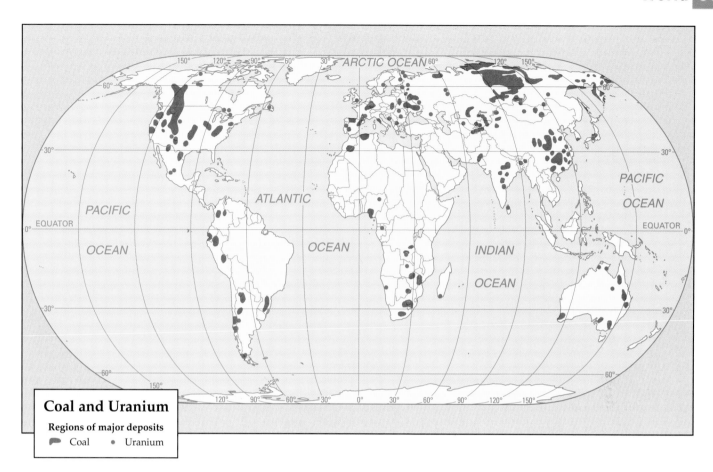

Coal and Uranium

Regions of major deposits

- Coal
- Uranium

Coal Production and Consumption

Leaders in World Production

- 29.3% **China**
- 23.1% **United States**
- 16.2% **former U.S.S.R.**
- 5.6% **India**
- 5.0% **South Africa**
- 20.8% **All other countries**

Leaders in World Consumption

- 28.9% **China**
- 20.8% **United States**
- 15.5% **former U.S.S.R.**
- 5.7% **India**
- 4.1% **Poland**
- 25.0% **All other countries**

Uranium Production and Consumption*

Leaders in World Production

- 30.3% **Canada**
- 17.9% **South Africa**
- 12.9% **United States**
- 10.0% **Australia**
- 8.9% **France**
- 20.0% **All other countries**

Leaders in World Consumption

- 28.9% **United States**
- 15.7% **France**
- 9.9% **Japan**
- 8.4% **Germany**
- 6.2% **former U.S.S.R.**
- 30.9% **All other countries**

*Includes only uranium used to generate electricity.

Lifetime of Fossil Fuels	Initial World Supply	Supply Consumed To Date	Remaining Known Reserves	Estimated Unknown Reserves	Estimated Year of Depletion*
Coal	7,600,000 million tons	190,000 million tons	7,410,000 million tons (known and unknown)		2200 to 5500
Oil (petroleum)	1,721,000 million barrels	560,320 million barrels	535,380 million barrels	525,300 million barrels	2035
Natural gas	255,400,000 million cubic meters	36,400,000 million cubic meters	97,300,000 million cubic meters	121,800,000 million cubic meters	2050

*given present rates of use

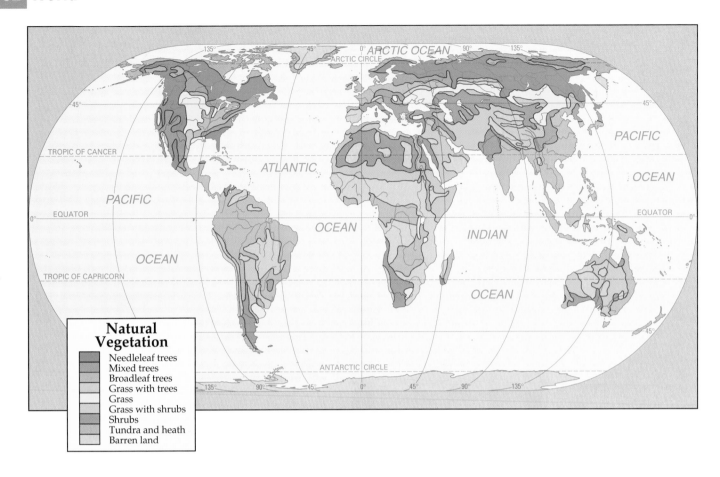

Natural Vegetation

- Needleleaf trees
- Mixed trees
- Broadleaf trees
- Grass with trees
- Grass
- Grass with shrubs
- Shrubs
- Tundra and heath
- Barren land

Natural Vegetation

The world can be divided into zones of natural vegetation. Several categories of vegetation are mapped above.

Most of the categories can be sub-divided. For example, there are several kinds of broadleaf trees: maples, oaks, birches, sycamores, cottonwoods, and so on.

Seven types of vegetation listed in the map key are shown here.

needleleaf trees

mixed trees

broadleaf trees

grass with trees

grass

shrubs

tundra and heath

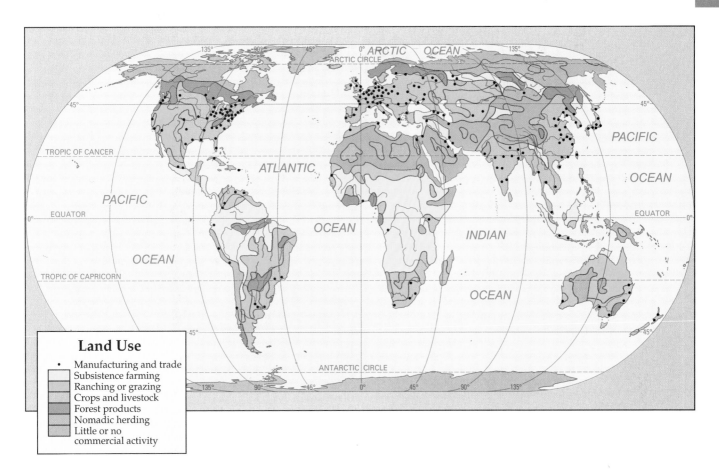

Land Use

- Manufacturing and trade
- Subsistence farming
- Ranching or grazing
- Crops and livestock
- Forest products
- Nomadic herding
- Little or no commercial activity

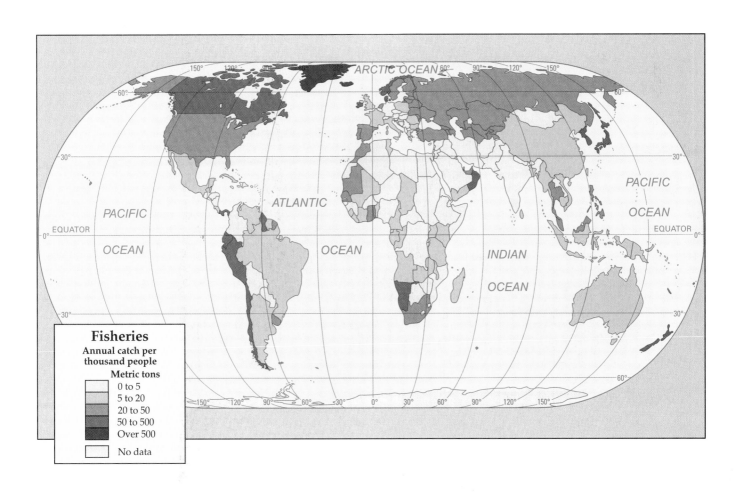

Fisheries

Annual catch per thousand people

Metric tons

- 0 to 5
- 5 to 20
- 20 to 50
- 50 to 500
- Over 500

- No data

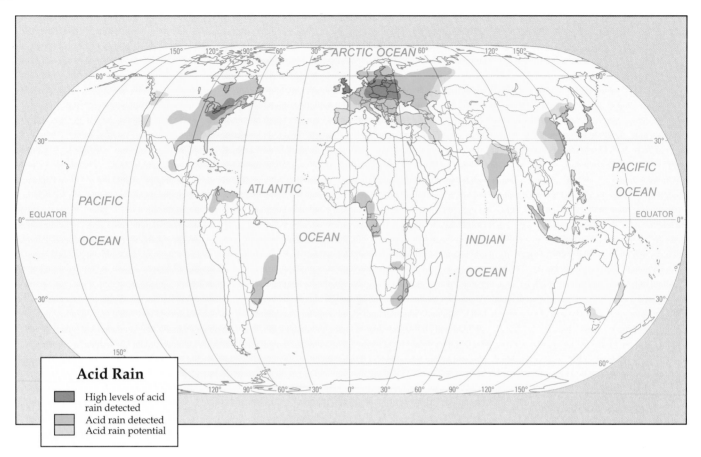

Acid Rain

- High levels of acid rain detected
- Acid rain detected
- Acid rain potential

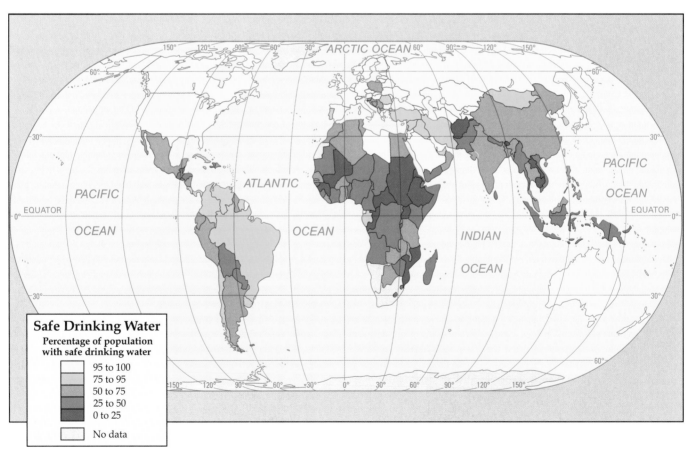

Safe Drinking Water

Percentage of population with safe drinking water

- 95 to 100
- 75 to 95
- 50 to 75
- 25 to 50
- 0 to 25
- No data

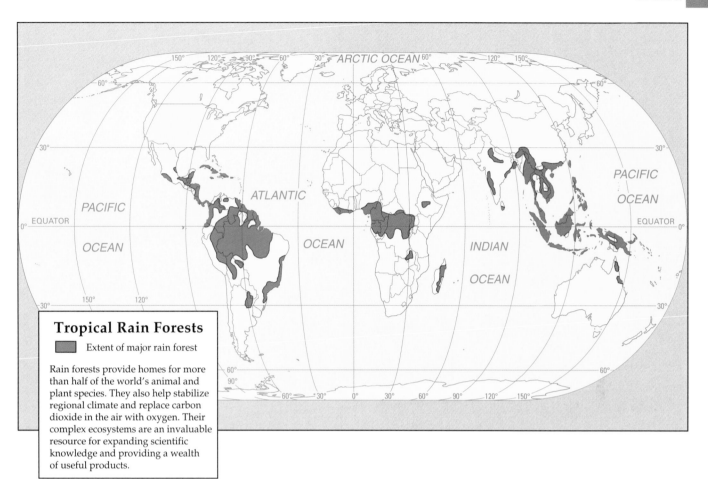

Tropical Rain Forests

Extent of major rain forest

Rain forests provide homes for more than half of the world's animal and plant species. They also help stabilize regional climate and replace carbon dioxide in the air with oxygen. Their complex ecosystems are an invaluable resource for expanding scientific knowledge and providing a wealth of useful products.

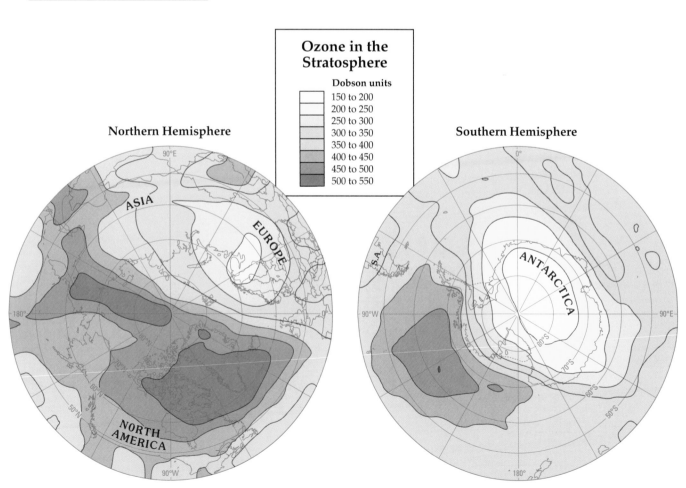

Ozone in the Stratosphere

Dobson units

150 to 200
200 to 250
250 to 300
300 to 350
350 to 400
400 to 450
450 to 500
500 to 550

Northern Hemisphere

Southern Hemisphere

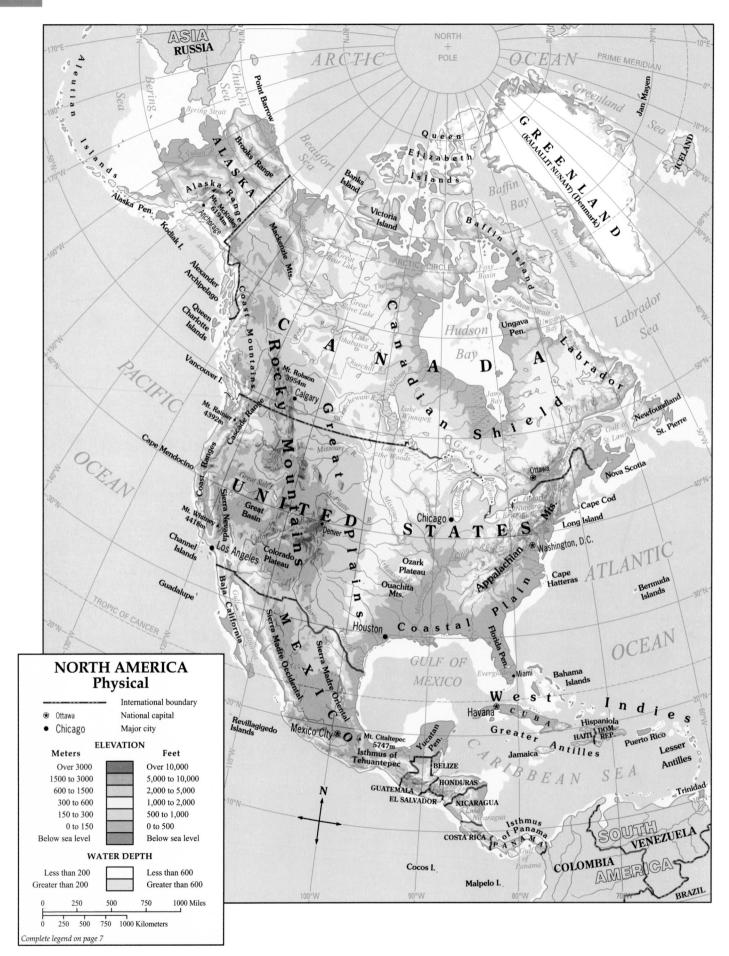

NORTH AMERICA
Physical

———	International boundary
⊛ Ottawa	National capital
● Chicago	Major city

ELEVATION

Meters		Feet
Over 3000		Over 10,000
1500 to 3000		5,000 to 10,000
600 to 1500		2,000 to 5,000
300 to 600		1,000 to 2,000
150 to 300		500 to 1,000
0 to 150		0 to 500
Below sea level		Below sea level

WATER DEPTH

Less than 200		Less than 600
Greater than 200		Greater than 600

0   250   500   750   1000 Miles
0   250   500   750   1000 Kilometers

Complete legend on page 7

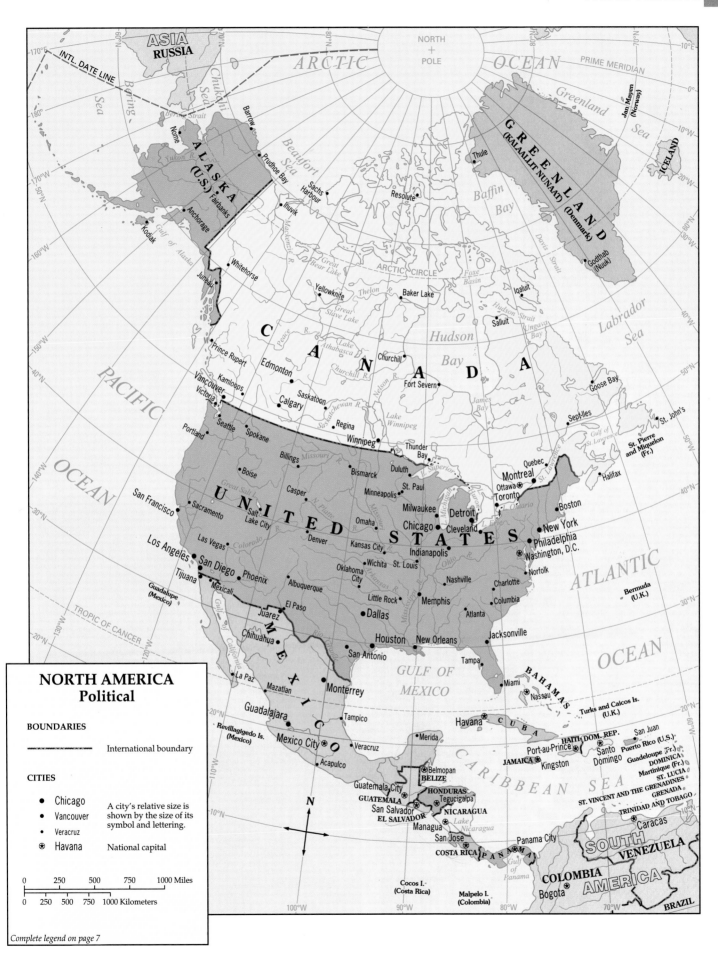

ASIA
RUSSIA

ARCTIC OCEAN

NORTH POLE

PRIME MERIDIAN

Greenland Sea

Jan Mayen (Norway)

ICELAND

INTL. DATE LINE

Bering Sea

Chukchi Sea

Beaufort Sea

Barrow

Nome

ALASKA (U.S.)

Prudhoe Bay

Sachs Harbour

Inuvik

Resolute

Baffin Bay

Thule

G R E E N L A N D (KALAALLIT NUNAAT) (Denmark)

Fairbanks

Anchorage

Kodiak

Gulf of Alaska

Juneau

Whitehorse

Mackenzie R.

Great Bear Lake

ARCTIC CIRCLE

Davis Strait

Godthab (Nuuk)

Foxe Basin

Iqaluit

Yellowknife

Great Slave Lake

Thelon

Baker Lake

Salluit

Hudson Strait

Ungava Bay

Labrador Sea

PACIFIC

Prince Rupert

Peace R.

Lake Athabasca

Churchill R.

Churchill

Fort Severn

C A N A D A

Hudson Bay

James Bay

Goose Bay

Edmonton

Kamloops

Vancouver

Victoria

Calgary

Saskatoon

Saskatchewan R.

Nelson R.

Lake Winnipeg

Sept-Iles

St. John's

Gulf of St. Lawrence

OCEAN

Portland

Seattle

Spokane

Regina

Winnipeg

Thunder Bay

L. Superior

St. Lawrence R.

Quebec

Montreal

Halifax

St. Pierre and Miquelon (Fr.)

Billings

Missouri

Bismarck

Duluth

St. Paul

L. Huron

Ottawa

Toronto

L. Ontario

Boston

Boise

Minneapolis

Milwaukee

L. Michigan

Detroit

Cleveland

L. Erie

New York

San Francisco

Sacramento

Casper

U N I T E D

Omaha

Missouri R.

Chicago

Indianapolis

Philadelphia

Washington, D.C.

Great Salt L.

Salt Lake City

N. Platte R.

Denver

S T A T E S

Kansas City

St. Louis

Ohio R.

Las Vegas

Colorado R.

Norfolk

Los Angeles

San Diego

Tijuana

Mexicali

Phoenix

Albuquerque

Oklahoma City

Wichita

Arkansas R.

Nashville

Memphis

Charlotte

Columbia

ATLANTIC

Guadalupe (Mexico)

Juarez

El Paso

Little Rock

Atlanta

Bermuda (U.K.)

Chihuahua

M E X I C O

Gulf of California

Rio Grande

Dallas

Houston

Mississippi R.

New Orleans

Jacksonville

TROPIC OF CANCER

San Antonio

Tampa

GULF OF MEXICO

OCEAN

La Paz

Mazatlan

Monterrey

Miami

BAHAMAS

Nassau

Guadalajara

Tampico

Havana

C U B A

Turks and Caicos Is. (U.K.)

Revillagigedo Is. (Mexico)

Merida

San Juan

HAITI DOM. REP.

Puerto Rico (U.S.)

Mexico City

Veracruz

Port-au-Prince

Santo Domingo

Guadeloupe (Fr.)

DOMINICA (Fr.)

Acapulco

JAMAICA

Kingston

ST. LUCIA

Martinique (Fr.)

Belmopan

BELIZE

C A R I B B E A N   S E A

ST. VINCENT AND THE GRENADINES

GRENADA

Guatemala City

GUATEMALA

HONDURAS

Tegucigalpa

NICARAGUA

TRINIDAD AND TOBAGO

San Salvador

EL SALVADOR

Managua

Lake Nicaragua

Caracas

SOUTH

VENEZUELA

San Jose

COSTA RICA

P A N A M A

Panama City

Gulf of Panama

Cocos I. (Costa Rica)

Malpelo I. (Colombia)

COLOMBIA

Bogota

AMERICA

BRAZIL

N

NORTH AMERICA
Political

BOUNDARIES

――――――― International boundary

CITIES

● Chicago

● Vancouver

• Veracruz

⊛ Havana

A city's relative size is shown by the size of its symbol and lettering.

National capital

| 0 | 250 | 500 | 750 | 1000 Miles |

| 0 | 250 | 500 | 750 | 1000 Kilometers |

Complete legend on page 7

100°W   90°W   80°W   70°W

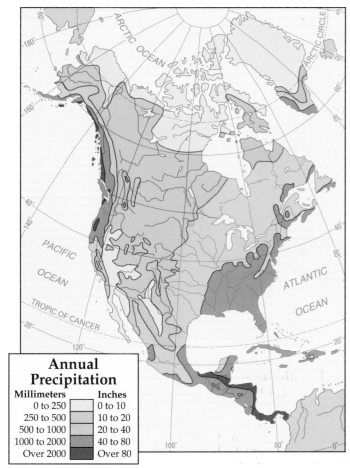

Annual Precipitation

Millimeters		Inches
0 to 250		0 to 10
250 to 500		10 to 20
500 to 1000		20 to 40
1000 to 2000		40 to 80
Over 2000		Over 80

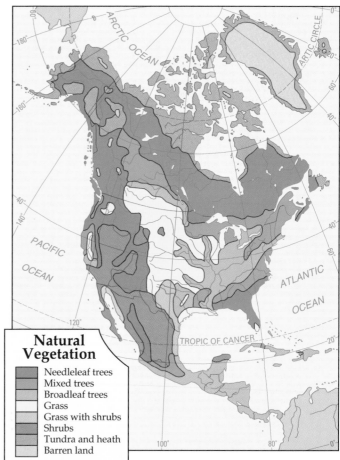

Natural Vegetation

- Needleleaf trees
- Mixed trees
- Broadleaf trees
- Grass
- Grass with shrubs
- Shrubs
- Tundra and heath
- Barren land

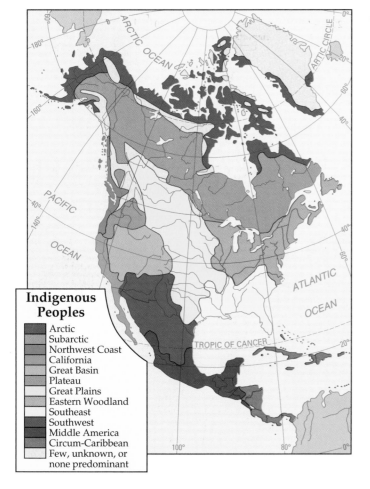

Indigenous Peoples

- Arctic
- Subarctic
- Northwest Coast
- California
- Great Basin
- Plateau
- Great Plains
- Eastern Woodland
- Southeast
- Southwest
- Middle America
- Circum-Caribbean
- Few, unknown, or none predominant

The Canadian Rockies stretch across British Columbia and Alberta. They are part of the Rocky Mountain chain, which extends from the southwestern United States to northern Alaska.

Yellowstone National Park in the western United States preserves over 2,000,000 acres (809 400 hectares) of evergreen forests and mountain meadows. Its natural wonders include 3,000 geysers and hot springs.

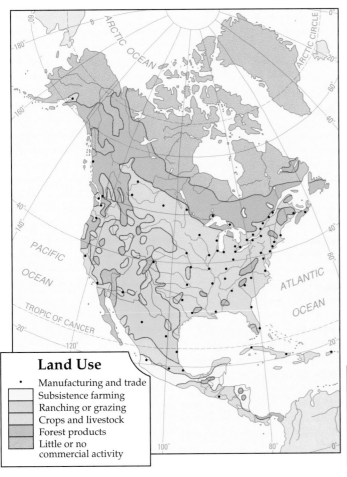

Land Use

- • Manufacturing and trade
- Subsistence farming
- Ranching or grazing
- Crops and livestock
- Forest products
- Little or no commercial activity

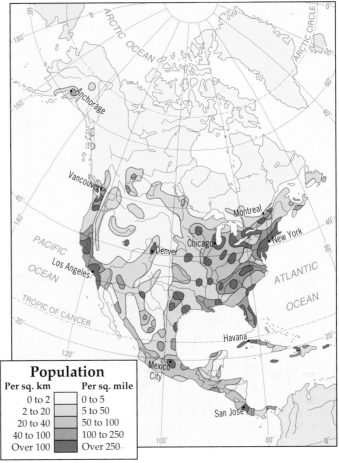

Population

Per sq. km	Per sq. mile
0 to 2	0 to 5
2 to 20	5 to 50
20 to 40	50 to 100
40 to 100	100 to 250
Over 100	Over 250

Canadian Trade in North America

Canadian trade is important, but not dominant, in many North American countries.

(See pages 128-129 for more about trade within NAFTA and the rest of the Pacific Rim.)

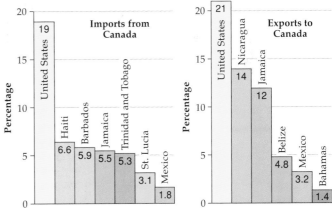

Imports from Canada

United States 19
Haiti 6.6
Barbados 5.9
Jamaica 5.5
Trinidad and Tobago 5.3
St. Lucia 3.1
Mexico 1.8

Exports to Canada

United States 21
Nicaragua 14
Jamaica 12
Belize 4.8
Mexico 3.2
Bahamas 1.4

MEXICO
Area Comparison

Mexico has about one-fourth the area of Canada but its population is three times as large.

Mexico	1 958 201 km²
Canada	9 970 610 km²

North America–the world's breadbasket–is a major producer and the leading exporter of wheat.

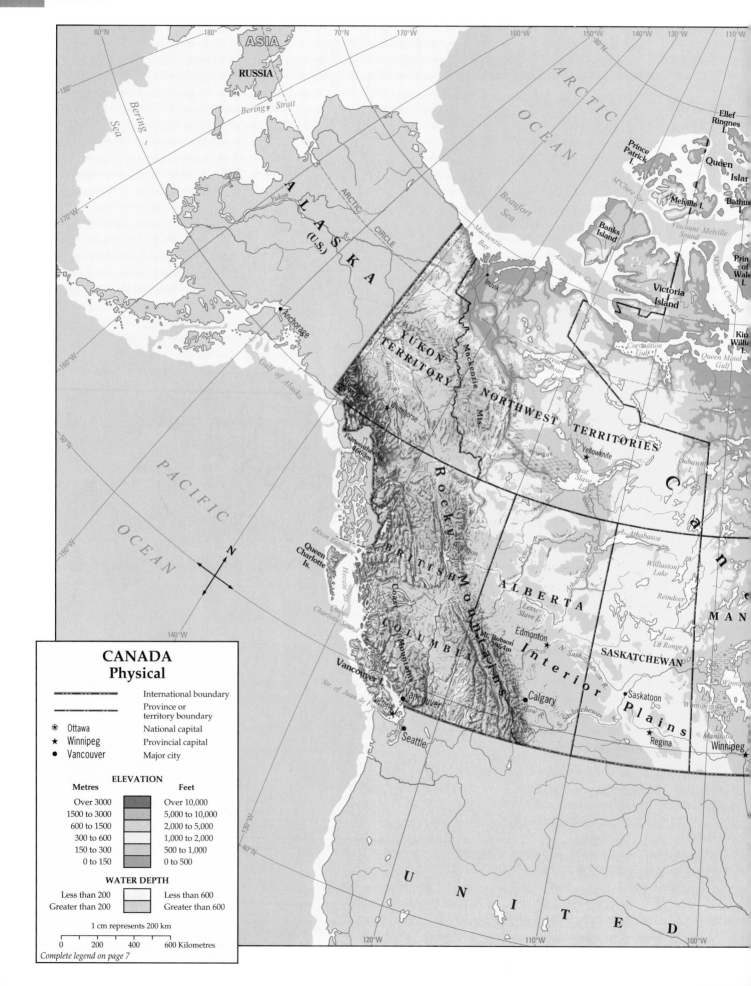

CANADA
Physical

———————	International boundary
———————	Province or territory boundary
⊛ Ottawa	National capital
★ Winnipeg	Provincial capital
● Vancouver	Major city

ELEVATION

Metres		Feet
Over 3000		Over 10,000
1500 to 3000		5,000 to 10,000
600 to 1500		2,000 to 5,000
300 to 600		1,000 to 2,000
150 to 300		500 to 1,000
0 to 150		0 to 500

WATER DEPTH

Less than 200		Less than 600
Greater than 200		Greater than 600

1 cm represents 200 km

| 0 | 200 | 400 | 600 Kilometres |

Complete legend on page 7

ICELAND

G R E E N L A N D
(KALAALLIT NUNAAD) (Denmark)

ARCTIC CIRCLE

Denmark Strait

ATLANTIC OCEAN

Axel Heiberg I.

Ellesmere Island

Kane Basin

abeth

Devon Island

Baffin Bay

Lancaster Sound

erset I.

othia en.

Gulf of Boothia

Baffin Island

Cumberland Sd.

Melville Peninsula

N U N A V U T

Foxe Basin

Foxe Peninsula

Iqaluit

Frobisher Bay

Southampton I.

Hudson Strait

Foxe Channel

Cape Chidley

Davis Strait

Cape Farewell

Labrador Sea

Chesterfield Inlet

Coats I.

Ungava Bay

Torngat Mts.

Mansel I.

Ungava Peninsula

R. aux Feuilles

Hudson Bay

Belcher Is.

James Bay

Smallwood Res.

Labrador

Happy Valley Goose Bay

Churchill

NEWFOUNDLAND

OBA

d i a n

Severn R.

L. Mistassini

R. Manicouagan

Strait of Belle Isle

Anticosti I.

Newfoundland

St. John's

Cape Race

ONTARIO

S h i e l d

Albany R.

QUEBEC

St. Lawrence R.

Gaspe Pen.

Gulf of St. Lawrence

Miquelon (Fr.)

St.-Pierre (Fr.)

Lake of the Woods

Thunder Bay

L. Nipigon

Quebec

NEW BRUNSWICK

Fredericton

PRINCE EDWARD ISLAND

Cape Breton Island

NOVA SCOTIA

Halifax

Sable I.

L. Superior

Sault Ste. Marie

L. Nipissing

Montreal

Ottawa

Bay of Fundy

NOVA

Cape Sable

ATLANTIC OCEAN

L. Michigan

L. Huron

Georgian Bay

L. Simcoe

Toronto

L. Ontario

Detroit

Windsor

L. Erie

Niagara Falls

S T A T E S

ASIA
RUSSIA

INTERNATIONAL DATE LINE

Bering Strait

ARCTIC OCEAN

Bering Sea

A L A S K A (U.S.)

ARCTIC CIRCLE

Yukon

Beaufort Sea

Mackenzie Bay

Amundsen Gulf

Ellef Ringnes I.

Prince Patrick I.

Queen Isla

Melville I.

Batt

Viscount Melville Sound

M'Clure Str.

M'Clintock Channel

Pri o Wa I.

Sachs Harbour

Banks I.

Victoria Island

Cambridge Bay

K WI

Old Crow

Inuvik

Coronation Gulf

Queen Maud Gulf

YUKON TERRITORY

Dawson

Pelly Crossing

Norman Wells

Great Bear Lake

Mackenzie R.

Anchorage

Gulf of Alaska

PACIFIC OCEAN

Yukon R.

Whitehorse

NORTHWEST TERRITORIES

Dubawnt L.

Juneau

Watson Lake

Liard R.

Fort Simpson

Yellowknife

Great Slave Lake

Hay River

Fort Smith

N

Fort Nelson

Slave R.

L. Athabasca

Dixon Entrance

Queen Charlotte Is.

Prince Rupert

Skeena R.

Hecate Str.

Kitimat

Williston Lake

B R I T I S H

Dawson Creek

Prince George

Fraser R.

Peace R.

Peace River

Grande Prairie

Lesser Slave L.

Athabasca R.

A L B E R T A

Fort McMurray

Wollaston Lake

Reindeer L.

Buffalo Narrows

Lac La Ronge

M A N

Thompson

Flin Flon

Queen Charlotte Sound

C O L U M B I A

Kamloops

Columbia R.

Edmonton

Red Deer

N. Saskatchewan R.

Prince Albert

S A S K A T C H E W A N

Saskatoon

Winnipeg

Vancouver I.

Str. of Juan de Fuca

Vancouver

Victoria

Calgary

Bow R.

Saskatchewan R.

Moose Jaw

Regina

Winnipegosis

Manitoba L.

Seattle

Medicine Hat

Lethbridge

Winnipeg

Brandon

Portland

U N I T E D

D

60°N 180° 70°N 170°W 160°W 150°W 140°W 130°W 110°W
80°N
50°N
40°N
180° 170°W 160°W 150°W 140°W 130°W 120°W 110°W 100°W

CANADA
Political

BOUNDARIES

International boundary

Province or territory boundary

CITIES

● Montreal

● Saskatoon

• Resolute

⊛ Ottawa National capital

★ Winnipeg Provincial capital

A city's relative size is shown by the size of its symbol and lettering.

1 cm represents 200 km

0 200 400 600 Kilometres

Complete legend on page 7

Axel
Heiberg
I.

Ellesmere
Island

Kane
Basin

Elizabeth

Devon I.

solute

Lancaster Sound

erset I.

Gulf
of
Boothia

Kugaaruk

N U N A V U T

Baffin
Bay

Clyde River

**Baffin
Island**

Davis
Strait

Foxe
Basin

Cumberland Sd.

Godthåb

Foxe Channel

Iqaluit

Frobisher Bay

Chesterfield
Inlet

Southampton
I.

Hudson
Strait

Coats I.

Salluit

Mansel I.

Ungava
Bay

G R E E N L A N D
(KALAALLIT NUNAAD) (Denmark)

Denmark
Strait

ICELAND

ARCTIC CIRCLE

ATLANTIC

OCEAN

Labrador
Sea

Cape Farewell

Churchill

Hudson

Belcher
Is.

Kuujjuarapik

R. aux Feuilles

Kuujjuaq

R. George

Smallwood
Res.

Happy Valley-
Goose Bay

Churchill

NEWFOUNDLAND

St. John's

OBA

Fort Severn

Severn R.

Bay

James
Bay

L.
Mistassini

Res.
Manicouagan

Labrador
City

Strait of Belle Isle

Corner
Brook

Newfoundland

Winisk R.

Albany R.

Moosonee

O N T A R I O

Q U E B E C

Sept-Îles

Anticosti
I.

**ST-PIERRE AND
MIQUELON**
(France)

Gulf of
St. Lawrence

Cape Breton I.

Sable I.
(Nova Scotia)

Kenora

Lake of
the Woods

L.
Nipigon

Thunder
Bay

L. Superior

Sault Ste.
Marie

Sudbury

Val-d'Or

L.
Nipissing

Hull

Quebec

St. Lawrence R.

St. John R.

**PRINCE
EDWARD
ISLAND**

Charlottetown

**NEW
BRUNSWICK**
Fredericton

**NOVA
SCOTIA**

Halifax

Minneapolis

L. Michigan

Georgian
Bay

L.
Simcoe

L. Huron

Kingston

Toronto

L. Ontario

Montreal

Ottawa

Saint John

Bay of Fundy

Yarmouth

Boston

Hamilton

London

Buffalo

Niagara
Falls

Detroit

Windsor

L. Erie

S   **T**   **A**   **T**   **E**   **S**

New York

Chicago

ATLANTIC

OCEAN

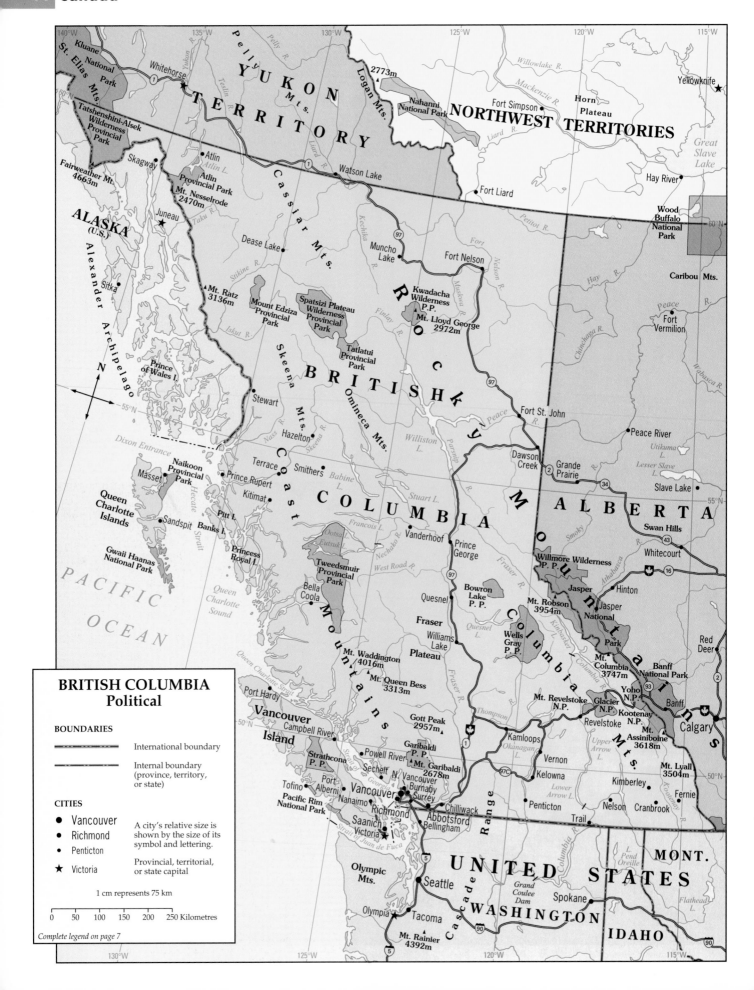

BRITISH COLUMBIA
Political

BOUNDARIES

———————— International boundary

———————— Internal boundary
(province, territory,
or state)

CITIES

● Vancouver

● Richmond

• Penticton

★ Victoria

A city's relative size is
shown by the size of its
symbol and lettering.

Provincial, territorial,
or state capital

1 cm represents 75 km

0   50   100   150   200   250 Kilometres

Complete legend on page 7

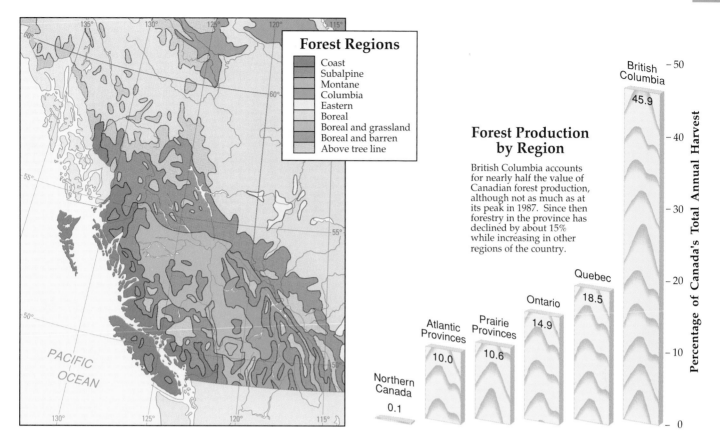

Forest Regions

	Coast
	Subalpine
	Montane
	Columbia
	Eastern
	Boreal
	Boreal and grassland
	Boreal and barren
	Above tree line

Forest Production by Region

British Columbia accounts for nearly half the value of Canadian forest production, although not as much as at its peak in 1987. Since then forestry in the province has declined by about 15% while increasing in other regions of the country.

Percentage of Canada's Total Annual Harvest

- British Columbia 45.9
- Quebec 18.5
- Ontario 14.9
- Prairie Provinces 10.6
- Atlantic Provinces 10.0
- Northern Canada 0.1

Energy in British Columbia

Sources of Electrical Energy
Total production: 63 064 GW·h

- Hydroelectric 94.2%
- Fossil Fuels 5.8%

Uses of Electrical Energy
Total consumption: 57 741 GW·h

- Other 26.3%
- Residential 22.6%
- Commercial 20.4%
- Mining and Manufacturing 30.7%

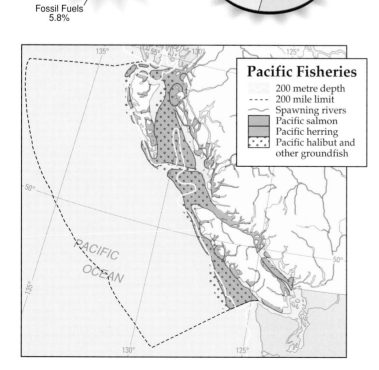

Pacific Fisheries

	200 metre depth
- - - -	200 mile limit
	Spawning rivers
	Pacific salmon
	Pacific herring
	Pacific halibut and other groundfish

PACIFIC OCEAN

Forests in the coastal mountains of British Columbia are valuable both as rich ecosystems and as sources of prized logs and lumber.

Vancouver is Canada's busiest port for exports. Half of all shipments from Canada to foreign countries depart from Vancouver or other ports in British Columbia.

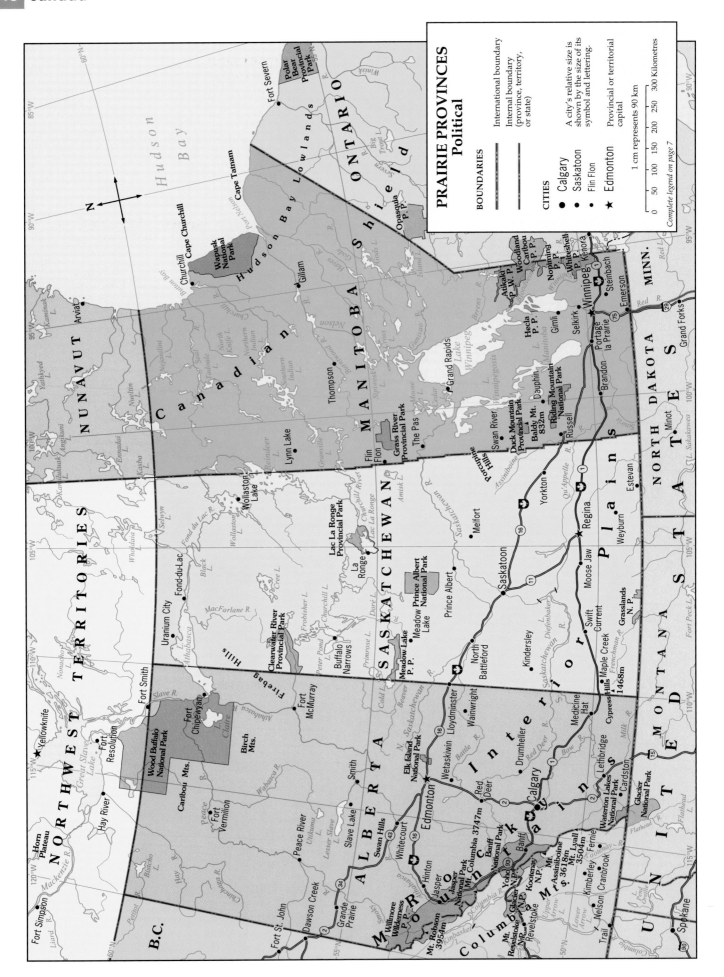

PRAIRIE PROVINCES
Political

BOUNDARIES

International boundary

Internal boundary
(province, territory,
or state)

CITIES

A city's relative size is
shown by the size of its
symbol and lettering.

● Calgary

• Saskatoon

• Flin Flon

★ Edmonton Provincial or territorial
capital

1 cm represents 90 km

0 50 100 150 200 250 300 Kilometres

Complete legend on page 7

NORTHWEST TERRITORIES

NUNAVUT

Hudson Bay

Canadian Shield

ONTARIO

MANITOBA

SASKATCHEWAN

ALBERTA

B.C.

UNITED STATES

NORTH DAKOTA

MINN.

MONTANA

Interior Plains

Rocky Mountains

Columbia

N

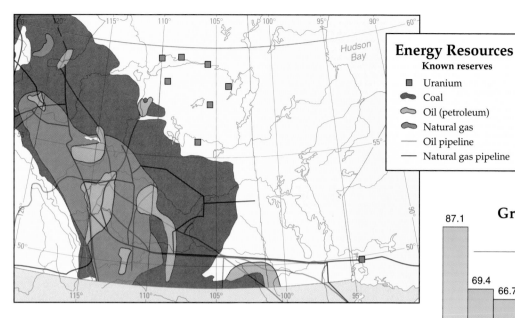

Energy Resources
Known reserves

- ■ Uranium
- 🖤 Coal
- 🖤 Oil (petroleum)
- 🖤 Natural gas
- — Oil pipeline
- — Natural gas pipeline

Canola, which is grown mainly for its oil, has become both valuable and widespread. The canola grown each year is now worth nearly 50% as much as Canada's entire annual wheat crop.

Growth of Prairie Cities 1971-1991

In recent decades, Census Metropolitan Areas (CMAs) in the Prairie Provinces have grown at a faster rate than those in other parts of Canada.

Percentage Increase in Population

- Calgary — 87.1
- Edmonton — 69.4
- Saskatoon — 66.7
- Vancouver — 48.2
- Toronto — 48.1
- Halifax — 43.9
- St. John's — 30.3
- Montreal — 14.0

Prairie CMAs | **Other Canadian CMAs**

Wheat Production by Province

The Prairie Provinces account for about 95% of Canada's wheat harvest each year.

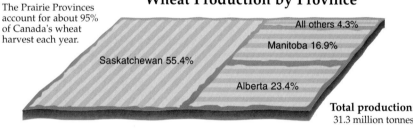

- All others 4.3%
- Manitoba 16.9%
- Saskatchewan 55.4%
- Alberta 23.4%

Total production: 31.3 million tonnes

Energy in the Prairie Provinces

Sources of Electrical Energy
Total production: 82 150 GW·h

- Fossil Fuels 65.1%
- Hydroelectric 34.9%

Uses of Electrical Energy
Total consumption: 76 187 GW·h

- Other 21.3%
- Residential 17.9%
- Commercial 27.1%
- Mining and Manufacturing 33.7%

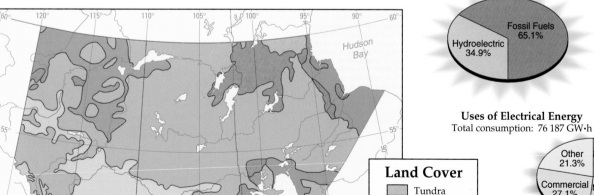

Land Cover

- Tundra
- Taiga
- Wetland
- Forest
- Ice
- Farmland
- Rangeland

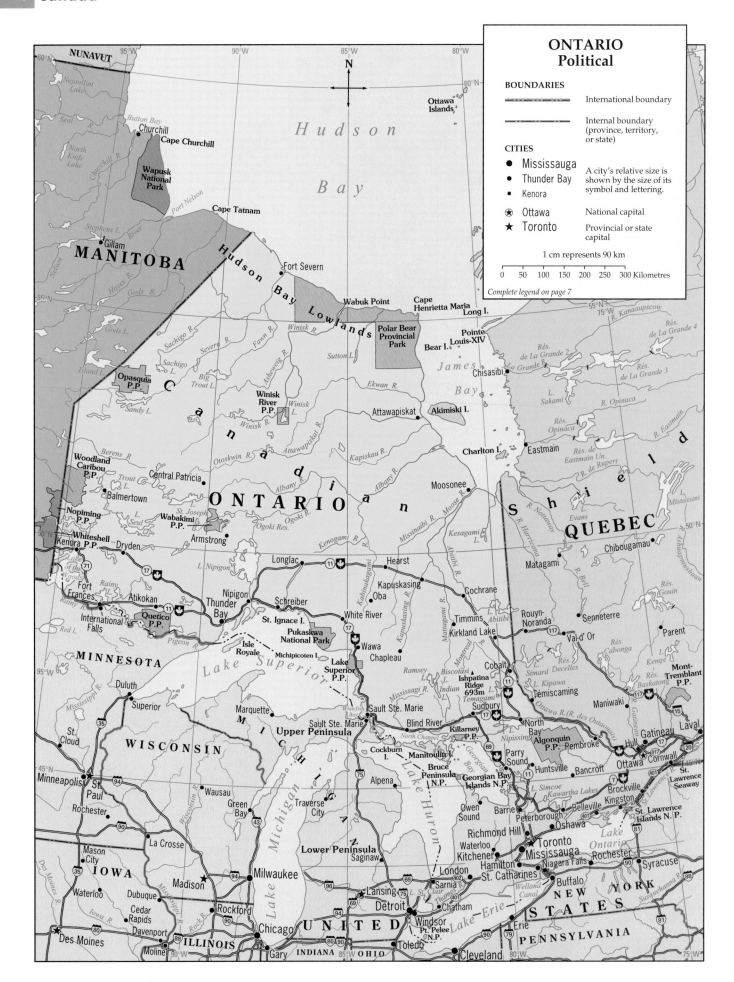

ONTARIO
Political

BOUNDARIES

International boundary

Internal boundary
(province, territory,
or state)

CITIES

● Mississauga

● Thunder Bay

• Kenora

A city's relative size is
shown by the size of its
symbol and lettering.

⊛ Ottawa — National capital

★ Toronto — Provincial or state
capital

1 cm represents 90 km

0 50 100 150 200 250 300 Kilometres

Complete legend on page 7

NUNAVUT

Nejanilini Lake

Seal R.

North Knife Lake

Churchill

Cape Churchill

Button Bay

Wapusk National Park

H u d s o n

B a y

Ottawa Islands

Cape Tatnam

Port Nelson

Stephens I.

Gillam

Nelson

MANITOBA

Hayes R.

Gods R.

Churchill R.

Fort Severn

Wabuk Point

Cape Henrietta Maria

Long I.

H u d s o n   B a y   L o w l a n d s

Polar Bear Provincial Park

Bear I.

Pointe Louis-XIV

R. Kanaaupscow

Rés. de La Grande 4

Gods L.

Island L.

Opasquia P.P.

Sachigo R.

Severn R.

Sachigo L.

Big Trout L.

Fawn R.

Asheweig R.

Winisk R.

Winisk River P.P.

Winisk L.

Sutton L.

Ekwan R.

Attawapiskat

Akimiski I.

J a m e s

B a y

Chisasibi

La Grande R.

Rés. de La Grande 2

Rés. de La Grande 3

L. Sakami

R. Opinaca

C

a

n

a

d

i

a

n

Sandy L.

Berens R.

Woodland Caribou P.P.

Trout L.

Central Patricia

Balmertown

Otoskwin R.

Albany R.

Kapiskau R.

Attawapiskat R.

Charlton I.

Eastmain

Rés. Opinaca

Rés. de Eastmain Un.

R. de Rupert

R. Eastmain

L. Mistassini

Nopiming P.P.

Whiteshell P.P.

Kenora

Lake of the Woods

Dryden

L. Seul

St. Joseph L.

Wabakimi P.P.

Ogoki Res.

Ogoki R.

Armstrong

ONTARIO

Albany R.

Kenogami R.

Missinabi R.

Moose R.

Moosonee

Kesagami L.

R. Nottaway

Evans L.

QUEBEC

Chibougamau

Matagami

R. Bell

Rés. Gouin

S h i e l d

Ashuapmushuan R.

Longlac

Hearst

L. Nipigon

Fort Frances

Rainy R.

Atikokan

Nipigon

Schreiber

Kapuskasing

Oba

Cochrane

Rouyn-Noranda

Senneterre

Parent

Red L.

International Falls

Quetico P.P.

11

17

71

Thunder Bay

St. Ignace I.

White River

Kabinakagami R.

Kapuskasing R.

Timmins

Kirkland Lake

Mattagami R.

Montreal R.

Val-d' Or

117

Rés. Cabonga

Rés. Kempt

MINNESOTA

Pigeon R.

Isle Royale

Pukaskwa National Park

Michipicoten I.

Wawa

Chapleau

Missisagi R.

Ramsey L.

Biscotasi L.

Kapuskasing R.

Cobalt

Rés. Simard Decelles

Mont-Tremblant P.P.

117

Duluth

Lake   S u p e r i o r

Lake Superior P.P.

Ishpatina Ridge 693m

Indian L.

L. Temagami

L. Abitibi

Témiscaming

L. Kipawa

Rés. Baskatong

15

Superior

Mississippi R.

Marquette

Sault Ste. Marie

Blind River

North Channel

Sudbury

North Bay

Algonquin P.P.

Ottawa R. (R. des Outaouais)

Maniwaki

Gatineau R.

35

St. Cloud

M

I

C

H

Whitefish Bay

Sault Ste. Marie

Upper Peninsula

Cockburn I.

Killarney P.P.

69

Parry Sound

L. Nipissing

Huntsville

Pembroke

Hull

Ottawa

Cornwall

17

417

20

WISCONSIN

I

G

A

75

Manitoulin I.

Bruce Peninsula N.P.

Georgian Bay

Georgian Bay Islands N.P.

Bancroft

7

Brockville

St. Lawrence Seaway

Minneapolis

St. Paul

94

Wausau

Alpena

69

Owen Sound

L. Simcoe

Kawartha Lakes

Barrie

Belleville

Kingston

St. Lawrence Islands N.P.

81

90

Rochester

Wisconsin R.

Green Bay

Traverse City

N

Georgian Bay

Peterborough

Oshawa

Richmond Hill

401

Lake Ontario

Rochester

43

La Crosse

Milwaukee

90

Mason City

35

IOWA

96

Saginaw

Lower Peninsula

Lake   M i c h i g a n

A

Waterloo

Kitchener

Hamilton

Toronto

Mississauga

Niagara Falls

Syracuse

90

Waterloo

Madison

94

Lansing

75

Thames R.

London

St. Catharines

Buffalo

Susquehanna R.

88

Dubuque

Cedar Rapids

Rockford

Rock R.

69

Detroit

Chatham

Welland Canal

Lake Erie

Erie

79

NEW YORK

Davenport

80

Des Moines

Iowa R.

Mississippi R.

Moline

ILLINOIS

88

Chicago

80 90

Gary

INDIANA

Rock R.

UNITED

Windsor

Pt. Pelee N.P.

L. St. Clair

401

Sarnia

STATES

Toledo

OHIO

90

Cleveland

PENNSYLVANIA

Des Moines

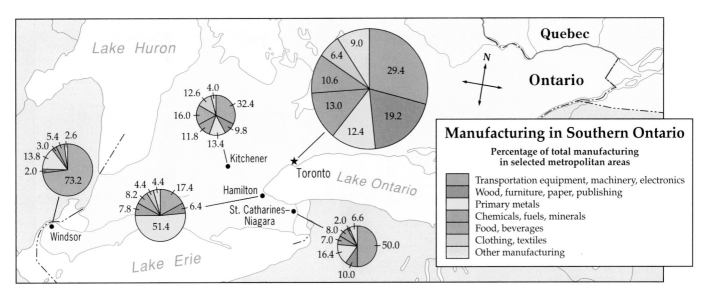

Manufacturing in Southern Ontario

Percentage of total manufacturing in selected metropolitan areas

- Transportation equipment, machinery, electronics
- Wood, furniture, paper, publishing
- Primary metals
- Chemicals, fuels, minerals
- Food, beverages
- Clothing, textiles
- Other manufacturing

Value of Manufacturing by Province

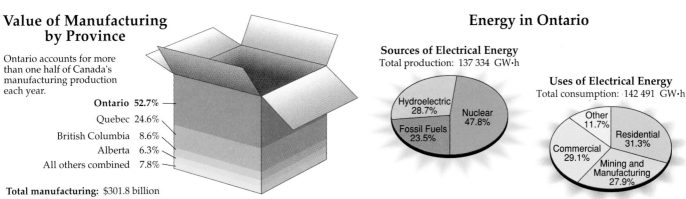

Ontario accounts for more than one half of Canada's manufacturing production each year.

Ontario	**52.7%**
Quebec	24.6%
British Columbia	8.6%
Alberta	6.3%
All others combined	7.8%

Total manufacturing: $301.8 billion

Energy in Ontario

Sources of Electrical Energy
Total production: 137 334 GW·h

- Hydroelectric 28.7%
- Nuclear 47.8%
- Fossil Fuels 23.5%

Uses of Electrical Energy
Total consumption: 142 491 GW·h

- Other 11.7%
- Residential 31.3%
- Commercial 29.1%
- Mining and Manufacturing 27.9%

Great Lakes and St. Lawrence Seaway

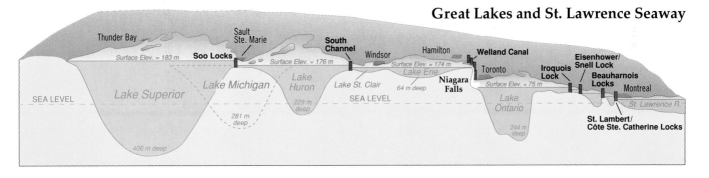

Thunder Bay — Sault Ste. Marie — Soo Locks — Surface Elev. = 183 m — South Channel — Windsor — Hamilton — Welland Canal — Toronto — Iroquois Lock — Eisenhower/Snell Lock — Beauharnois Locks — Montreal

Lake Superior — Lake Michigan — Lake Huron — Lake St. Clair — Lake Erie — Niagara Falls — Lake Ontario — St. Lawrence R.

Surface Elev. = 176 m — Surface Elev. = 174 m — 64 m deep — Surface Elev. = 75 m

SEA LEVEL

229 m deep — 281 m deep — 406 m deep — 244 m deep

St. Lambert/Côte Ste. Catherine Locks

Nearly 30% of all Canadian shipping occurs on the Great Lakes. The Soo Locks, between Ontario and Michigan at Sault Ste. Marie, permit freighters to reach Lake Superior from the lower Great Lakes.

Surface mines in the vicinity of Sudbury yield ore from one of the world's richest deposits of nickel.

85°W 80°W 75°W 70°W 65°W

QUEBEC Political

BOUNDARIES
International boundary
Internal boundary (province, territory, or state)

CITIES
● Montreal
● Longueuil
• Kuujjuaq
A city's relative size is shown by the size of its symbol and lettering.
⊛ Ottawa — National capital
★ Quebec — Provincial, territorial or state capital

1 cm represents 100 km
0 50 100 150 200 250 300 Kilometres
Complete legend on page 7

N U N A V U T

Southampton Island
Salisbury Island
Nottingham Island
Iqaluit
Baffin Island
Coats Island
Mansel Island
Salluit
Resolution Island
Ungava
Akpatok Island
Killiniq Island
Cape Chidley
Peninsula
Ottawa Islands
Povungnituk
60°N
Torngat Mts.

H u d s o n
Bay
Inukjuak
Ungava Bay
Mt. d'Iberville (Mt. Caubvick) 1652m
Sleeper Is.
King George Is.
Kuujjuaq
L. Payne
L. Minto
R. aux Feuilles
R. aux Mélèzes
R. Vachon
R. de Povungnituk

Belcher Islands
L. à l'Eau Claire
R. Caniapiscau
R. George
R. de la Baleine

Cape Henrietta Maria
Long I.
Kuujjuarapik
Grande R. de la Baleine
L. Bienville
55°N
Schefferville
Rigolet
L a b r a d o r
Polar Bear P.P.
Pointe Louis-XIV
R. Kanaaupscow
Smallwood Res.
Lake Melville
Mealy Mts.
Bear I.
Q U E B E C
Rès. de la Grande 2
Rès. de Cuniapiscau
Menihek Lakes
Churchill Falls
Vaskaupi R.
Eagle R.
Chisasibi
Grande R.
Rès. de la Grande 4
Ross Bay Junction
Twin Falls
Churchill Falls
Churchill R.
Happy Valley-Goose Bay
James
Akimiski I.
Rès. de la Grande 3
L. Opiscotéo
Labrador City
L. Brûlé
NEWFOUNDLAND
Bay
Rès. Opinaca
R. Opinaca
Eastmain
L. Sakami
L. Naococane
Ashuanipi L.
St. Augustin
Charlton I.
Rès. de Eastmain Un
R. Eastmain
Otish Mts.
R. Sainte-Marguerite

Moosonee
Rès. de Rupert
Gagnon
R. aux Outardes
R. Moisie
R. Magpie
R. Romaine
R. Natashquan
R. du Petit Mécatina
Moose R.
R. Broadback
R. Nottaway
L. Evans
L. Mistassini
R. Péribonka
Rès. Manouane
Rès. Manicouagan
Havre-Saint-Pierre
Kesagami L.
C a n a d i a n
Mingan Archipelago N.P. Reserve
Gros Morne National Park
Matagami
Chibougamau
Baie-Comeau
Sept-Îles
Anticosti Island
Corner Brook
Cochrane
Pointe des Monts
Chic-Choc Mts.
Stephenville
Timmins
Alma
Matane
Gaspé
Forillon N.P.
Newfoundland
Rouyn-Noranda
Senneterre
R. Pipmuacan
St-Jean
Saguenay R.
Gaspésie P.P.
Rimouski
Gulf of St. Lawrence
Channel-Port aux Basques
Val-d'Or
Rès. Gouin
Jonquière
Chicoutimi
Tadoussac
Gaspe Peninsula
Chandler
Cabot Strait
Cobalt
Parent
La Tuque
Rivière-du-Loup
Chaleur Bay
Campbellton
Madeleine Is.
Cape Breton Highlands N.P.
Rès. Cabonga
Beauport
Edmundston
Grand Falls
Bathurst
Témiscaming
Maniwaki
La Mauricie National Park
Charlesbourg
Montmagny
Sydney
North Bay
Mont-Tremblant P.P.
Joliette
Quebec
Trois-Rivières
NEW BRUNSWICK
Kouchibouguac N.P.
PRINCE EDWARD ISLAND
Charlottetown
Cape Breton Island
Parry Sound
Algonquin P.P.
Pembroke
Laval
Drummondville
Fredericton
Moncton
New Glasgow
Port Hawkesbury
Huntsville
ONTARIO
Oka
Longueuil
Granby
Sherbrooke
UNITED STATES
Saint John
Fundy N.P.
Truro
SCOTIA
Canso
Bancroft
Hull
Ottawa
Montreal
MAINE
Amherst
Halifax
Barrie
Brockville
Kingston
St. Lawrence Seaway
Mooshead L.
Grand Manan I.
Digby
Lunenburg
Sable I.
Richmond Hill
Peterborough
St. Lawrence Islands N.P.
Montpelier
NEW YORK
Augusta
NOVA
Kejimkujik National Park
Oshawa
Lake Ontario
VERMONT
NEW HAMPSHIRE
Yarmouth
ATLANTIC OCEAN
Toronto
Mississauga
Niagara Falls
Syracuse
Portland
Cape Sable
Buffalo
Concord

ATLANTIC OCEAN

Hydroelectric Energy

Capacity of generating station in megawatts

- 3 000 to 5 000
- 1 000 to 3 000
- 100 to 1 000
- Hydroelectric dam

Quebec's growing industrial strength is partly due to its hydroelectric power. High-voltage lines carry electricity from dams in the north to cities near the St. Lawrence River.

Manufacturing in Quebec

Percentage of total value	
21.8	Wood, furniture, paper, publishing
18.1	Transportation equipment, machinery, electronics
15.6	Chemicals, fuels, minerals
14.8	Metals
14.7	Food, beverages
10.6	Clothing, textiles
4.4	Other

Annual value:
$74.4 billion

Manufacturing in Quebec is not dominated by any one sector. As a result, the province has a more flexible economy.

Energy in Quebec

Sources of Electrical Energy
Total production: 142 204 GW·h

- Hydroelectric 96.2%
- Nuclear 2.9%
- Fossil Fuels 0.9%

Uses of Electrical Energy
Total consumption: 161 485 GW·h

- Other 18.1%
- Residential 29.6%
- Commercial 18.9%
- Mining and Manufacturing 33.4%

Ethnic Composition of Quebec

Quebec

- 2.7%
- 11.4%
- 7.1%
- 4.2%
- 74.6%

Remainder of Canada

- 5.3%
- 26.4%
- 18.1%
- 6.9%
- 43.3%

- French
- English
- Other European
- Asian
- Other, mixed

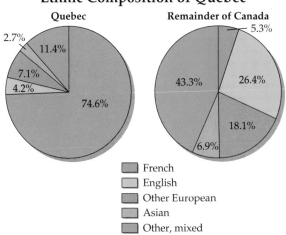

Founded in 1642, Montreal is one of the oldest and largest cities in Canada. Today Montreal remains a major financial centre and the principal city of French-speaking Canada.

ATLANTIC PROVINCES
Political

BOUNDARIES

International boundary

Internal boundary
(province or territory)

CITIES

● Laval — A city's relative size is shown by the size of its symbol and lettering.

● Sydney

★ St. John's — Provincial or territorial capital

1 cm represents 80 km

0   50   100   150   200   250   300 Kilometres

Complete legend on page 7

R. Vachon
R. aux Feuilles
R. aux Mélèzes
R. Caniapiscau

Akpatok Island
Killiniq Island
Cape Chidley

Ungava Bay

Torngat Mts.
Mt.Caubvick
(Mt. d'Iberville)
1652m

Labrador Sea

Kuujjuaq

R. George
R. à la Baleine

Hebron

QUEBEC

Nain
Fraser R.

Scheffervile

Rés. de Caniapiscau

Menihek Lakes

Smallwood Res.

Adlatok R.

Makkovik

Naskaupi R.

Labrador

Kanairiktok R.

Hamilton Inlet

Rigolet

Lake Melville

Mealy Mts.

Lake Opiscotéo

Churchill Falls
Churchill Falls
Twin Falls

Ross Bay Junction

Churchill R.

Shield

Happy Valley-Goose Bay

Eagle R.

ATLANTIC OCEAN

Labrador City

Lake Ashuanipi

Little Mecatina R.

Lake Brûlé

Canadian

NEWFOUNDLAND

Alexis R.

Port Hope Simpson

Otish Mts.

Gagnon

R. Ste-Marguerite

R. Moisie

R. Aguanish

R. Natashquan

R. Romaine

R. du Petit Mécatina

R. St-Augustin

R. St. Paul

St. Anthony

Rés. Manicouagan

R. aux Outardes

Sept-Îles

Havre-Saint-Pierre

Mingan Archipelago N.P. Reserve

Strait of Belle Isle

White Bay

Long Range Mts.

Baie-Comeau

Pointe des Monts

Anticosti Island

Gros Morne National Park

Notre Dame Bay

St. Lawrence River

Chic-Choc Mts.

Gaspé
Forillon N.P.
Gaspésie P.P.

Gulf of St. Lawrence

Windsor
Bay of Islands

Gander

Bonavista Bay

Matane

Rimouski

Gaspe Peninsula

Chaleur Bay

Chandler

Corner Brook

Grand Lake

Terra Nova National Park

Stephenville

Grand Falls

Campbellton
Mount Carleton P.P.
820m

Bathurst

Madeleine Islands

St. George's Bay

Long Range Mts.

Newfoundland

Clarenville

Trinity Bay

Edmundston

Grand Falls

Miramichi

NEW

Kouchibouguac N.P.

Cabot Strait

Lloyds R.

Conception Bay

Cape Spear
St. John's

St. John R.

**MAINE
(U.S.)**

Fredericton

BRUNSWICK

Miramichi R.

PRINCE EDWARD ISLAND

Cape Breton Highlands N.P.
532m

Channel-Port aux Basques

ST.-PIERRE AND MIQUELON (France)

Argentia
Avalon Peninsula

Fortune Bay

Placentia Bay

St. Mary's Bay

Cape Race

Moncton

Prince Edward Island N.P.

Charlottetown

St. Ann's Bay

Sydney
Cape Breton Island
Louisbourg

Amherst

Fundy N.P.

Northumberland Str.

Saint John

New Glasgow

Port Hawkesbury

Canso

Truro

SCOTIA

Sherbrooke

Bay of Fundy

Grand Manan I.
Digby

Kejimkujik National Park

NOVA

Dartmouth

Halifax

Lunenburg

L. Rossignol

Yarmouth

Shelburne

Sable I.

Cape Sable

Gulf of Maine

ATLANTIC OCEAN

Bras d'Or L.

Bonne Bay

N

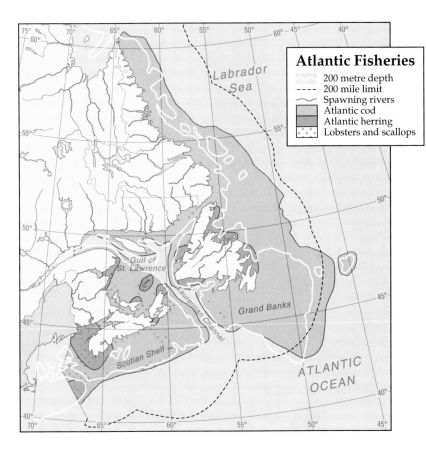

Atlantic Fisheries

〰〰	200 metre depth
- - -	200 mile limit
〜〜	Spawning rivers
▨	Atlantic cod
▦	Atlantic herring
⠿	Lobsters and scallops

Labrador Sea

Gulf of St. Lawrence

Laurentian Channel

Grand Banks

Scotian Shelf

ATLANTIC OCEAN

Productivity in the Atlantic Provinces

Geographic isolation helps diminish the value of goods and services produced in the Atlantic Provinces, measured as gross domestic product (GDP).

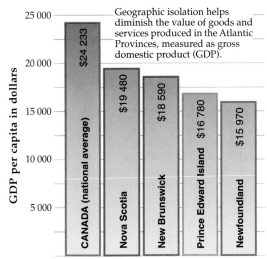

GDP per capita in dollars

- CANADA (national average) $24 233
- Nova Scotia $19 480
- New Brunswick $18 590
- Prince Edward Island $16 780
- Newfoundland $15 970

Recent drops in fish populations have led many fishing villages to adopt new ways to survive. Some attract tourists. Many others have turned to *aquaculture* (growing fish domestically, often in offshore enclosures).

Atlantic Cod

In July 1992, a sharp decline in stocks of cod led the Government of Canada to declare a two-year moratorium on the Atlantic cod fishery.

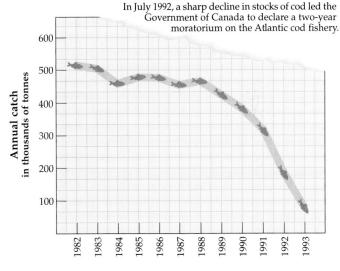

Annual catch in thousands of tonnes

(years 1982–1993)

Halifax is one of Canada's busiest cargo ports. Unlike most other eastern ports in Canada, it usually is free of ice and open to shipping all winter long.

Energy in the Atlantic Provinces

Sources of Electrical Energy
Total production: 62 539 GW·h

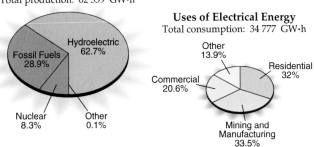

- Hydroelectric 62.7%
- Fossil Fuels 28.9%
- Nuclear 8.3%
- Other 0.1%

Uses of Electrical Energy
Total consumption: 34 777 GW·h

- Other 13.9%
- Residential 32%
- Commercial 20.6%
- Mining and Manufacturing 33.5%

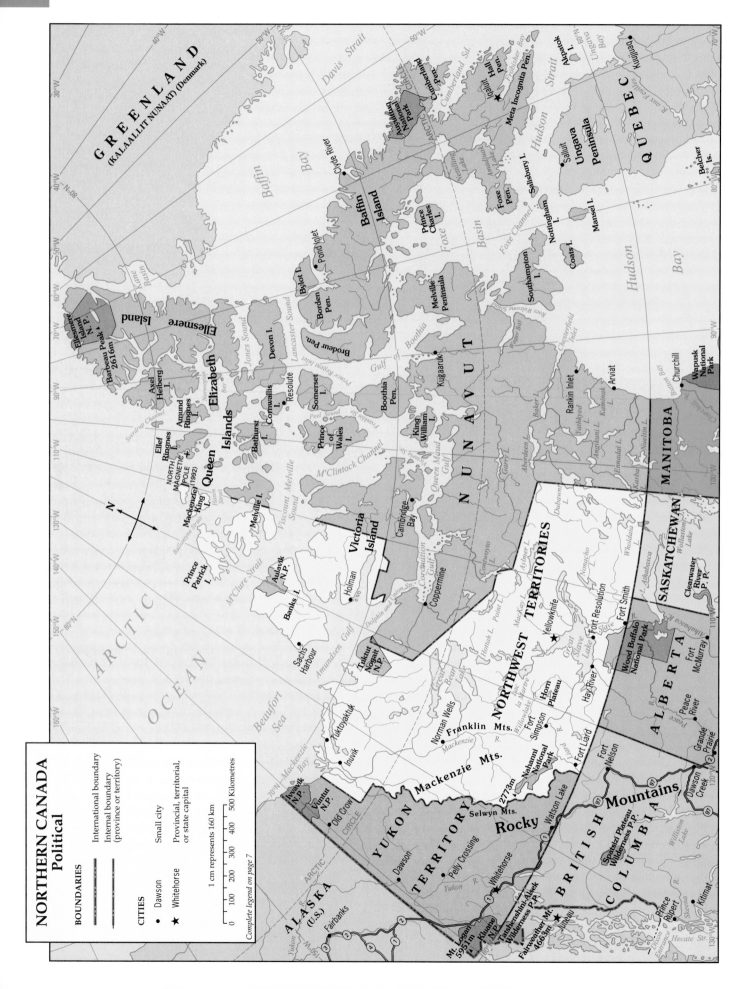

GREENLAND
(KALAALLIT NUNAAT) (Denmark)

Davis Strait

Baffin

Bay

Clyde River

Auyuittuq National Park

Cumberland Pen.

Igaluit Hall Pen.

Meta Incognita Pen.

Frobisher Bay

Hudson Strait

Akpatok I.

Ungava Bay

Kuujjuaq

QUEBEC

Saluit

Ungava Peninsula

Belcher Is.

Pond Inlet

Bylot I.

Borden Pen.

Baffin Island

Prince Charles I.

Foxe Pen.

Salisbury I.

Foxe Basin

Nottingham I.

Mansel I.

Hudson

Melville Peninsula

Coats I.

Southampton I.

Roes Welcome Sound

Bay

Devon I.

Lancaster Sound

Brodeur Pen.

Gulf of Boothia

Kugaaruk

Chesterfield Inlet

Churchill

Wapusk National Park

Ellesmere Island

Barbeau Peak 2616m

Ellesmere Island N. P.

Kane Basin

Jones Sound

Norwegian Bay

Axel Heiberg I.

Amund Ringnes I.

Queen Elizabeth Islands

Somerset I.

Boothia Pen.

NUNAVUT

Rankin Inlet

Arviat

Baker L.

Yathkyed L.

Kaminak L.

Angikuni L.

Ennadai L.

Nueltin L.

MANITOBA

Ellef Ringnes I.

NORTH MAGNETIC POLE (1992)

King Christian I.

Bathurst I.

Cornwallis I.

Resolute

Prince of Wales I.

King William I.

Queen Maud Gulf

Aberdeen L.

Garry L.

Wholdaia L.

SASKATCHEWAN

Wollaston Lake

Clearwater River P. P.

Mackenzie King I.

Hazen Strait

Melville I.

Viscount Melville Sound

M'Clintock Channel

Cambridge Bay

Contwoyto L.

Dubawnt L.

Victoria Island

Coronation Gulf

Coppermine

Point L.

MacKay L.

Aylmer L.

Nonacho L.

L. Athabasca

Fort Smith

Wood Buffalo National Park

ALBERTA

Fort McMurray

Peel Sound

Prince Regent Inlet

Franklin Str.

Dolphin and Union Str.

Holman

Aulavik N.P.

Banks I.

Prince Patrick I.

M'Clure Strait

Ballantyne Strait

Sverdrup Channel

Sachs Harbour

Amundsen Gulf

Tuktut Nogait N.P.

Yellowknife

Fort Resolution

Great Slave Lake

Hay River

Peace River

Grande Prairie

NORTHWEST TERRITORIES

Hottah L.

la Martre

Fort Simpson

Horn Plateau

Fort Liard

Fort Nelson

Dawson Creek

ARCTIC

OCEAN

Beaufort Sea

Mackenzie Bay

Tuktoyaktuk

Inuvik

Norman Wells

Franklin Mts.

Willowlake R.

Liard R.

Mackenzie R.

Great Bear Lake

Great Bear R.

Bear L.

Mackenzie Mts.

2773m

Nahanni National Park

Watson Lake

British Mountains

Ivvavik N.P.

Vuntut N.P.

Old Crow

Selwyn Mts.

YUKON TERRITORY

Pelly Crossing

Dawson

Whitehorse

Rocky

Williston Lake

Spatsizi Plateau Wilderness P.P.

Prince Rupert

BRITISH COLUMBIA

ALASKA (U.S.)

Fairbanks

Mt. Logan 5951m

Kluane N.P.

Tatshenshini-Alsek Wilderness P.P.

Mt. Fairweather 4663m

Juneau

Skeena R.

Kitimat

Hecate Str.

Yukon R.

N

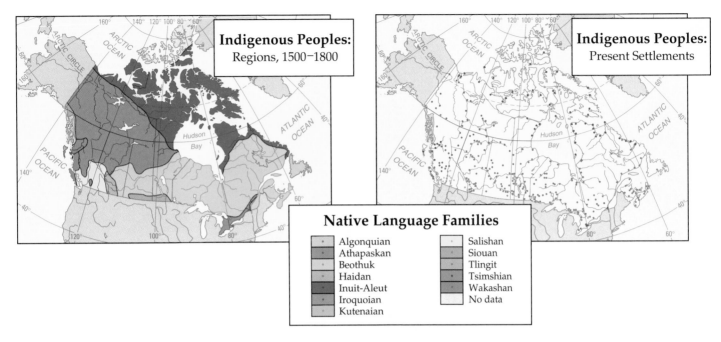

Indigenous Peoples:
Regions, 1500–1800

Indigenous Peoples:
Present Settlements

Native Language Families

- Algonquian
- Athapaskan
- Beothuk
- Haidan
- Inuit-Aleut
- Iroquoian
- Kutenaian
- Salishan
- Siouan
- Tlingit
- Tsimshian
- Wakashan
- No data

Tungsten and copper come from this mine in the western Northwest Territories. Other mines in Northern Canada yield gold, silver, uranium, lead, zinc, and cadmium.

Some Inuit continue in traditional occupations involving local natural resources. Even so, mechanized transportation, telecommunications, and modern dwellings have changed Inuit life greatly in recent decades.

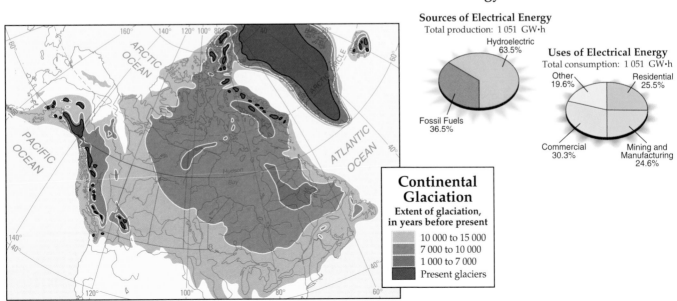

Energy in Northern Canada

Sources of Electrical Energy
Total production: 1 051 GW·h

Hydroelectric 63.5%
Fossil Fuels 36.5%

Uses of Electrical Energy
Total consumption: 1 051 GW·h

Other 19.6%
Residential 25.5%
Commercial 30.3%
Mining and Manufacturing 24.6%

Continental Glaciation
Extent of glaciation, in years before present

- 10 000 to 15 000
- 7 000 to 10 000
- 1 000 to 7 000
- Present glaciers

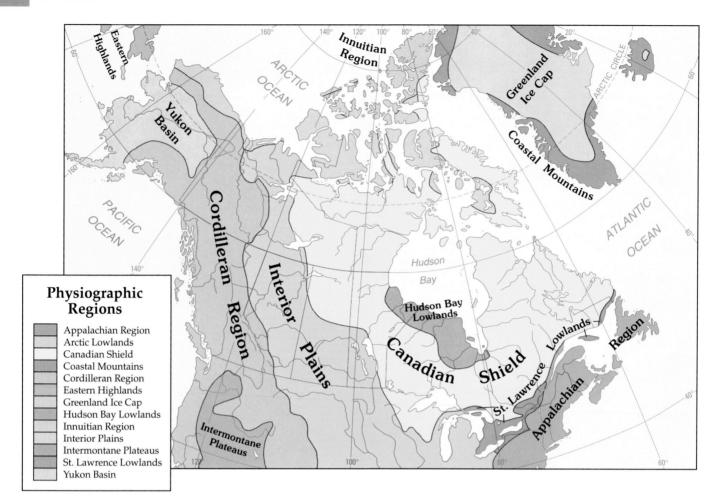

Physiographic Regions

- Appalachian Region
- Arctic Lowlands
- Canadian Shield
- Coastal Mountains
- Cordilleran Region
- Eastern Highlands
- Greenland Ice Cap
- Hudson Bay Lowlands
- Innuitian Region
- Interior Plains
- Intermontane Plateaus
- St. Lawrence Lowlands
- Yukon Basin

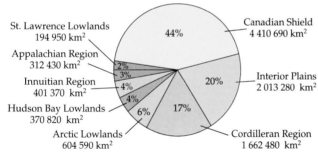

St. Lawrence Lowlands 194 950 km²

Appalachian Region 312 430 km²

Innuitian Region 401 370 km²

Hudson Bay Lowlands 370 820 km²

Arctic Lowlands 604 590 km²

Canadian Shield 4 410 690 km² — 44%

Interior Plains 2 013 280 km² — 20%

Cordilleran Region 1 662 480 km² — 17%

2% 3% 4% 4% 6%

Total Area of Canada: 9 970 610 km²

One of Canada's most level regions is the Hudson Bay Lowlands. It was part of the floor of Hudson Bay until the continent rose after being freed from the weight of glacial ice.

Cross Section of Canada

ELEVATION
Metres

- Over 3000
- 1500 to 3000
- 600 to 1500
- 300 to 600
- 150 to 300
- 0 to 150
- Below sea level

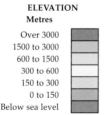

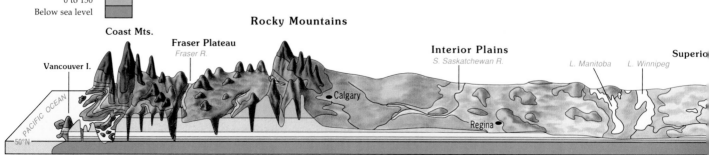

Vancouver I. — Coast Mts. — Fraser Plateau (Fraser R.) — Rocky Mountains — Interior Plains (S. Saskatchewan R.) — L. Manitoba — L. Winnipeg — Superior

Calgary — Regina

PACIFIC OCEAN — 50°N

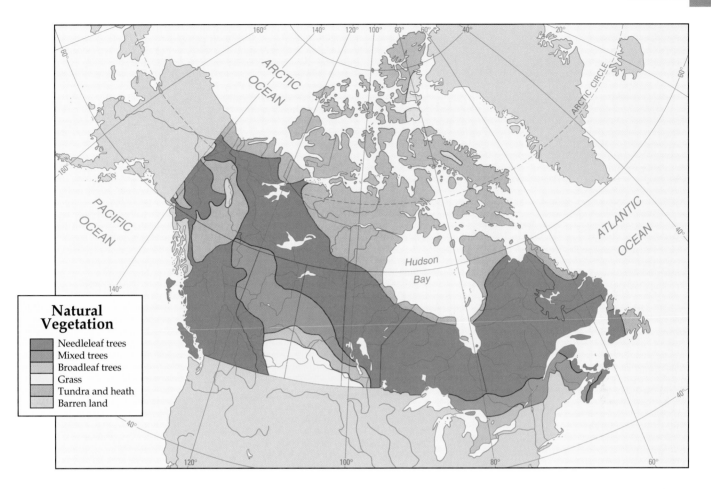

Natural Vegetation

- Needleleaf trees
- Mixed trees
- Broadleaf trees
- Grass
- Tundra and heath
- Barren land

Lake Superior, one of the Great Lakes, is located on the Canadian Shield. It is the world's largest body of fresh water.

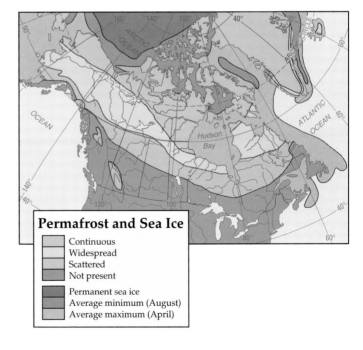

Permafrost and Sea Ice

- Continuous
- Widespread
- Scattered
- Not present

- Permanent sea ice
- Average minimum (August)
- Average maximum (April)

...plands
L. Nipigon

Canadian   Shield
Hudson Bay Lowlands
James Bay

Laurentide Scarp
R. Manicouagan

Newfoundland

Strait of Belle Isle

ATLANTIC OCEAN

50°N

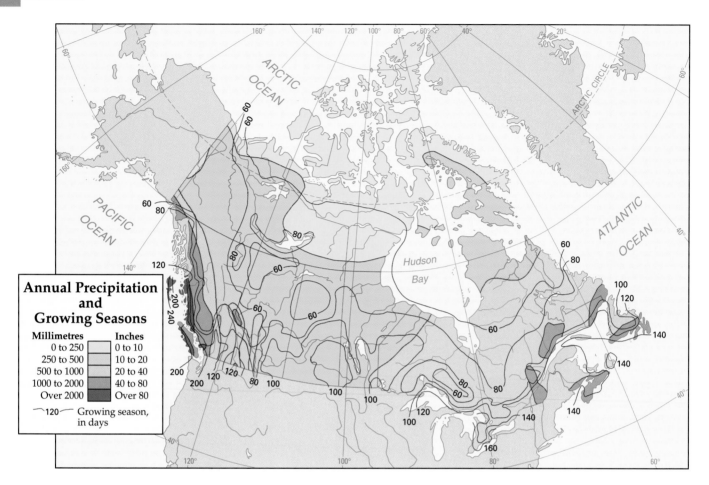

Annual Precipitation and Growing Seasons

Millimetres	Inches
0 to 250	0 to 10
250 to 500	10 to 20
500 to 1000	20 to 40
1000 to 2000	40 to 80
Over 2000	Over 80

—120— Growing season, in days

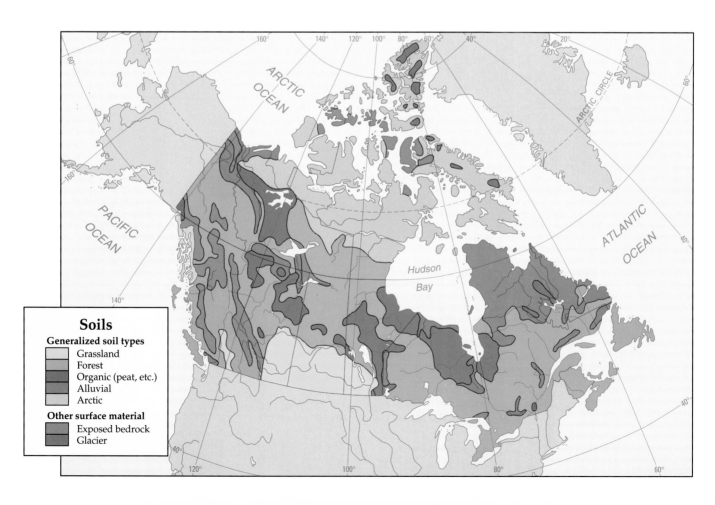

Soils

Generalized soil types

- Grassland
- Forest
- Organic (peat, etc.)
- Alluvial
- Arctic

Other surface material

- Exposed bedrock
- Glacier

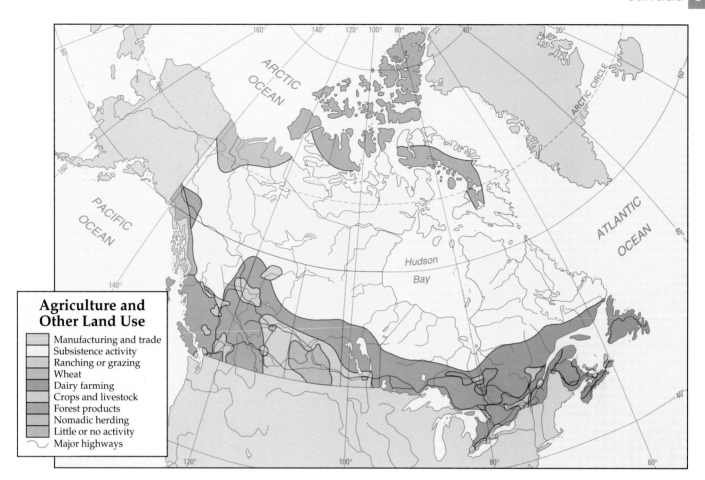

Agriculture and Other Land Use

- Manufacturing and trade
- Subsistence activity
- Ranching or grazing
- Wheat
- Dairy farming
- Crops and livestock
- Forest products
- Nomadic herding
- Little or no activity
- Major highways

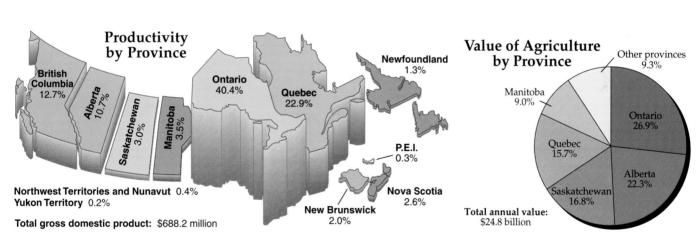

Productivity by Province

British Columbia 12.7%
Alberta 10.7%
Saskatchewan 3.0%
Manitoba 3.5%
Ontario 40.4%
Quebec 22.9%
Newfoundland 1.3%
P.E.I. 0.3%
Nova Scotia 2.6%
New Brunswick 2.0%

Northwest Territories and Nunavut 0.4%
Yukon Territory 0.2%

Total gross domestic product: $688.2 million

Value of Agriculture by Province

Other provinces 9.3%
Ontario 26.9%
Manitoba 9.0%
Quebec 15.7%
Alberta 22.3%
Saskatchewan 16.8%

Total annual value: $24.8 billion

Change in Canadian Farms

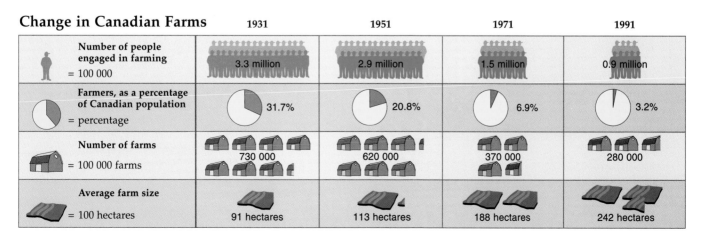

		1931	1951	1971	1991
Number of people engaged in farming = 100 000		3.3 million	2.9 million	1.5 million	0.9 million
Farmers, as a percentage of Canadian population = percentage		31.7%	20.8%	6.9%	3.2%
Number of farms = 100 000 farms		730 000	620 000	370 000	280 000
Average farm size = 100 hectares		91 hectares	113 hectares	188 hectares	242 hectares

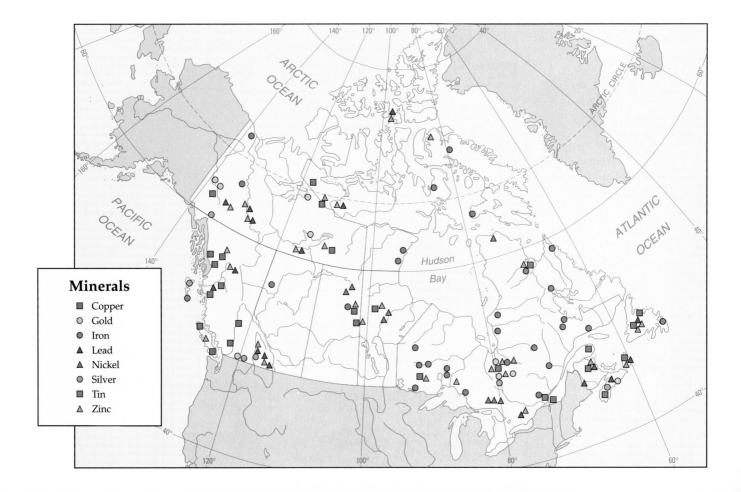

Energy Resources
Known reserves

- ■ Uranium
- ⬤ Coal
- ⬤ Oil (petroleum)
- ⬤ Natural gas
- — Oil pipeline
- — Natural gas pipeline

Minerals

- ■ Copper
- ⬤ Gold
- ⬤ Iron
- ▲ Lead
- ▲ Nickel
- ⬤ Silver
- ■ Tin
- ▲ Zinc

Economic Comparisons

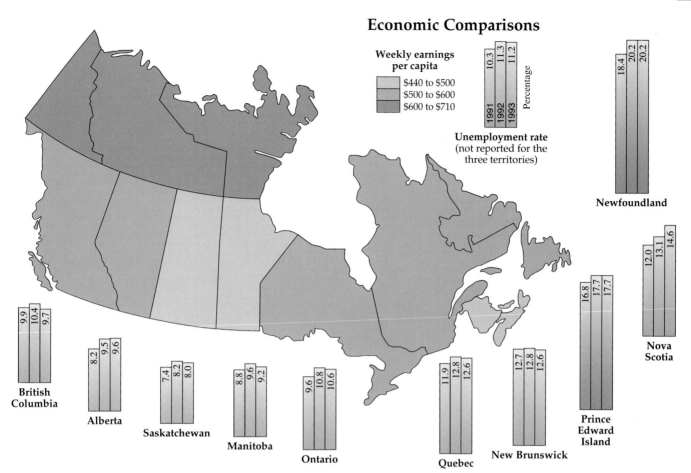

Weekly earnings
per capita

$440 to $500
$500 to $600
$600 to $710

Unemployment rate
(not reported for the
three territories)

1991 10.3
1992 11.3
1993 11.2

Percentage

Newfoundland 18.4 20.2 20.2

Nova Scotia 12.0 13.1 14.6

British Columbia 9.9 10.4 9.7

Alberta 8.2 9.5 9.6

Saskatchewan 7.4 8.2 8.0

Manitoba 8.8 9.6 9.2

Ontario 9.6 10.8 10.6

Quebec 11.9 12.8 12.6

New Brunswick 12.7 12.8 12.6

Prince Edward Island 16.8 17.7 17.7

Forestry Exports

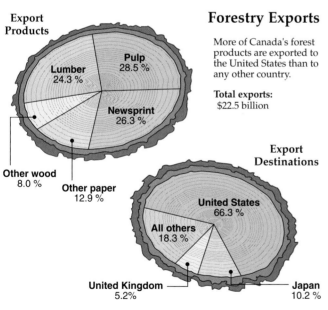

Export Products

Pulp 28.5 %
Lumber 24.3 %
Newsprint 26.3 %
Other wood 8.0 %
Other paper 12.9 %

More of Canada's forest
products are exported to
the United States than to
any other country.

Total exports:
$22.5 billion

Export Destinations

United States 66.3 %
All others 18.3 %
United Kingdom 5.2%
Japan 10.2 %

CANADA Balance of Trade

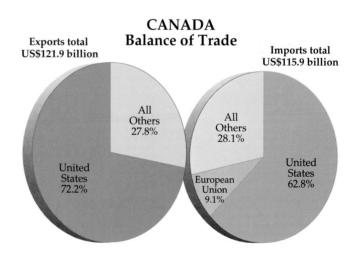

Exports total
US$121.9 billion

All Others 27.8%
United States 72.2%

Imports total
US$115.9 billion

All Others 28.1%
United States 62.8%
European Union 9.1%

Value of Mining by Region

Annual value:
$17.7 billion

Ontario 30.3%
Prairie Provinces 19.9%
British Columbia 16.2%
Quebec 16.2%
Others 17.4%

Export Destinations		Import Sources	
United States	72.2%	United States	62.8%
Japan	5.6%	Japan	6.8%
United Kingdom	2.3%	United Kingdom	3.4%
Germany	1.5%	Germany	2.7%
Italy	1.2%	France	1.7%
South Korea	1.1%	South Korea	1.7%
Netherlands	1.1%	Taiwan	1.5%
All others	15.0%	All others	19.4%

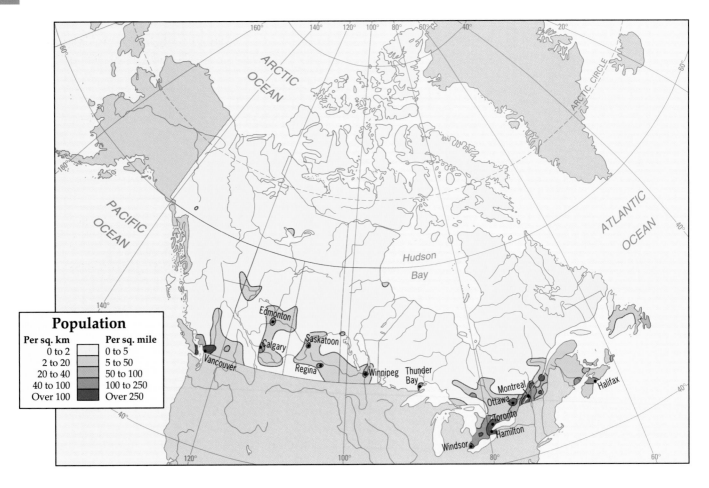

Population

Per sq. km	Per sq. mile
0 to 2	0 to 5
2 to 20	5 to 50
20 to 40	50 to 100
40 to 100	100 to 250
Over 100	Over 250

CANADA Urban Population

Canadian cities continue to grow, but the proportion of Canadians living in or near cities hardly changed between 1971 and 1991.

62% URBAN

1951
Total of 14 million

75% URBAN

1971
Total of 21.6 million

76% URBAN

1991
Total of 27.3 million

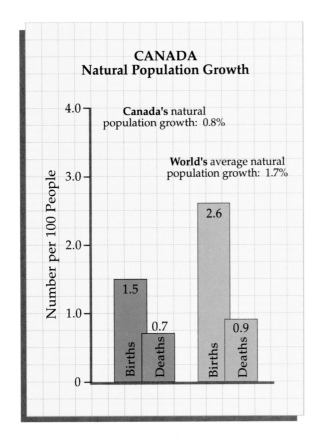

CANADA
Natural Population Growth

Canada's natural population growth: 0.8%

World's average natural population growth: 1.7%

Number per 100 People

4.0

3.0

2.0

2.6

1.5

1.0

0.7

0.9

0

Births | Deaths | Births | Deaths

Toronto dominates the cultural and economic life of Canada. Its growing metropolitan area now extends to the horizon and beyond.

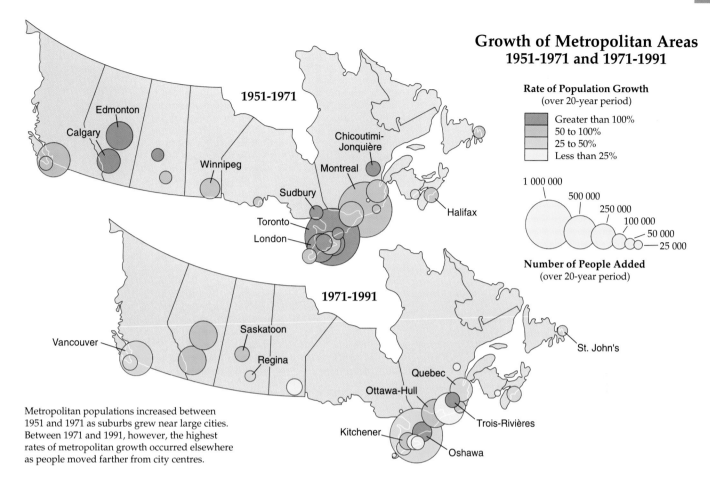

Growth of Metropolitan Areas
1951-1971 and 1971-1991

1951-1971

1971-1991

Rate of Population Growth
(over 20-year period)

Greater than 100%
50 to 100%
25 to 50%
Less than 25%

1 000 000
500 000
250 000
100 000
50 000
25 000

Number of People Added
(over 20-year period)

Metropolitan populations increased between 1951 and 1971 as suburbs grew near large cities. Between 1971 and 1991, however, the highest rates of metropolitan growth occurred elsewhere as people moved farther from city centres.

Metropolitan Toronto in 1931

1 cm represents 11 km
0   10   20   30 km

Metropolitan Toronto in 1951

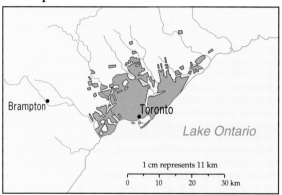

1 cm represents 11 km
0   10   20   30 km

Metropolitan Toronto in 1971

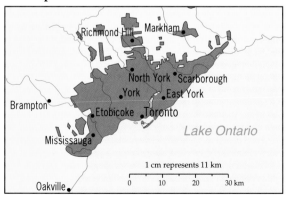

1 cm represents 11 km
0   10   20   30 km

Metropolitan Toronto in 1998

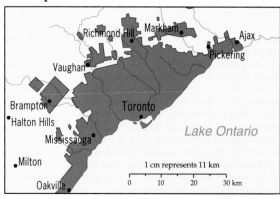

1 cm represents 11 km
0   10   20   30 km

Urbanization

• Cities, and towns with 30 000 residents or more

■ Extent of Toronto's metropolitan area

Since World War II, growth of metropolitan areas has occurred away from central cities. Outlying towns and rural land have been transformed by new residential and business development.

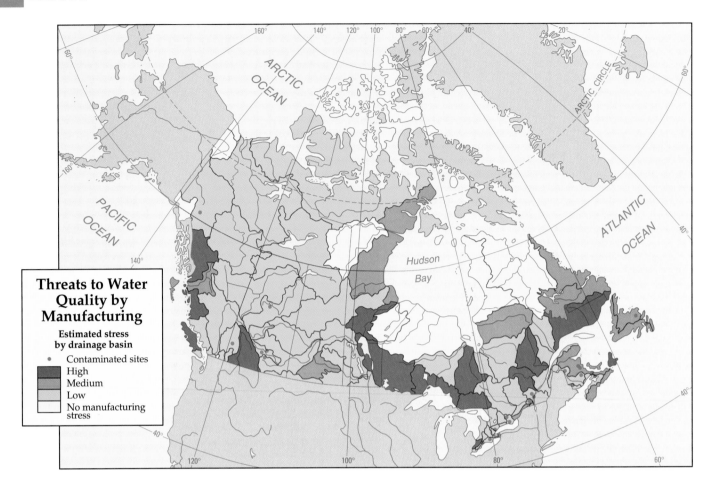

Threats to Water Quality by Manufacturing

Estimated stress by drainage basin

- Contaminated sites
- High
- Medium
- Low
- No manufacturing stress

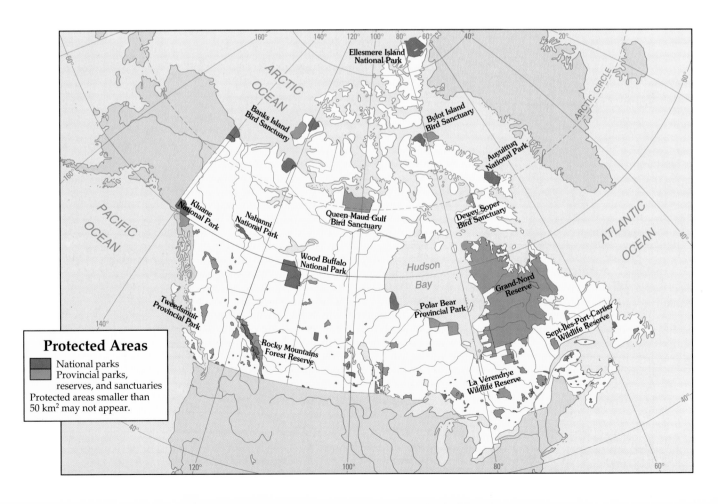

Ellesmere Island National Park

Banks Island Bird Sanctuary

Bylot Island Bird Sanctuary

Auyuittuq National Park

Kluane National Park

Nahanni National Park

Queen Maud Gulf Bird Sanctuary

Dewey Soper Bird Sanctuary

Wood Buffalo National Park

Grand-Nord Reserve

Tweedsmuir Provincial Park

Polar Bear Provincial Park

Sept-Îles-Port-Cartier Wildlife Reserve

Rocky Mountains Forest Reserve

La Vérendrye Wildlife Reserve

Protected Areas

- National parks
- Provincial parks, reserves, and sanctuaries

Protected areas smaller than 50 km^2 may not appear.

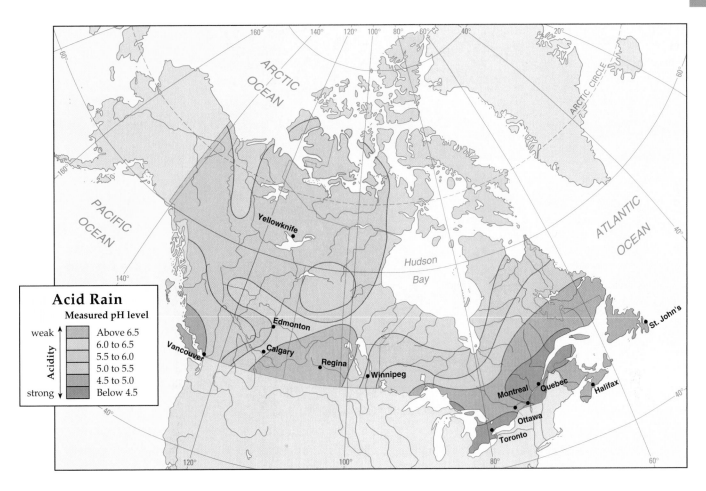

Acid Rain

Measured pH level

weak — Acidity — strong

Above 6.5	
6.0 to 6.5	
5.5 to 6.0	
5.0 to 5.5	
4.5 to 5.0	
Below 4.5	

Domestic Water Use

In Canada, a family of four uses 1360 litres of water indoors each day. Only 70 litres, or 5 percent, are used for preparing food or drinking.

Flushing toilet: 610 L — 45%

Brushing teeth and bathing: 410 L — 30%

Laundering clothes: 270 L — 20%

Drinking and kitchen uses: 70 L — 5%

Sulphur Dioxide Emissions

Emissions of sulphur dioxide (SO_2), a major source of acid rain in Canada, come mostly from the United States. Both countries have successfully reduced emissions since 1970.

Thousands of metric tonnes of SO_2 per year

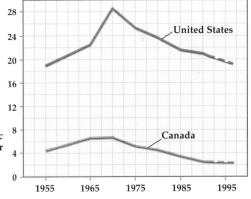

United States

Canada

The future of the Beaufort Sea beluga whale is uncertain, and the St. Lawrence beluga is endangered. Many other marine mammals have been threatened and even made extinct by hunting and by degradation of habitat.

Success in convincing consumers to recycle aluminum beverage cans has helped establish public awareness of the need to use resources responsibly.

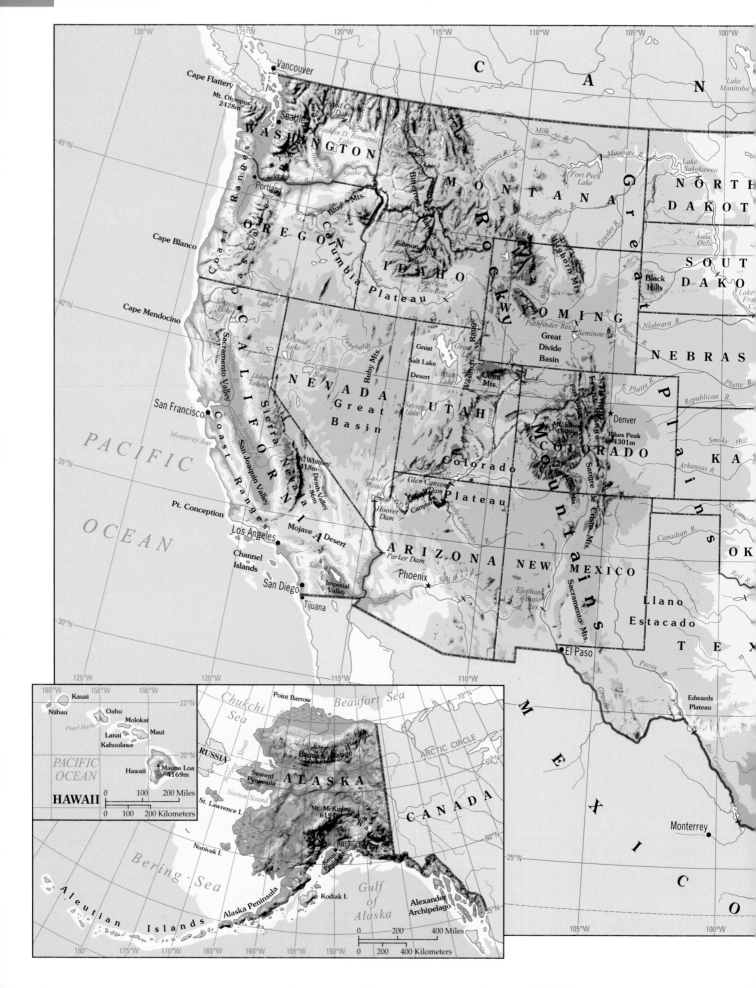

C A N A D A

Lake Manitoba

Vancouver

Cape Flattery
Mt. Olympus
2428m

Strait of Juan de Fuca

Seattle

W A S H I N G T O N

Grand Coulee Dam

Franklin D. Roosevelt Lake

Columbia R.

Portland

Snake R.

Blue Mts.

M O N T A N A

Milk R.

Missouri R.

Fort Peck Lake

Lake Sakakawea

N O R T H D A K O T

Cape Blanco

O R E G O N

Columbia Plateau

Bitterroot Range

Salmon River

I D A H O

Salmon River Mts.

American Falls Res.

Snake R.

Yellowstone R.

Bighorn R.

Bighorn Mts.

Powder R.

Lake Oahe

S O U T H D A K O

Black Hills

Cape Mendocino

Shasta Lake

Goose Lake

Pyramid Lake

Humboldt R.

Great Salt Lake Desert

Great Salt Lake

Utah Lake

Wasatch Range

Uinta Mts.

Pathfinder Res.

Seminoe Res.

W Y O M I N G

Great Divide Basin

Platte R.

Niobrara R.

N E B R A S

P A C I F I C

Sacramento Valley

Lake Tahoe

Carson Sink

N E V A D A

Great Basin

Ruby Mts.

Sevier Lake

U T A H

Green R.

C O L O R A D O

Park Range

Mt. Elbert 4399m

Front Range

Denver

Pikes Peak 4301m

S. Platte R.

Republican R.

Platte R.

Smoky Hill

K A

San Francisco

Monterey Bay

Coast Ranges

Sierra Nevada

San Joaquin Valley

C A L I F O R N I A

Mt. Whitney 4418m

Death Valley -86m

Lake Mead

Colorado Plateau

Glen Canyon Dam

Grand Canyon

Colorado R.

Little Colorado R.

Sangre de Cristo Mts.

M O U N T A I N S

Arkansas R.

Canadian R.

N. Canadian R.

O K

Pt. Conception

Los Angeles

Channel Islands

San Diego

Tijuana

Mojave Desert

Salton Sea

Imperial Valley

Hoover Dam

Parker Dam

Colorado R.

A R I Z O N A

Gila R.

Phoenix

Salt R.

N E W M E X I C O

Elephant Butte Res.

Sacramento Mts.

Llano Estacado

Pecos R.

T E X

El Paso

Rio Grande

M E X I C O

Edwards Plateau

Monterrey

Point Barrow

Chukchi Sea

Beaufort Sea

RUSSIA

Bering Strait

Brooks Range

ARCTIC CIRCLE

Seward Peninsula

Norton Sound

St. Lawrence I.

A L A S K A

CANADA

Nunivak I.

Mt. McKinley 6194m

Alaska Range

Anchorage

Kenai Peninsula

Bering Sea

Kodiak I.

Gulf of Alaska

Alexander Archipelago

Alaska Peninsula

A l e u t i a n   I s l a n d s

0   200   400 Miles
0   200   400 Kilometers

UNITED STATES
Physical

International boundary
State boundary
⊛ Washington, D.C. — National capital
★ Atlanta — State capital
● Detroit — Major city

ELEVATION

Meters		Feet
Over 3000		Over 10,000
1500 to 3000		5,000 to 10,000
600 to 1500		2,000 to 5,000
300 to 600		1,000 to 2,000
150 to 300		500 to 1,000
0 to 150		0 to 500
Below sea level		Below sea level

WATER DEPTH

Less than 200		Less than 600
Greater than 200		Greater than 600

0   100   200   300 Miles
0   100   200   300 Kilometers

Complete legend on page 7

CANADA

Calgary

Vancouver
Bellingham
Olympia • Seattle • Spokane
Tacoma
WASHINGTON
Astoria • Vancouver
Portland
Salem
Eugene • OREGON
Coos Bay
Medford • Klamath Falls

Moscow
Lewiston
Walla Walla
Pendleton
Baker
Ontario
IDAHO
Boise
Twin Falls
Idaho Falls
Pocatello

Missoula
MONTANA
Butte • Helena
Great Falls
Billings

Calgary
Minot
NORTH DAKOTA
Bismarck

WYOMING
Sheridan
Casper
Rock Springs
Laramie • Cheyenne

SOUTH DAKOTA
Rapid City • Pierre
Aberdeen

NEBRASKA
North Platte
Grand Is

Eureka
Shasta Lake
Goose Lake
Winnemucca
Pyramid Lake
Reno • Carson Sink
Carson City
Sacramento
Oakland
San Francisco
San Jose
Monterey Bay
Monterey
Fresno
Bakersfield
Santa Barbara
Los Angeles • Pasadena
Long Beach • San Bernardino
Riverside
San Diego
Tijuana

NEVADA
Elko
Humboldt R.
Lake Tahoe
CALIFORNIA
San Joaquin R.

Great Salt Lake
Ogden
Salt Lake City
Provo
Utah Lake
UTAH
Sevier Lake
Lake Powell

Fort Collins
Boulder • Greeley
Denver
Grand Junction
Moab
COLORADO
Colorado Springs
Pueblo
Durango • Trinidad

KANSAS
Goodland
Dodge City

PACIFIC OCEAN

Las Vegas
Lake Mead
Boulder City
Salton Sea
Yuma
ARIZONA
Phoenix
Tucson
Nogales
Nogales

Flagstaff
Prescott
Gallup
NEW MEXICO
Albuquerque
Santa Fe
Silver City
Las Cruces
Roswell
Carlsbad
El Paso
Juarez

Amarillo
Lubbock
TEXAS
Abilene
Brownwood

MEXICO

San Antonio
Del Rio
Laredo
Nuevo Laredo
Monterrey

Rio Grande
Pecos R.

HAWAII
Lihue
Honolulu
Wailuku
Hilo
Pahala
PACIFIC OCEAN
0 100 200 Miles
0 100 200 Kilometers

INTERNATIONAL DATE LINE

Chukchi Sea
Beaufort Sea
Prudhoe Bay
RUSSIA
Kotzebue
Nome
ALASKA
Bethel
Fairbanks
Anchorage
Valdez
Seward
Kodiak
Dutch Harbor
Bering Sea
Yukon R.
Kuskokwim R.
Norton Sound
Gulf of Alaska
Sitka
Juneau
CANADA
ARCTIC CIRCLE

0 200 400 Miles
0 200 400 Kilometers

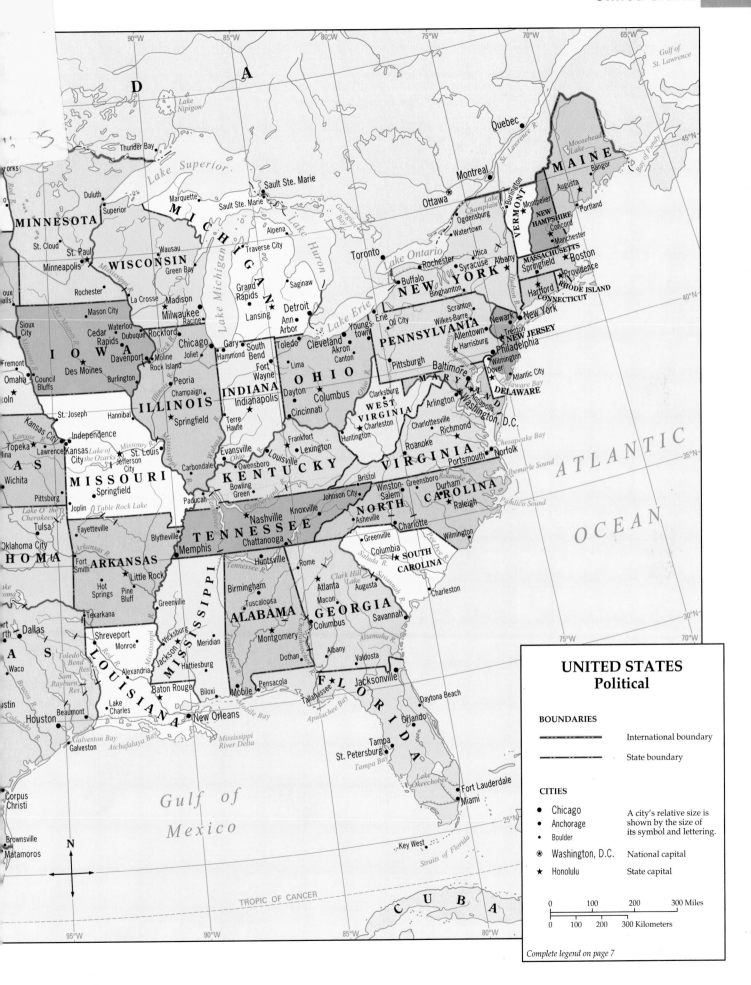

UNITED STATES
Political

BOUNDARIES

———————— International boundary

———————— State boundary

CITIES

● Chicago

● Anchorage

• Boulder

A city's relative size is shown by the size of its symbol and lettering.

⊗ Washington, D.C.   National capital

★ Honolulu   State capital

0   100   200   300 Miles

0 100   200 300 Kilometers

Complete legend on page 7

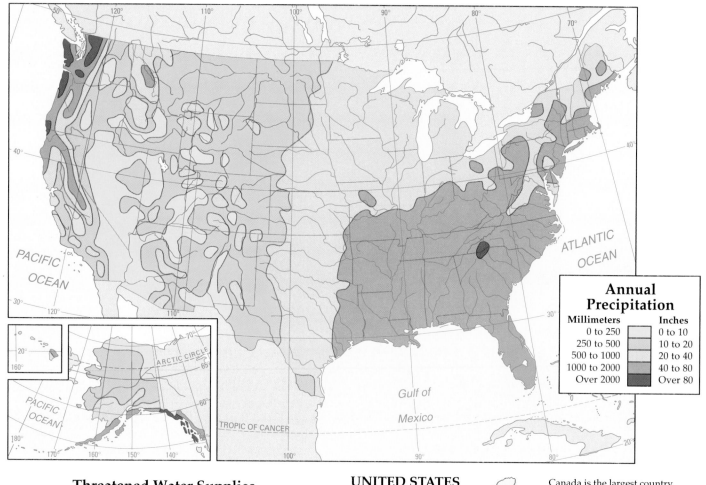

Annual Precipitation

Millimeters		Inches
0 to 250		0 to 10
250 to 500		10 to 20
500 to 1000		20 to 40
1000 to 2000		40 to 80
Over 2000		Over 80

Threatened Water Supplies

Rivers and aquifers in the arid regions of the West and Great Plains are being drained to supply water for farm and ranch irrigation, hydroelectric plants, flood-control dams, and industrial and residential needs.

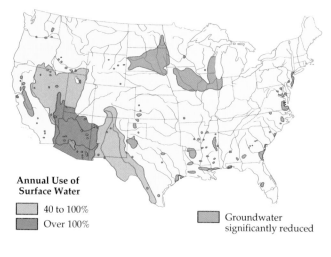

Annual Use of Surface Water

- 40 to 100%
- Over 100%
- Groundwater significantly reduced

UNITED STATES Area Comparison

Canada is the largest country in the Western Hemisphere. It extends farther from east to west and from north to south than the 48 contiguous states of the United States.

Contiguous U.S.	7 825 112 km²
Canada	9 970 610 km²

Cross Section of the United States

ELEVATION		
Meters		**Feet**
Over 3000		Over 10,000
1500 to 3000		5,000 to 10,000
600 to 1500		2,000 to 5,000
300 to 600		1,000 to 2,000
150 to 300		500 to 1,000
0 to 150		0 to 500
Below sea level		Below sea level

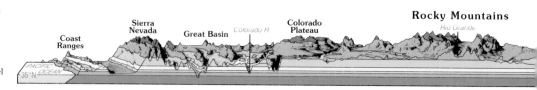

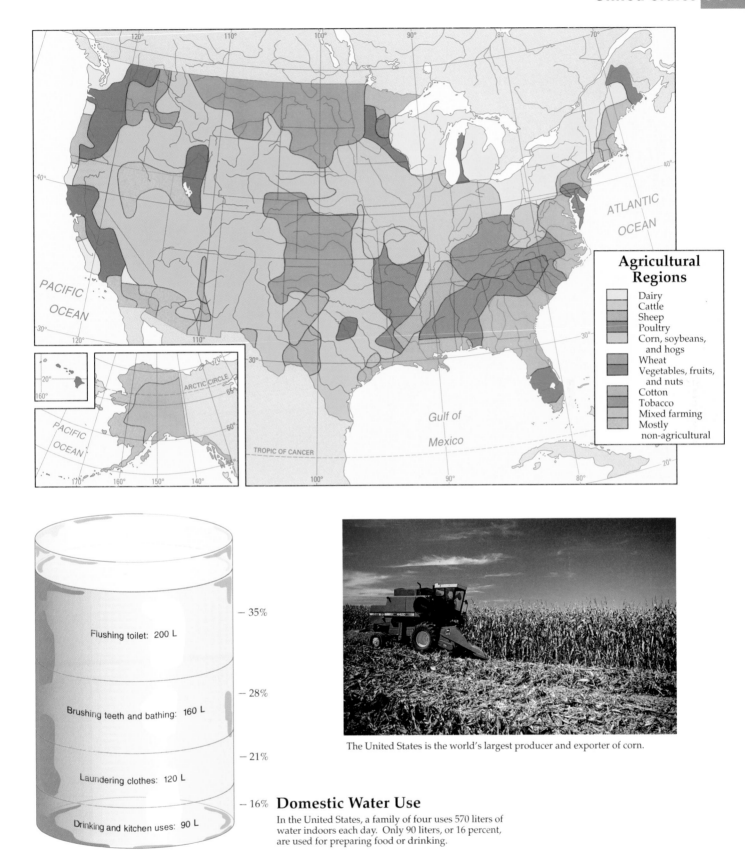

Agricultural Regions

- Dairy
- Cattle
- Sheep
- Poultry
- Corn, soybeans, and hogs
- Wheat
- Vegetables, fruits, and nuts
- Cotton
- Tobacco
- Mixed farming
- Mostly non-agricultural

PACIFIC OCEAN

ATLANTIC OCEAN

Gulf of Mexico

TROPIC OF CANCER

ARCTIC CIRCLE

Flushing toilet: 200 L — 35%

Brushing teeth and bathing: 160 L — 28%

Laundering clothes: 120 L — 21%

Drinking and kitchen uses: 90 L — 16%

The United States is the world's largest producer and exporter of corn.

Domestic Water Use

In the United States, a family of four uses 570 liters of water indoors each day. Only 90 liters, or 16 percent, are used for preparing food or drinking.

Great Plains | Ozark Plateau | Central Lowland — Mississippi R. — Tennessee R. | Appalachian Mountains | Atlantic Coastal Plain

ATLANTIC OCEAN — 35°N

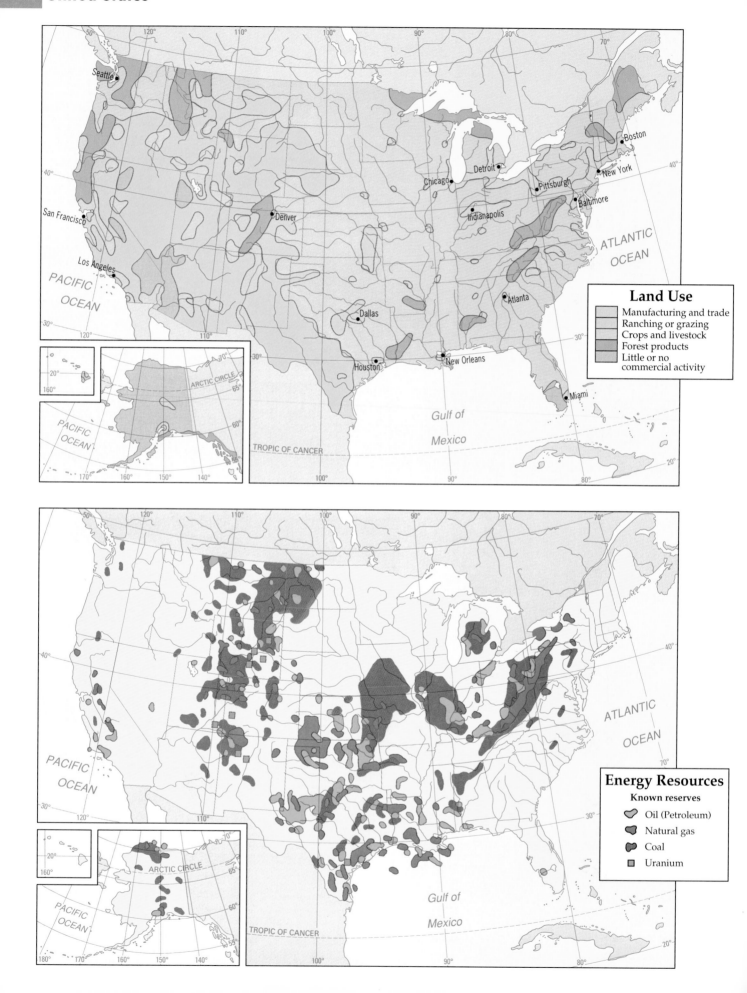

Land Use

- Manufacturing and trade
- Ranching or grazing
- Crops and livestock
- Forest products
- Little or no commercial activity

Energy Resources

Known reserves

- Oil (Petroleum)
- Natural gas
- Coal
- Uranium

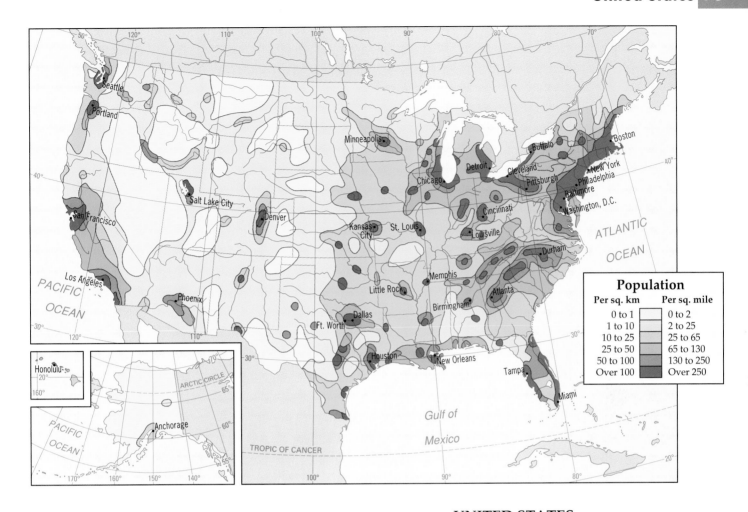

Population

Per sq. km	Per sq. mile
0 to 1	0 to 2
1 to 10	2 to 25
10 to 25	25 to 65
25 to 50	65 to 130
50 to 100	130 to 250
Over 100	Over 250

UNITED STATES
Natural Population Growth

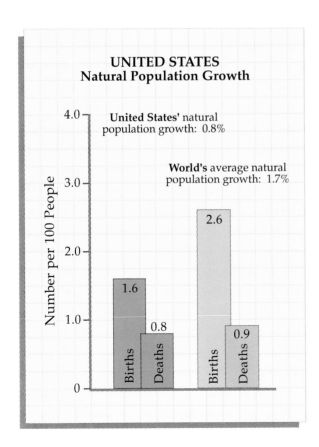

United States' natural population growth: 0.8%

World's average natural population growth: 1.7%

Number per 100 People

- Births 1.6
- Deaths 0.8
- Births 2.6
- Deaths 0.9

UNITED STATES
Balance of Trade

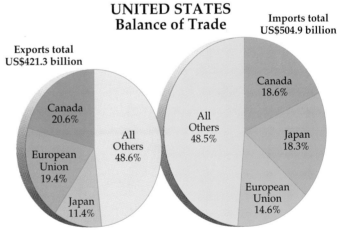

Exports total US$421.3 billion

- Canada 20.6%
- European Union 19.4%
- Japan 11.4%
- All Others 48.6%

Imports total US$504.9 billion

- Canada 18.6%
- Japan 18.3%
- European Union 14.6%
- All Others 48.5%

New York City, with a metropolitan population of more than 16 million people, is the largest city in the United States. It is the country's leading centre of finance, trade, telecommunications, and the arts.

**CENTRAL AMERICA
AND CARIBBEAN SEA
Physical**

⊛ Havana	International boundary
⊛ Havana	National capital
● Monterrey	Major city

ELEVATION

Meters		Feet
Over 3000		Over 10,000
1500 to 3000		5,000 to 10,000
600 to 1500		2,000 to 5,000
300 to 600		1,000 to 2,000
150 to 300		500 to 1,000
0 to 150		0 to 500

WATER DEPTH

Less than 200		Less than 600
Greater than 200		Greater than 600

0   100   200   300   400 Miles
0   100   200   300   400 Kilometers

Complete legend on page 7

UNITED STATES

NORTH AMERICA

Los Angeles

Guadalupe I.

Angel de
la Guardia I.

Cedros I.

Tiburon I.

Cape
Eugenia

TROPIC OF CANCER

Santa
Margarita I.

San Jose I.

Cape San Lucas

Tres Marias Is.

Cape Corrientes

Revillagigedo Is.

PACIFIC

OCEAN

Colorado R.

Gulf
Sea

Gulf of
California
(Cortes)

Sebastian
Vizcaino Bay

Rio Grande

Sierra Madre Occidental

Sierra Madre Oriental

Plateau
of
Mexico

MEXICO

Monterrey

Houston

New Orleans

Amistad
Res.

Rio Grande

GULF   OF

MEXICO

Madre
Lagoon

Cape Rojo

Bay of
Campeche

Yucatan

Peninsula

Terminos
Lagoon

L. Chapala

Paricutin
Volcano
2808m

Popocatepetl
Volcano
5452m

Mexico City

Orizaba
5700m

Lerma R.

Miguel
Aleman Res.

Sierra Madre del Sur

Acapulco

Gulf of
Tehuantepec

Isthmus of
Tehuantepec

El Chicon
1060m

GUATEMALA

Tajumulco
4211m

Guatemala
City

EL SALVADOR

Gulf of
Fonse

BEL

N

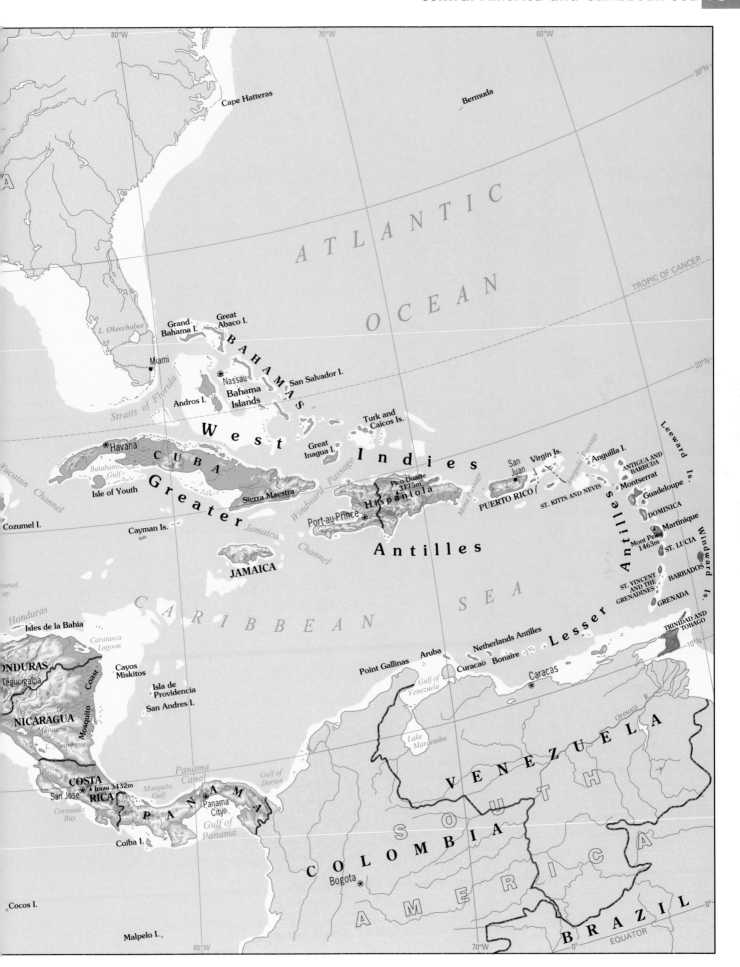

ATLANTIC

OCEAN

TROPIC OF CANCER

Cape Hatteras

Bermuda

L. Okeechobee

Grand Bahama I.

Great Abaco I.

B A H A M A S

Miami

Nassau

San Salvador I.

Andros I.

Bahama Islands

W e s t

Straits of Florida

Yucatan Channel

Havana

C U B A

Batabano Gulf

Isle of Youth

Sierra Maestra

G r e a t e r

Cozumel I.

Cayman Is.

Jamaica Channel

JAMAICA

Turk and Caicos Is.

Great Inagua I.

I n d i e s

Windward Passage

Hispaniola

Pico Duarte 3175m

Port-au-Prince

A n t i l l e s

San Juan

Virgin Is.

Mona Passage

PUERTO RICO

Anegada Passage

Anguilla I.

ANTIGUA AND BARBUDA

Montserrat

ST. KITTS AND NEVIS

Guadeloupe

DOMINICA

Mont Pelée 1463m

Martinique

ST. LUCIA

ST. VINCENT AND THE GRENADINES

BARBADOS

GRENADA

Leeward Is.

L e s s e r

A n t i l l e s

Windward Is.

TRINIDAD AND TOBAGO

C A R I B B E A N

S E A

Honduras

Isles de la Bahia

Caratasca Lagoon

Cayos Miskitos

ONDURAS

Tegucigalpa

Mosquito Coast

NICARAGUA

Managua

L. Nicaragua

San Juan R.

Isla de Providencia

San Andres I.

Point Gallinas

Aruba

Netherlands Antilles

Curacao

Bonaire

Caracas

Gulf of Venezuela

Lake Maracaibo

V E N E Z U E L A

Orinoco R.

COSTA

Irazu 3432m

San Jose

RICA

Coronada Bay

Mosquito Gulf

P A N A M A

Panama Canal

Panama City

Gulf of Darien

Gulf of Panama

Coiba I.

C O L O M B I A

S

O

U

T

H

A

M

E

R

I

C

A

Cocos I.

Bogota

Malpelo I.

EQUATOR

B R A Z I L

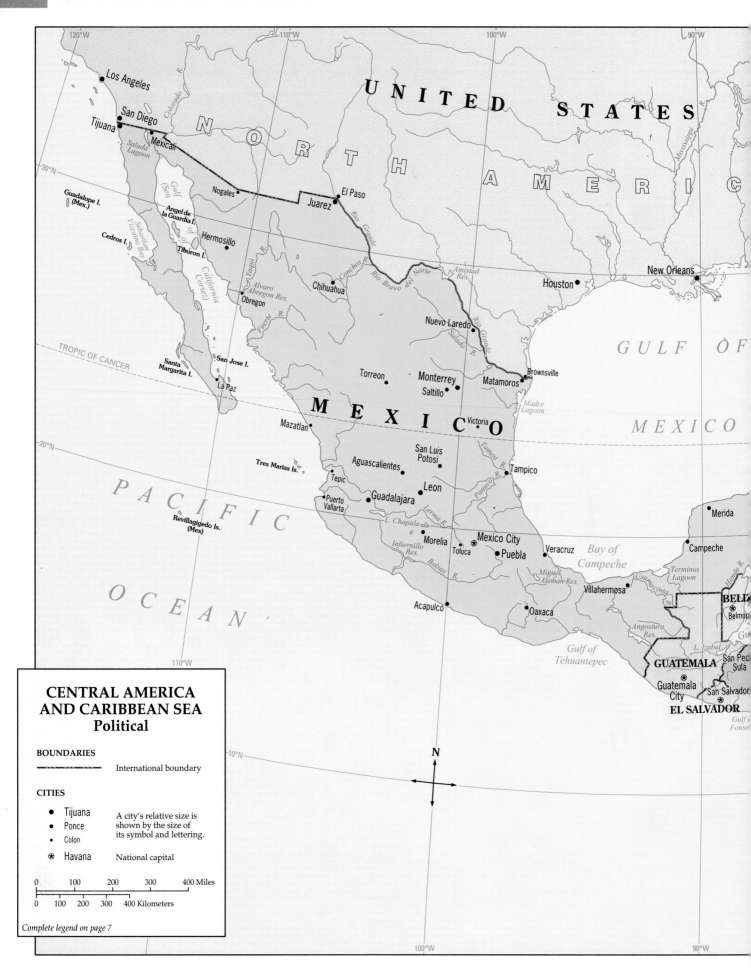

120°W

110°W

100°W

90°W

UNITED STATES

Los Angeles

San Diego
Tijuana
Mexicali

Salada
Lagoon

30°N

Guadalupe I.
(Mex.)

Nogales

El Paso

Juarez

Colorado R.

NORTH

Angel de
la Guardia I.

Hermosillo

Tiburon I.

Cedros I.

Sebastian
Vizcaino Bay

Gulf
(Sea)

Yaqui R.

Alvaro
Abregon Res.

Obregon

Chihuahua

Conchos R.

Rio Grande

Rio Bravo del Norte

Amistad
Res.

Houston

New Orleans

A M E R I C A

TROPIC OF CANCER

Santa
Margarita I.

San Jose I.

La Paz

Fuerte R.

Torreon

Monterrey
Saltillo

Nuevo Laredo

Salado R.

Matamoros

Brownsville

GULF OF

MEXICO

Madre
Lagoon

M E X I C O

Victoria

20°N

Mazatlan

Tres Marias Is.

Tepic

Aguascalientes

San Luis
Potosi

Leon

Tampico

Tamesi R.

Panuco R.

Puerto
Vallarta

Guadalajara

L. Chapala

Lerma R.

Morelia

Infiernillo
Res.

Toluca

Mexico City

Puebla

Veracruz

Bay of
Campeche

Merida

Campeche

P A C I F I C

Revillagigedo Is.
(Mex)

Balsas R.

Miguel
Aleman Res.

Terminos
Lagoon

Usumacinta R.

Honda R.

O C E A N

Acapulco

Oaxaca

Villahermosa

Angostura
Res.

BELI

Belmo

110°W

Gulf of
Tehuantepec

L. Izabal

Gu

GUATEMALA

San Pe
Sula

Guatemala
City

San Salvador

EL SALVADOR

Gulf
Fonse

10°N

N

CENTRAL AMERICA AND CARIBBEAN SEA
Political

BOUNDARIES

International boundary

CITIES

● Tijuana   A city's relative size is
● Ponce   shown by the size of
· Colon   its symbol and lettering.

⊛ Havana   National capital

| 0 | 100 | 200 | 300 | 400 Miles |

| 0 | 100 | 200 | 300 | 400 Kilometers |

Complete legend on page 7

100°W

90°W

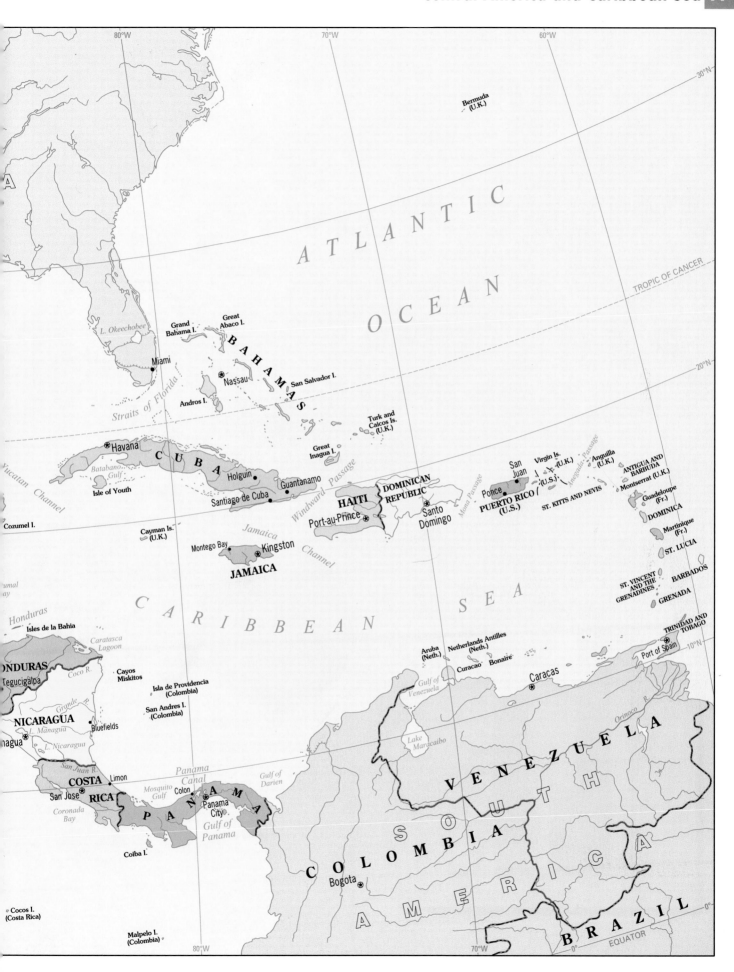

ATLANTIC

OCEAN

TROPIC OF CANCER

30°N

20°N

10°N

0°

EQUATOR

80°W

70°W

60°W

Bermuda
(U.K.)

L. Okeechobee

Miami

Grand
Bahama I.

Great
Abaco I.

BAHAMAS

Nassau

San Salvador I.

Andros I.

Straits of Florida

Turk and
Caicos Is.
(U.K.)

Great
Inagua I.

Havana

CUBA

Batabano
Gulf

Yucatan Channel

Isle of Youth

Holguin

Guantanamo

Santiago de Cuba

Windward Passage

HAITI

Port-au-Prince

DOMINICAN
REPUBLIC

Santo
Domingo

Mona Passage

San
Juan

PUERTO RICO
(U.S.)

Ponce

Virgin Is.
(U.K.)
(U.S.)

Anegada Passage

Anguilla
(U.K.)

ANTIGUA AND
BARBUDA

Montserrat (U.K.)

ST. KITTS AND NEVIS

Guadeloupe
(Fr.)

DOMINICA

Martinique
(Fr.)

ST. LUCIA

ST. VINCENT
AND THE
GRENADINES

BARBADOS

GRENADA

Cozumel I.

Cayman Is.
(U.K.)

Jamaica

Montego Bay

Kingston

JAMAICA

Jamaica
Channel

CARIBBEAN

SEA

umal
ay

Honduras

Isles de la Bahia

Caratasca
Lagoon

ONDURAS

Tegucigalpa

Coco R.

Cayos
Miskitos

Isla de Providencia
(Colombia)

San Andres I.
(Colombia)

Grande

NICARAGUA

Bluefields

agua

L. Managua

L. Nicaragua

San Juan R.

COSTA

Limon

RICA

San Jose

Mosquito
Gulf

Colon

Panama
Canal

PANAMA

Panama
City

Gulf of
Darien

Gulf of
Panama

Coronada
Bay

Coiba I.

Aruba
(Neth.)

Netherlands Antilles
(Neth.)

Curacao

Bonaire

TRINIDAD AND
TOBAGO

Port of Spain

Gulf of
Venezuela

Caracas

VENEZUELA

Lake
Maracaibo

Orinoco R.

SOUTH

COLOMBIA

AMERICA

Bogota

Cocos I.
(Costa Rica)

Malpelo I.
(Colombia)

BRAZIL

80°W

70°W

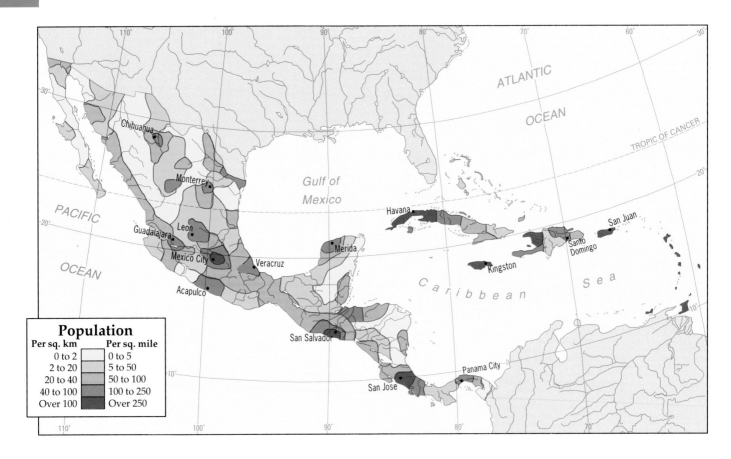

Population

Per sq. km	Per sq. mile
0 to 2	0 to 5
2 to 20	5 to 50
20 to 40	50 to 100
40 to 100	100 to 250
Over 100	Over 250

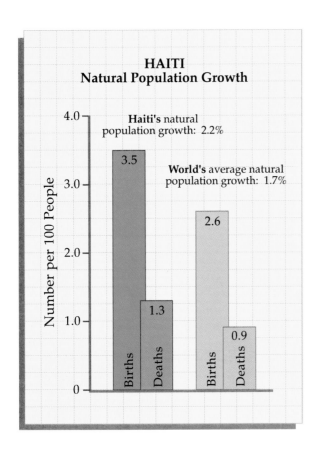

HAITI
Natural Population Growth

Haiti's natural population growth: 2.2%

World's average natural population growth: 1.7%

Number per 100 People

Births 3.5
Deaths 1.3
Births 2.6
Deaths 0.9

MEXICO
Balance of Trade

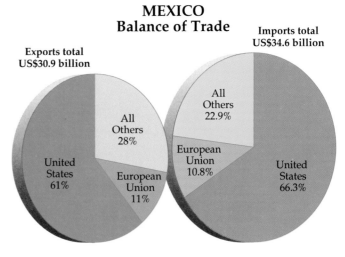

Exports total US$30.9 billion

United States 61%
European Union 11%
All Others 28%

Imports total US$34.6 billion

United States 66.3%
European Union 10.8%
All Others 22.9%

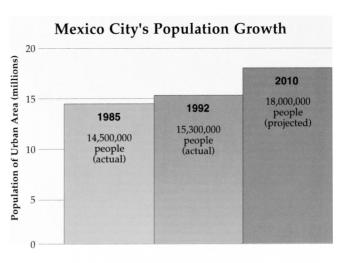

Mexico City's Population Growth

Population of Urban Area (millions)

1985 14,500,000 people (actual)

1992 15,300,000 people (actual)

2010 18,000,000 people (projected)

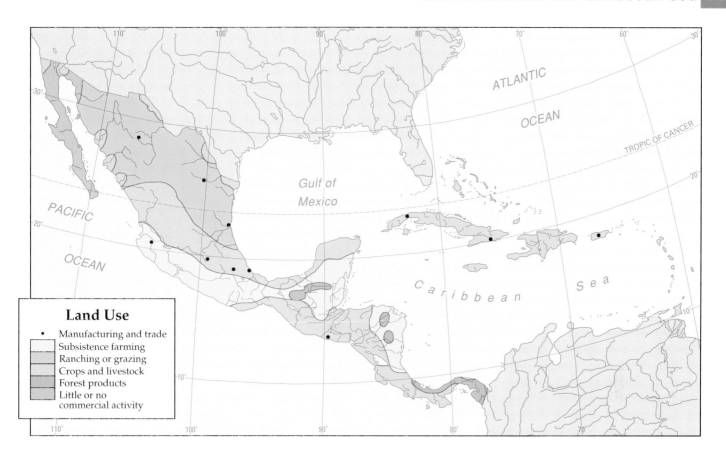

Land Use

- Manufacturing and trade
- Subsistence farming
- Ranching or grazing
- Crops and livestock
- Forest products
- Little or no commercial activity

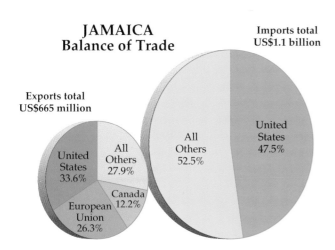

JAMAICA
Balance of Trade

Exports total
US$665 million

United States 33.6%

All Others 27.9%

European Union 26.3%

Canada 12.2%

Imports total
US$1.1 billion

All Others 52.5%

United States 47.5%

Latin America

- Spanish
- Portuguese
- French
- Other (non-Latin)

Central America is part of a larger culture region called Latin America, which includes 33 countries. Most of the people in this region speak one of the Latin-based languages of Spanish, Portuguese, or French.

Caribbean people enjoy daily visits to open-air markets that offer a variety of fresh tropical produce.

SOUTH AMERICA
Physical

—————— International boundary
⊛ Lima   National capital
● Recife   Major city

ELEVATION

Meters		Feet
Over 6000		Over 20,000
3000 to 6000		10,000 to 20,000
1500 to 3000		5,000 to 10,000
600 to 1500		2,000 to 5,000
300 to 600		1,000 to 2,000
150 to 300		500 to 1,000
0 to 150		0 to 500

WATER DEPTH

Less than 200		Less than 600
Greater than 200		Greater than 600

0   250   500   750   1000 Miles
0 250 500 750 1000 Kilometers

Complete legend on page 7

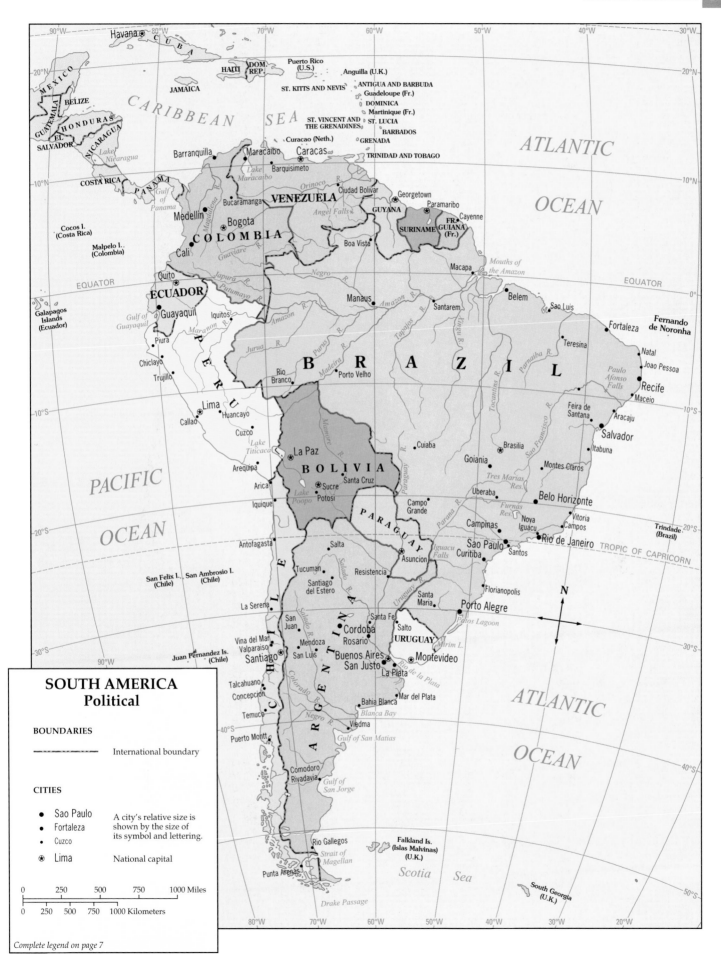

SOUTH AMERICA
Political

BOUNDARIES

International boundary

CITIES

● Sao Paulo
● Fortaleza
· Cuzco   A city's relative size is shown by the size of its symbol and lettering.
⊛ Lima   National capital

0   250   500   750   1000 Miles

0   250   500   750   1000 Kilometers

Complete legend on page 7

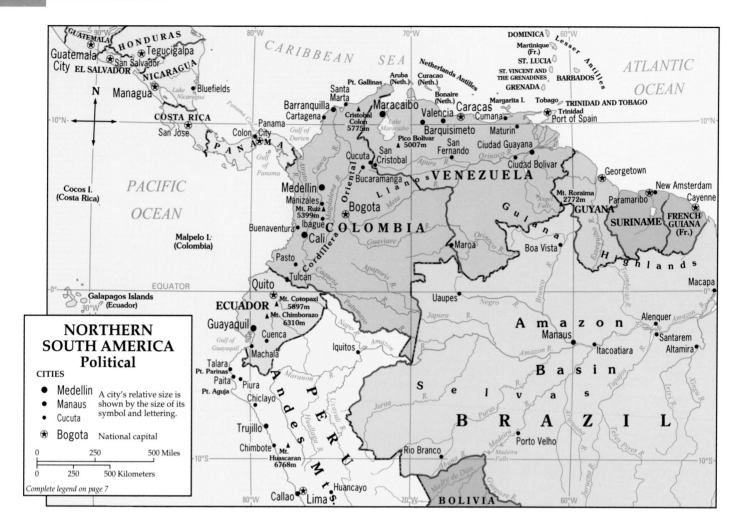

NORTHERN SOUTH AMERICA
Political

CITIES

● **Medellin**   A city's relative size is
● **Manaus**   shown by the size of its
• Cucuta   symbol and lettering.

✪ **Bogota**   National capital

0	250	500 Miles
0	250	500 Kilometers

Complete legend on page 7

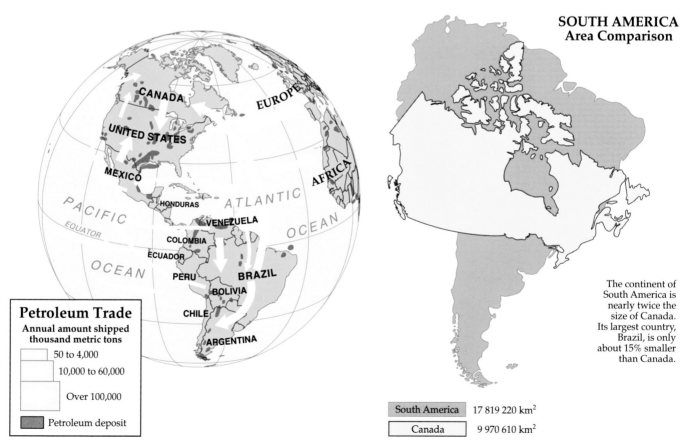

Petroleum Trade

**Annual amount shipped
thousand metric tons**

- 50 to 4,000
- 10,000 to 60,000
- Over 100,000

■ Petroleum deposit

SOUTH AMERICA
Area Comparison

The continent of
South America is
nearly twice the
size of Canada.
Its largest country,
Brazil, is only
about 15% smaller
than Canada.

South America	17 819 220 km²
Canada	9 970 610 km²

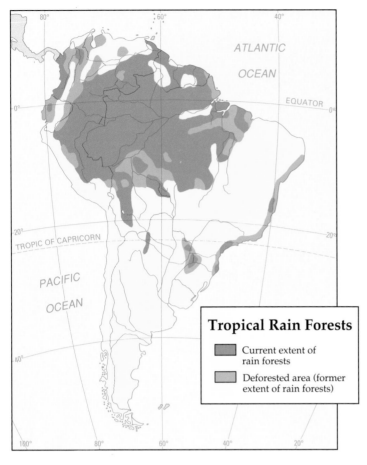

Tropical Rain Forests

- Current extent of rain forests
- Deforested area (former extent of rain forests)

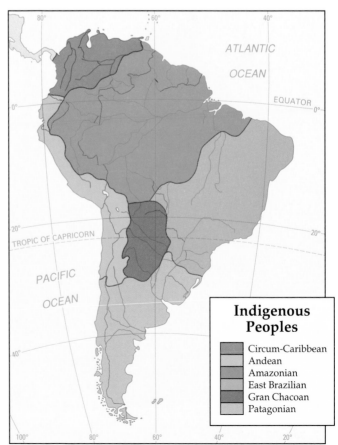

Brazil's economic development often comes at the expense of the Amazon rain forest. Deforestation increases annually as trees are cut down to make way for farms and highways.

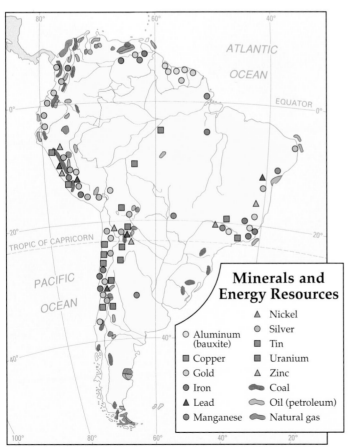

Minerals and Energy Resources

- ○ Aluminum (bauxite)
- ■ Copper
- ● Gold
- ● Iron
- ▲ Lead
- ● Manganese
- ▲ Nickel
- ● Silver
- ■ Tin
- ■ Uranium
- ▲ Zinc
- ～ Coal
- ～ Oil (petroleum)
- ～ Natural gas

Indigenous Peoples

- Circum-Caribbean
- Andean
- Amazonian
- East Brazilian
- Gran Chacoan
- Patagonian

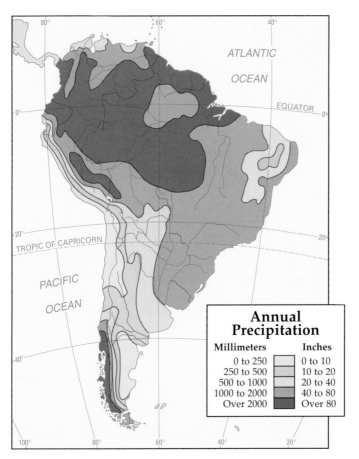

Annual Precipitation

Millimeters		Inches
0 to 250		0 to 10
250 to 500		10 to 20
500 to 1000		20 to 40
1000 to 2000		40 to 80
Over 2000		Over 80

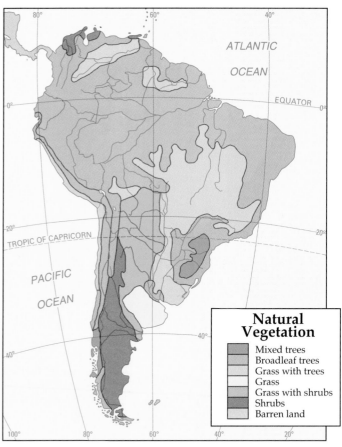

Natural Vegetation

- Mixed trees
- Broadleaf trees
- Grass with trees
- Grass
- Grass with shrubs
- Shrubs
- Barren land

Brazil's urban population is a diverse mixture of European, African, and Indian ancestry.

VENEZUELA
Balance of Trade

Exports total US$15.5 billion

United States 46.5%

All Others 53.5%

Imports total US$6.8 billion

All Others 34.6%

United States 44.3%

European Union 21.1%

Cross Section of South America

ELEVATION

Meters		Feet
Over 6000		Over 20,000
3000 to 6000		10,000 to 20,000
1500 to 3000		5,000 to 10,000
600 to 1500		2,000 to 5,000
300 to 600		1,000 to 2,000
150 to 300		500 to 1,000
0 to 150		0 to 500
Below sea level		Below sea level

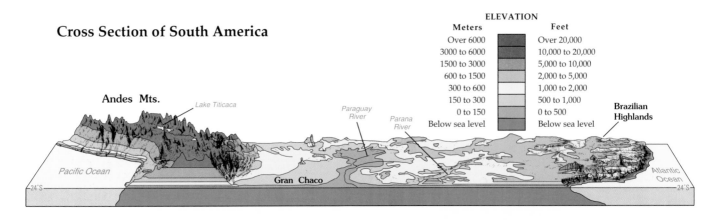

Andes Mts. · Lake Titicaca · Paraguay River · Parana River · Brazilian Highlands · Pacific Ocean · Gran Chaco · Atlantic Ocean

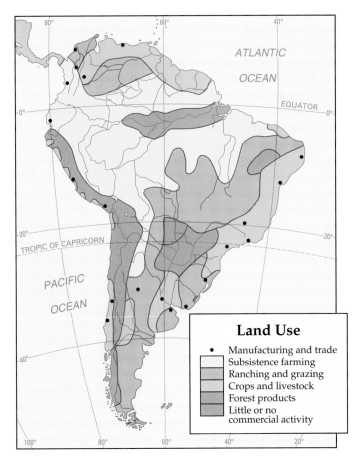

Land Use

- • Manufacturing and trade
- Subsistence farming
- Ranching and grazing
- Crops and livestock
- Forest products
- Little or no commercial activity

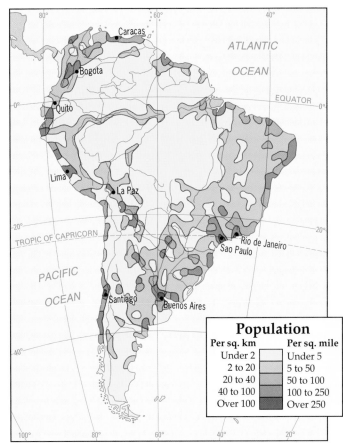

Population

Per sq. km	Per sq. mile
Under 2	Under 5
2 to 20	5 to 50
20 to 40	50 to 100
40 to 100	100 to 250
Over 100	Over 250

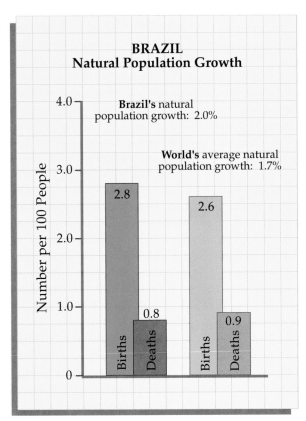

BRAZIL
Natural Population Growth

Brazil's natural population growth: 2.0%

World's average natural population growth: 1.7%

Number per 100 People

4.0

3.0

2.8 (Births)

2.6 (Births)

2.0

1.0

0.8 (Deaths)

0.9 (Deaths)

0

CHILE
Balance of Trade

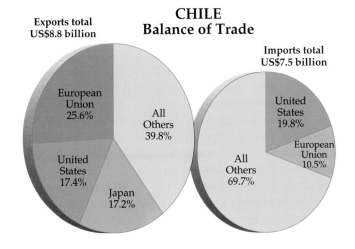

Exports total US$8.8 billion

European Union 25.6%

United States 17.4%

Japan 17.2%

All Others 39.8%

Imports total US$7.5 billion

United States 19.8%

European Union 10.5%

All Others 69.7%

More Indians live in Peru than in any other South American country. Many still farm and bring goods to market in the highlands where their ancestors, the Incas, once reigned.

ATLANTIC

OCEAN

ICELAND

Reykjavik

Surtsey I.   Hekla
              1491m

ARCTIC CIRCLE

PRIME MERIDIAN

ARCTIC

N

NORWEGIAN

SEA

Faeroe
Islands

Rockall

Shetland
Islands

Hebrides

Orkney Is.

Grampian Mts.

IRELAND

Irish Sea

UNITED
KINGDOM

Cambrian Mts.

Great Britain

London

NORTH

SEA

Lofoten
Is.

Trondheims Fiord

Sogne Fiord

Hardanger Fiord

Bokna Fiord

NORWAY

SWEDEN

Oslo

Skagerrak

Kattegat

L. Malaren

L. Vanern

L. Vattern

Gotaland

Gotland

Baltic

DENMARK

Jutland

Copenhagen

Bornholm

TO
RUSSIA

British Isles

Celtic
Sea

English Channel

Channel Is.

Strait of Dover

Frisian Is.

NETHERLANDS

BELGIUM

LUXEMBOURG

GERMANY

Northern

Elbe R.

POLA

Warsa

Vistula

Cape Finisterre

Bay of
Biscay

Paris

Paris Basin

FRANCE

Loire R.

Seine R.

Ore
Mts.

Elbe R.

CZECH REPUBLIC

Danube R.

Carpa
SLOVAKI

Cantabrian Mts.

Douro R.

Duero R.

Aquitaine
Basin

Massif
Central

Rhone R.

Mt. Blanc
4807m

SWITZERLAND

Munich

LIECH.

AUSTRIA

A l p s

HUNGARY

Great Hungar

Lisbon

PORTUGAL

SPAIN

Tagus R.

Madrid

Ebro R.

Pyrenees

ANDORRA

Gulf of
Lion

MONACO

SAN
MARINO

Ligurian
Sea

SLOVENIA

CROATIA

Adriatic

BOSNIA

Dinari

YUGOSLAVIA

Alp

Cape St. Vincent

Guadiana

Iberian

Peninsula

Guadalquivir

Corsica

VATICAN CITY

Rome

Apennines

Tiber R.

Sea

MACEDON

Balearic Sea

Balearic Islands

Sardinia

ITALY

Vesuvius
1277m

Tyrrhenian
Sea

Gulf of
Taranto

Pindus

ALBANIA

GRE

Strait of
Gibraltar

GIBRALTAR (U.K.)

MEDITERRA

Ionian
Sea

Ionian Is.

Algiers

MOROCCO

A
F
R
I
C
A

ALGERIA

TUNISIA

Tunis

Sicily

MALTA
Maltese Islands

Peloponnesus

Peloponnesus

WESTERN
SAHARA
(adm. Morocco)

OCEAN

North Cape

Novaya Zemlya

Kolguyev I.

Barents Sea

Kanin
Pen.

P e c h o r a

B a s i n

Kola
Pen.

Archangel

White
Sea

L.
Inari

a p l a n d

Kola
Pen.

L.
Onega

U r a l s   M o u n t a i n s

R U S S I A

Ob R.

Kamskoye
Res.

K a m a
U p l a n d

Vyatka R. Kama R.

Sukhona R.

Northern Dvina R.

FINLAND

Lake
Region

Bothnia

Lake
Ladoga

L.
Onega

St. Petersburg
(Leningrad)

ESTONIA

Riga   LATVIA

L.
Peipus

Gulf of Finland

Rybinsk
Res.

Moscow

Gorki
Res.

Volga R.

Oka R.

Kuybyshev
Res.

Volga R.

LITHUANIA

E u r o p e a n

P l a i n

C e n t r a l

R u s s i a n

U p l a n d

Oka-Don

P l a i n

V o l g a   U p l a n d

S t e p p e s

BELARUS

Dnepr R.

Pripyat Marshes

Neman R.

Dvina R.

Bug R.

Dnestr R.

Desna R.

Don R.

Volgograd
Res.

KAZAKHSTAN

Ural R.

A S I A

Syr   Darya

Aral
Sea

UKRAINE

Dnepr

Lowland

Dnestr R.

Prut R.

Black   Sea   Lowland

Sea of Azov

Caspian
Depression

Volga R. Delta

UZBEKISTAN

Amu   Darya

MOLDOVA

Mountains

Bug R.

OMANIA

Transylvanian Alps

Bucharest

Danube R.

Black   Odessa

Crimea
Pen.

Caucasus   Mountains

Mt. Elbrus
5642m

GEORGIA

Baku

C a s p i a n

S e a

TURKMENISTAN

Balkan Mts.

BULGARIA

B a l k a n

P e n i n s u l a

Danube R.

B l a c k   S e a

ARMENIA   AZERBAIJAN

E

Olympus
2917m

Bosporus

Istanbul

Sea of Marmara

Dardanelles

T U R K E Y

Lake
Van

Lake Urmia

Tehran

I R A N

Euboea

Cyclades

Rhodes

Crete

S E A

SYRIA

IRAQ

CYPRUS   LEBANON

EUROPE Physical		
International boundary		
Other boundary		
⊛ Copenhagen	National capital	
● Odessa	Major city	

ELEVATION

Meters		Feet
Over 3000		Over 10,000
1500 to 3000		5,000 to 10,000
600 to 1500		2,000 to 5,000
300 to 600		1,000 to 2,000
150 to 300		500 to 1,000
0 to 150		0 to 500
Below sea level		Below sea level

WATER DEPTH

Less than 200		Less than 600
Greater than 200		Greater than 600

0   100   200   300   400   500 Miles

0   100   200   300   400   500 Kilometers

Complete legend on page 7

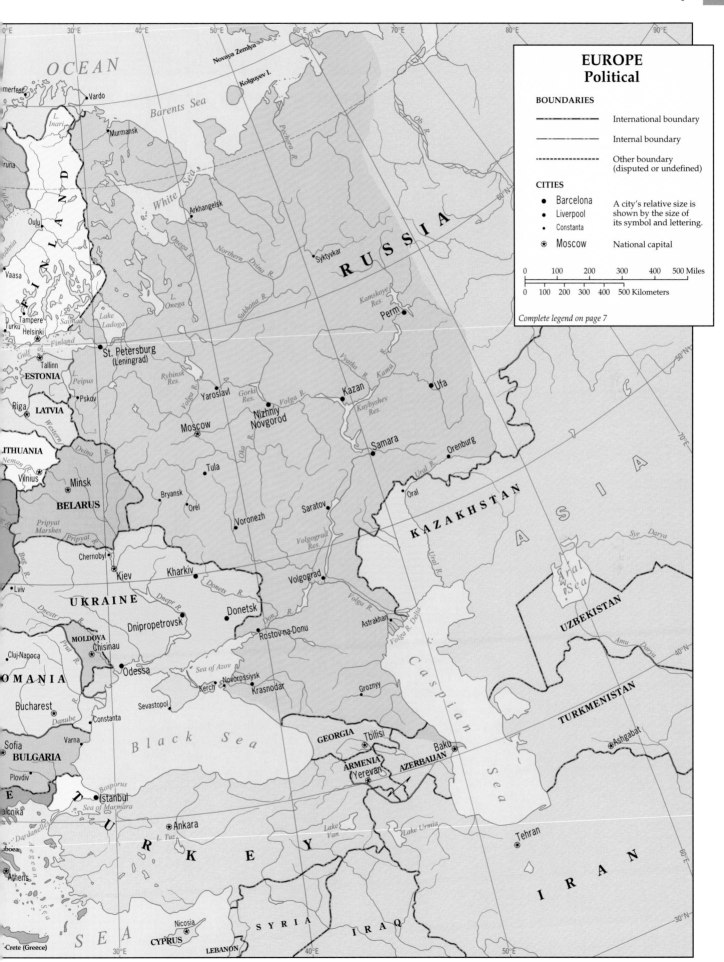

EUROPE
Political

BOUNDARIES

International boundary

Internal boundary

Other boundary
(disputed or undefined)

CITIES

● Barcelona

● Liverpool

• Constanta

A city's relative size is
shown by the size of
its symbol and lettering.

⊛ Moscow   National capital

| 0 | 100 | 200 | 300 | 400 | 500 Miles |

| 0 | 100 | 200 | 300 | 400 | 500 Kilometers |

Complete legend on page 7

OCEAN

merfest

Vardo

Novaya Zemlya

Kolguyev I.

Barents Sea

Murmansk

Pechora R.

Ob R.

L. Inari

FINLAND

runa

Oulu

White Sea

Arkhangelsk

Onega R.

Northern Dvina R.

Syktyvkar

RUSSIA

Vaasa

Tampere

Turku
Helsinki

L. Saimaa

Lake Ladoga

L. Onega

Sukhona R.

Kamskoye Res.

Perm

Estonia

Riga

LATVIA

St. Petersburg
(Leningrad)

Tallinn

L. Peipus

Rybinsk Res.

Pskov

Yaroslavl

Gorki Res.

Volga R.

Nizhniy
Novgorod

Kazan

Kuybyshev Res.

Kama R.

Vyatka R.

Ufa

Gulf of Finland

LITHUANIA

Vilnius

Neman R.

Western Dvina R.

Minsk

BELARUS

Moscow

Oka R.

Tula

Samara

Orenburg

Ural R.

Oral

Pripyat Marshes

Pripyat R.

Chernobyl

Bryansk

Orel

Voronezh

Saratov

KAZAKHSTAN

Lviv

Kiev

Kharkiv

UKRAINE

Donets R.

Dnepr R.

Dnipropetrovsk

Donetsk

Don R.

Volgograd

Volgograd Res.

Volga R.

Astrakhan

Ural R.

Aral Sea

Syr Darya

UZBEKISTAN

Amu Darya

Bug R.

Dnestr R.

Prut R.

MOLDOVA
Chisinau

Cluj-Napoca

OMANIA

Bucharest

Danube

Constanta

Sofia

BULGARIA

Plovdiv

Varna

Odessa

Rostov-na-Donu

Kerch

Novorossiysk

Krasnodar

Sevastopol

Sea of Azov

Black Sea

Volga R. Delta

Caspian Sea

Groznyy

GEORGIA

Tbilisi

ARMENIA
Yerevan

AZERBAIJAN

Baku

TURKMENISTAN

Ashgabat

E

Istanbul

Bosporus

Sea of Marmara

alonika

TURKEY

Ankara

L. Tuz

Lake Van

Lake Urmia

Tehran

IRAN

boea

Athens

Dardanelles

Aegean Sea

SEA

Nicosia

CYPRUS

SYRIA

IRAQ

LEBANON

Crete (Greece)

ASIA

WESTERN EUROPE
Political

BOUNDARIES

—————— International boundary

—————— Internal boundary

CITIES

● London

• Cologne

· Limerick

⊛ Paris

A city's relative size is shown by the size of its symbol and lettering.

National capital

0   50   100   150   200 Miles

0 50 100 150 200 Kilometers

Complete legend on page 7

CENTRAL EUROPE Political

BOUNDARIES

— · · — · · — International boundary

——————— Internal boundary (republic or territory)

CITIES

● Milan

● Leipzig

• Salzburg

✪ Warsaw — National capital

A city's relative size is shown by the size of its symbol and lettering.

0 50 100 150 200 Miles

0 50 100 150 200 Kilometers

Complete legend on page 7

North Sea

DENMARK

SWEDEN

Skagerrak

Kattegat

Goteborg
Jonkoping
Visby
Gotland (Sweden)
Oland

Baltic Sea

Gulf of Riga

ESTONIA

LATVIA

LITHUANIA

Riga

Alborg
Arhus
Helsingborg
Malmo
Esbjerg
Copenhagen
Odense
Fyn
Sjaelland
Schleswig
Kiel
Jutland
Bornholm (Den.)

Neman R.
Kaunas
Vilnius

Kaliningrad TO RUSSIA
Gdynia
Gdansk
Elblag
Hrodna
Bialystok

BELARUS

W. Frisian Is.
E. Frisian Is.
Bremerhaven
Lubeck
Rostock
Rugen
Pomerania
European Plain
Szczecin
Bydgoszcz
Vistula R.
Wloclawek
Warta R.
Poznan

NETHERLANDS
Amsterdam
The Hague
Rotterdam
Mittelland Canal
Hannover
Elbe R.
Bremen
Hamburg
Northern
Brandenburg
Berlin
Potsdam
Spree R.
Bielefeld
Braunschweig
Magdeburg
Halle
Oder R.

POLAND
Warsaw
Lublin
Bug R.
Kalisz
Lodz
Radom
Wroclaw
Ostrowiec
Czestochowa
Katowice
Krakow
Przemysl

Munster
Dortmund
Essen
Kassel
Dusseldorf
Cologne
Bonn
Aachen
Liege
Wiesbaden

BELGIUM

LUXEMBOURG
Luxembourg

GERMANY
Erfurt
Leipzig
Dresden
Chemnitz
Frankfurt
Main R.

Ore Mts.
Elbe R.
Prague
Plzen
Bohemia

CZECH REPUBLIC
Ostrava
Brno
Moravia
Moravia R.

UKRAINE
Lviv
Zhytomyr
Dnepr Lowland
Dnepr R.

FRANCE
Bayreuth
Nurnberg
Regensberg
Danube R.
Mannheim
Stuttgart
Rhine R.
Alsace
Ulm
Augsburg
Black Forest
Basel

Carpathian Mountains

SLOVAKIA
Bratislava
Kosice
Miskolc

Dnestr R.

MOLDOVA
Chernivtsi
Chisinau
Prut R.
Iasi

Zurich
Bern
Vaduz
LIECHTENSTEIN
Innsbruck

SWITZERLAND
Geneva
L. Geneva
Rhone R.
Rhine R.
Alps

Linz
Salzburg
Vienna

AUSTRIA
Graz
Klagenfurt

Budapest

HUNGARY
Great Hungarian Plain
Debrecen
Satu Mare
Oradea
Cluj-Napoca
Szeged
Mures R.
Timisoara
Subotica

ROMANIA
Brasov
Galati
Braila
Ploiesti

Black Sea Lowland
Odessa

Mt. Blanc 4807m
L. Constance
L. Como
Bolzano
Brescia
Padua
Turin
Verona
Po R.
Milan
Venice
Trieste
Rijeka

SLOVENIA
Maribor
Ljubljana
Zagreb
Drava R.

CROATIA
Osijek
Sava R.
Novi Sad
VOJVODINA

Transylvanian Alps

Bucharest
Danube Delta
Constanta

Genoa
Parma
Modena
Bologna
Ferrara
Carrara
Pisa
Florence
Riviera
Ligurian Sea
MONACO
Nice
Leghorn
Rimini
SAN MARINO
Ancona
Perugia

Dinaric Alps
Banja Luka

BOSNIA AND HERZEGOVINA
Sarajevo
Zadar
Split
Mostar
Dalmatia
Dubrovnik

Belgrade

YUGOSLAVIA
SERBIA
Cacak
Krusevac
Nis
Morava R.

Craiova
Olt R.
Danube
Ruse
Varna

Black Sea

Corsica (Fr.)
Bastia
Elba
Ajaccio

VATICAN CITY
Rome
Tiber R.
Apennines

ITALY
Foggia
Bari
Brindisi
Taranto

Sassari
Sardinia
Naples
Mt. Vesuvius 1277m
Salerno

Adriatic Sea

MONTENEGRO
Podgorica
Pec
KOSOVO
Pristina

Tirana

ALBANIA
Korce

MACEDONIA
Skopje
Bitola
Florina
Mt. Olympus 2917m

Balkan Mountains

Sofia

BULGARIA
Plovdiv
Rhodope Mts.
Serrai
Xanthi
Edirne
Burgas

Maritsa R.

Istanbul
Sea of Marmara
Bursa

TURKEY
Izmir

Cagliari

Tyrrhenian Sea

Cosenza
Catanzaro

Lipari Is.
Palermo
Messina
Reggio di Calabria
Sicily
Mt. Etna 3390m
Catania
Strait of Messina

Gulf of Taranto

Ionian Sea

Ionian Islands
Corfu

Pindus Mts.
Vardar R.

Larisa
Volos
Sporades
Lamia
Agrinion

GREECE
Patras
Piraeus
Athens
Peloponnesus

Aegean Sea
Thasos
Samothrace
Lemnos
Lesbos
Chios
Euboea
Samos
Cyclades
Dodecanese
Rhodes

Annaba
Carthage
Tunis

ALGERIA

TUNISIA
Sfax

Strait of Bonifacio

Mediterranean Sea

Pantelleria (It.)

Maltese Is.
Valletta
MALTA
Lampedusa (It.)

Sea of Crete
Khania
Iraklion
Crete

N

55°N
50°N
45°N
40°N
35°N

5°E 10°E 15°E 20°E 25°E 30°E

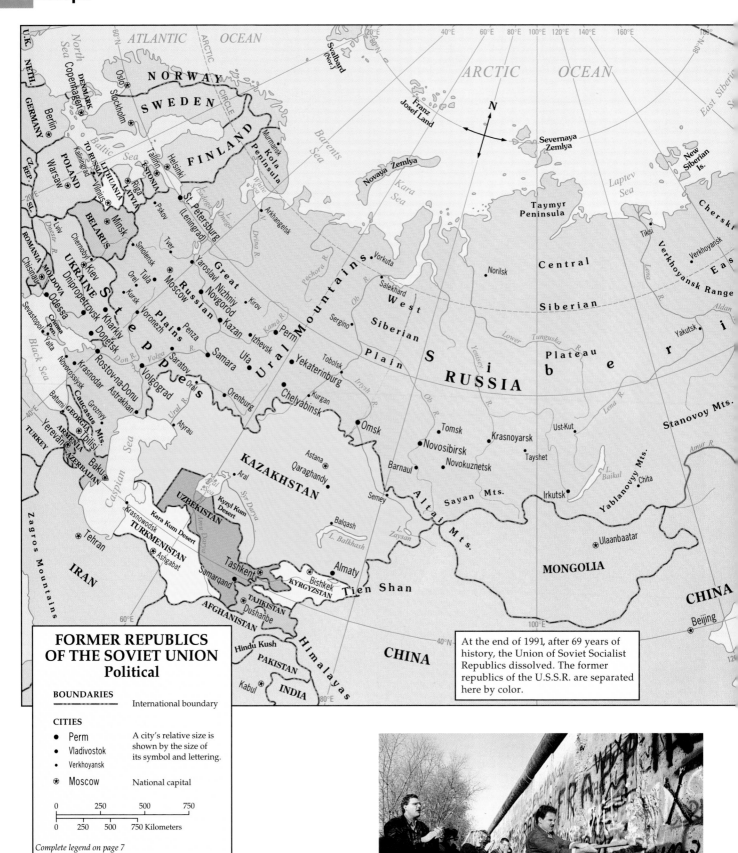

ATLANTIC OCEAN

ARCTIC OCEAN

U.K.
NETH.
GERMANY
Berlin
CZ. REP.
SL.
POLAND
Warsaw
DENMARK
Copenhagen
Oslo
NORWAY
SWEDEN
Stockholm
FINLAND
Helsinki
North Sea
Baltic Sea
TO RUSSIA
Kaliningrad
LITHUANIA
Vilnius
LATVIA
Riga
ESTONIA
Tallinn
Pskov
Svalbard (Nor.)
Barents Sea
Murmansk
Kola Peninsula
White Sea
Arkhangelsk
Franz Josef Land
N
Novaya Zemlya
Kara Sea
Severnaya Zemlya
New Siberian Is.
Laptev Sea
Taymyr Peninsula
Tiksi
Verkhoyansk
Verkhoyansk Range
Cherski
East S

BELARUS
Minsk
Chernobyl
UKRAINE
Kiev
Lviv
ROMANIA
MOLDOVA
Chisinau
Odessa
Dnipropetrovsk
Kharkiv
Donetsk
Sevastopol
Yalta
Crimea
Kerch
Novorossiysk
Batumi
GEORGIA
Tbilisi
ARMENIA
Yerevan
AZERBAIJAN
Baku
TURKEY
Black Sea
Caucasus Mts.
Krasnodar
Rostov-na-Donu
Groznyy
St. Petersburg (Leningrad)
L. Ladoga
L. Onega
Tver
Smolensk
Moscow
Yaroslavl
Nizhniy Novgorod
Orel
Tula
Kursk
Voronezh
Penza
Saratov
Volgograd
Astrakhan
Kazan
Samara
Ufa
Perm
Izhevsk
Great Russian Plains
Russian Steppes
Dnister R.
Dnipro R.
Don R.
Volga R.
Kama R.
Ural R.
Caspian Sea
Atyrau
Orenburg
Kirov
Ural Mountains
Vorkuta
Pechora R.
Ob R.
Salekhard
West Siberian Plain
Sergino
Tobolsk
Yekaterinburg
Chelyabinsk
Kurgan
Omsk
Irtysh R.
Ob R.
Norilsk
Central Siberian Plateau
RUSSIA
Lower Tunguska R.
Yenisey R.
Yakutsk
Lena R.
Aldan R.
Stanovoy Mts.
Amur R.
Tomsk
Novosibirsk
Krasnoyarsk
Ust-Kut
Tayshet
Barnaul
Novokuznetsk
Semey
Irkutsk
L. Baikal
Yablanovyy Mts.
Chita
IRAN
Tehran
Zagros Mountains
TURKMENISTAN
Ashgabat
Krasnowodsk
Kara Kum Desert
Amu Darya R.
UZBEKISTAN
Samarqand
Tashkent
Syr Darya R.
KAZAKHSTAN
Astana
Qaraghandy
Aral
Aral Sea
Kyzyl Kum Desert
Balqash
L. Balkhash
L. Zaysan
Altai Mts.
Sayan Mts.
Ulaanbaatar
MONGOLIA
CHINA
Beijing
AFGHANISTAN
Dushanbe
TAJIKISTAN
Bishkek
KYRGYZSTAN
Almaty
Tien Shan
Hindu Kush
PAKISTAN
Kabul
INDIA
Himalayas
CHINA

FORMER REPUBLICS OF THE SOVIET UNION
Political

BOUNDARIES

—————————   International boundary

CITIES

● Perm

• Vladivostok

· Verkhoyansk

⊛ Moscow

A city's relative size is shown by the size of its symbol and lettering.

National capital

| 0 | 250 | 500 | 750 |

| 0 | 250 | 500 | 750 Kilometers |

Complete legend on page 7

At the end of 1991, after 69 years of history, the Union of Soviet Socialist Republics dissolved. The former republics of the U.S.S.R. are separated here by color.

In November 1989, Germans tore down the Berlin Wall. It was an event that symbolized the collapse of over 40 years of Communist rule in Eastern Europe.

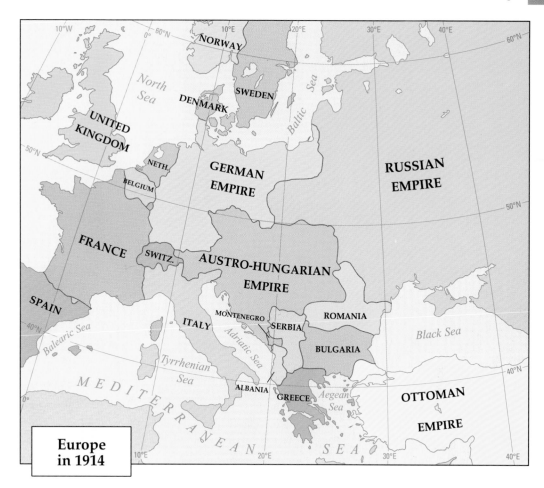

Europe in 1914

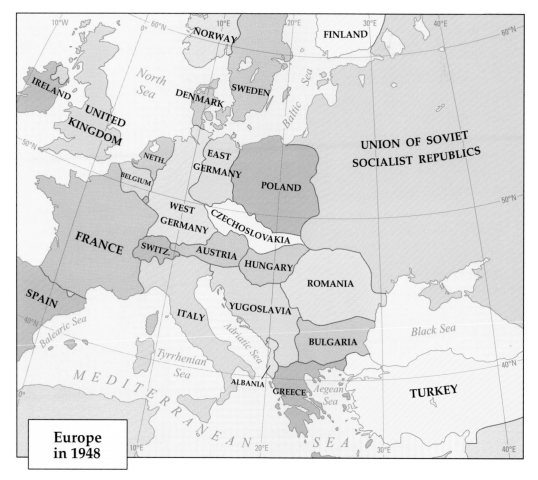

Twentieth-century Europe has seen radical changes in governments and boundaries. World War I brought the break-up of imperialistic monarchies and the formation of new, smaller states. Some of these, like Czechoslovakia, acquired democratic governments only to fall to Communism after World War II. Then, between 1989 and 1992, all the Communist governments of Europe were overthrown, and again new nations were formed.

Europe in 1948

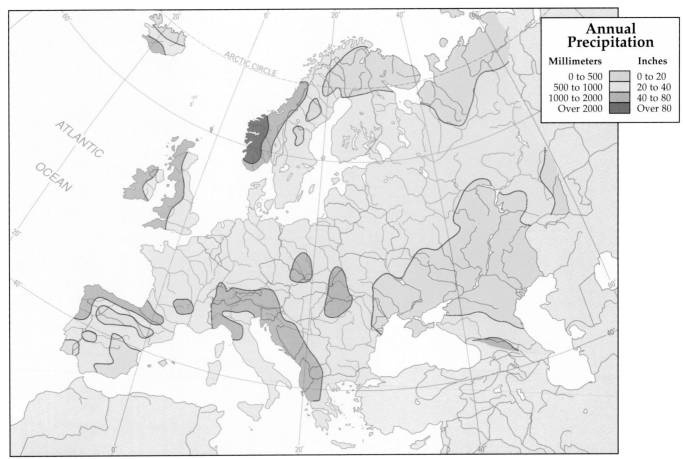

Annual Precipitation

Millimeters	Inches
0 to 500	0 to 20
500 to 1000	20 to 40
1000 to 2000	40 to 80
Over 2000	Over 80

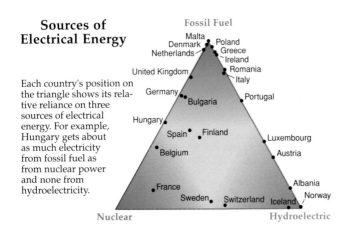

Vienna, Austria's capital, is the most prosperous city in Central Europe. Austria stands at the crossroads between former Communist states and democratically governed countries.

UNITED KINGDOM Area Comparison

The United Kingdom has more than twice as many people as Canada. Even so, it is smaller than the province of Newfoundland.

United Kingdom	244 110 km²
Canada	9 970 610 km²

Sources of Electrical Energy

Each country's position on the triangle shows its relative reliance on three sources of electrical energy. For example, Hungary gets about as much electricity from fossil fuel as from nuclear power and none from hydroelectricity.

Fossil Fuel

Malta
Denmark — Poland
Netherlands — Greece
— Ireland
United Kingdom — Romania
— Italy
Germany
Bulgaria — Portugal
Hungary
Spain — Finland
— Luxembourg
Belgium — Austria
France — Albania
Sweden — Switzerland — Iceland — Norway

Nuclear   Hydroelectric

The Alps are an important region for farming and industry as well as a major tourist attraction. Railways crisscross the mountains that were a barrier to travel for centuries.

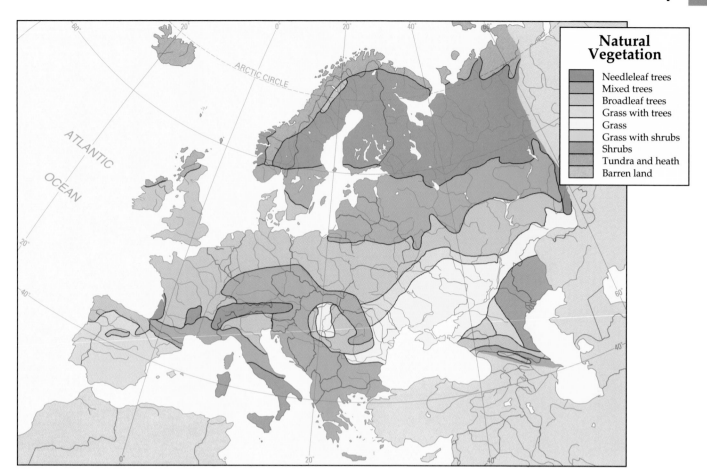

Natural Vegetation

- Needleleaf trees
- Mixed trees
- Broadleaf trees
- Grass with trees
- Grass
- Grass with shrubs
- Shrubs
- Tundra and heath
- Barren land

ARCTIC CIRCLE

ATLANTIC OCEAN

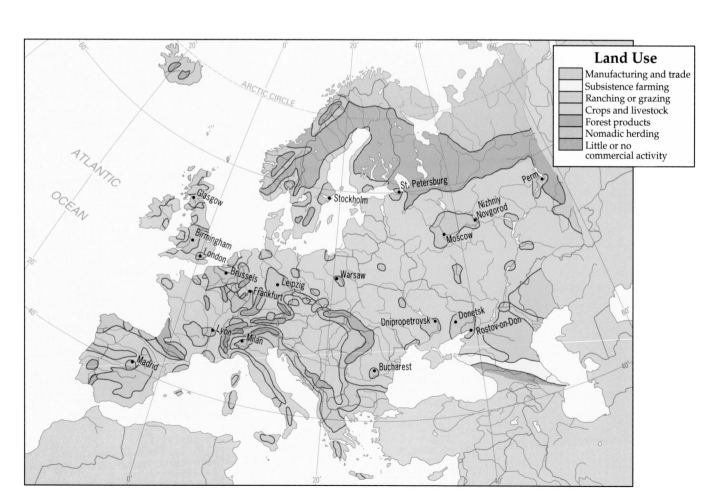

Land Use

- Manufacturing and trade
- Subsistence farming
- Ranching or grazing
- Crops and livestock
- Forest products
- Nomadic herding
- Little or no commercial activity

ARCTIC CIRCLE

ATLANTIC OCEAN

Glasgow
Birmingham
London
Brussels
Frankfurt
Leipzig
Lyon
Milan
Madrid
Stockholm
St. Petersburg
Perm
Nizhniy Novgorod
Moscow
Warsaw
Dnipropetrovsk
Donetsk
Rostov-on-Don
Bucharest

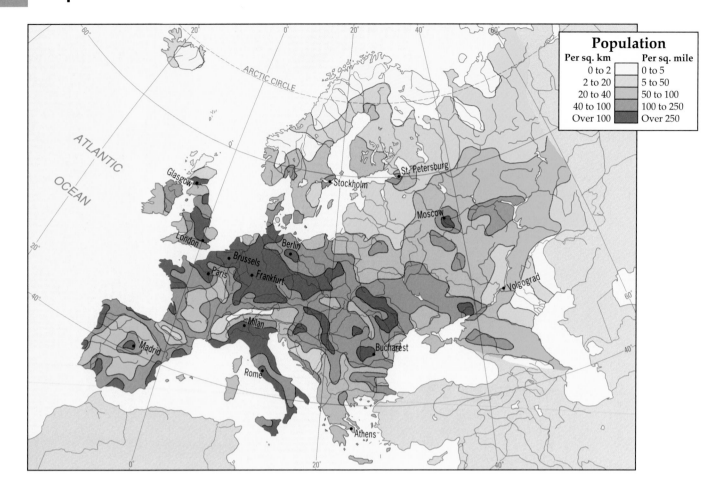

GREECE
Balance of Trade

Imports total
US$19.1 billion

Exports total
US$7.7 billion

All Others 42%

European Union 58%

All Others 42.5%

European Union 57.5%

BULGARIA
Balance of Trade

Exports total
US$3.1 billion

Imports total
US$3.1 billion

Commonwealth of Independent States 24.9%

European Union 15.1%

All Others 60%

All Others 42.3%

Commonwealth of Independent States 33.7%

European Union 24%

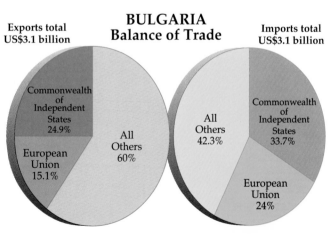

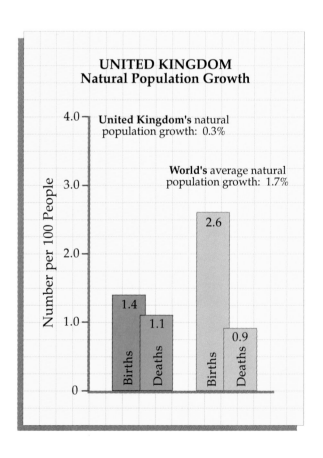

UNITED KINGDOM
Natural Population Growth

United Kingdom's natural
population growth: 0.3%

World's average natural
population growth: 1.7%

Number per 100 People

4.0

3.0

2.0 — 2.6

1.0 — 1.4 — 1.1 — 0.9

0

Births   Deaths   Births   Deaths

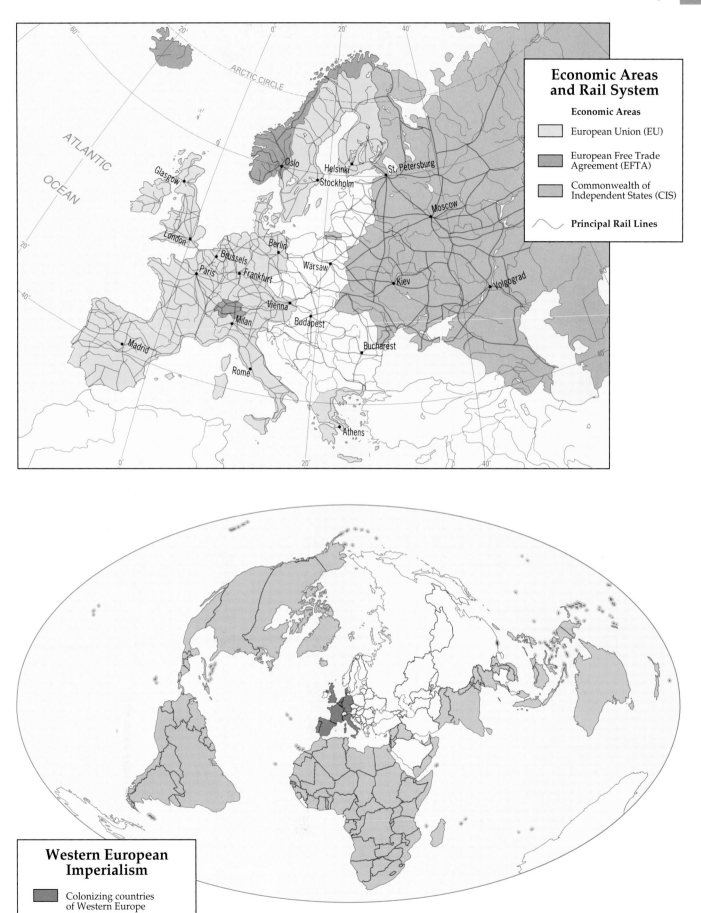

Economic Areas and Rail System

Economic Areas

European Union (EU)

European Free Trade Agreement (EFTA)

Commonwealth of Independent States (CIS)

Principal Rail Lines

Western European Imperialism

Colonizing countries of Western Europe

Past and present colonies and other territories of Western European countries

ATLANTIC OCEAN

FRANCE
GERMANY
CZ.
SL.
SWITZ.
AUS.
HUNGARY
SLOV.
CRO.
BOS.
YUGO.
MAC.
ALB.
ROMANIA
BULGARIA
MOLDOVA
UKRAINE
RUSSIA

ANDORRA
PORTUGAL
SPAIN
ITALY
GREECE

KAZAKHSTAN
Aral Sea
Caspian Sea
GEORGIA
ARMENIA
AZER.
UZBEKISTAN
TURKMENISTAN
AFGHANISTAN

Azores
Madeira Is.
Casablanca
MOROCCO
Atlas Mountains
TUNISIA
Black Sea
TURKEY
CYPRUS
SYRIA
LEBANON
ISRAEL
JORDAN
IRAQ
IRAN

Canary Is.
WESTERN SAHARA (adm. Morocco)
ALGERIA
Igidi Desert
LIBYA
EGYPT
Gulf of Sidra
Suez Canal
Sinai Pen.
KUWAIT
BAHRAIN
QATAR
Persian Gulf
UNITED ARAB EMIRATES
OMAN

Cape Blanc
S
Ahaggar Mts.
Mt. Tahat 3003m
Qattara Depression -133m
Cairo
Red Sea
Nile R.
SAUDI ARABIA
TROPIC OF CANCER

MAURITANIA
a
Air Mts.
Tibesti Mts.
Emi Koussi 3415m
Libyan Desert
Lake Nasser
Nubian Desert
YEMEN
Socotra
Cape Guardafui

Cape Verde
SENEGAL
GAMBIA
GUINEA-BISSAU
MALI
h
NIGER
Niger R.
Lake Chad
CHAD
Chari R.
e
SUDAN
Blue Nile
White Nile
ERITREA
Ras Dashen 4620m
DJIBOUTI
Gulf of Aden
Somali Pen.

SIERRA LEONE
GUINEA
LIBERIA
BURKINA FASO
CÔTE D'IVOIRE (IVORY COAST)
GHANA
TOGO
BENIN
Lake Volta
NIGERIA
Jos Plateau
l
Sudd
Ethiopian Highlands
ETHIOPIA
SOMALIA

Cape Palmas
Lagos
Cameroon Mtn. 4095m
Bioko
CAMEROON
CENTRAL AFRICAN REPUBLIC
Ubangi R.
Congo R.
UGANDA
Lake Albert
Lake Turkana
KENYA
Mt. Kenya 5199m
Mogadishu

EQUATORIAL GUINEA
Principe
Sao Tome
Gulf of Guinea
GABON
Congo Basin
CONGO REPUBLIC
Congo R.
Margherita 5109m
RWANDA
Lake Victoria
EQUATOR

Annobon
CONGO (ZAIRE)
Kasai R.
BURUNDI
Mt. Kilimanjaro 5895m
Seychelles

ATLANTIC OCEAN
CABINDA
Cuanza R.
Lake Tanganyika
TANZANIA
Pemba I.
Zanzibar
Amirante Is.

Ascension I.
Katanga Plateau
Lake Mweru
Lake Bangweulu
Aldabra Is.
Cerf I.

ANGOLA
Bie Plateau
ZAMBIA
Lake Nyasa
MALAWI
Lake Nyasa
Comoros Islands
Agalega Is.

St. Helena
Cuando R.
Victoria Falls
Zambezi R.
Kariba L.
MOZAMBIQUE
Mozambique Channel
MADAGASCAR

Cape Fria
Etosha Pan
Makgadikgadi Pans
ZIMBABWE
Limpopo R.
Mauritius
Reunion
Mascarene Is.

NAMIBIA
Namib Desert
BOTSWANA
Kalahari Desert
TROPIC OF CAPRICORN

SWAZILAND
Orange R.
SOUTH AFRICA
Drakensberg
LESOTHO
INDIAN OCEAN

Cape Town
Cape of Good Hope
Cape Agulhas
N

Prince Edward Islands
Crozet Islands

PRIME MERIDIAN

AFRICA
Physical

————	International boundary
- - - -	Other boundary
⊛ Mogadishu	National capital
● Casablanca	Major city

ELEVATION

Meters		Feet
Over 3000		Over 10,000
1500 to 3000		5,000 to 10,000
600 to 1500		2,000 to 5,000
300 to 600		1,000 to 2,000
150 to 300		500 to 1,000
0 to 150		0 to 500
Below sea level		Below sea level

WATER DEPTH

Less than 200		Less than 600
Greater than 200		Greater than 600

0   250   500   750   1000 Miles

0   250 500 750 1000 Kilometers

Complete legend on page 7

ATLANTIC
OCEAN

GERMANY
CZ. REP.
SL.
FRANCE SWITZ. AUS. HUNGARY
SLOV. CRO. ROMANIA
ITALY BOS. YUGO.
MAC. BULGARIA
ALB.
GREECE

UKRAINE
MOLDOVA

RUSSIA

Black Sea

GEORGIA
ARMENIA AZER.

KAZAKHSTAN

Aral
Sea

UZBEKISTAN

TURKMENISTAN

Caspian
Sea

ANDORRA
PORTUGAL SPAIN

TURKEY

CYPRUS
SYRIA
LEBANON
ISRAEL

IRAQ

IRAN

AFGHANISTAN

Azores
(Portugal)

Strait of Gibraltar
Rabat
Casablanca Tangier
Oran
Algiers
Constantine
Tunis
Sfax
TUNISIA

MEDITERRANEAN SEA

Tripoli

Gulf
of
Sidra

Benghazi

Alexandria
Cairo

Suez
Canal

JORDAN
KUWAIT

BAHRAIN
QATAR
SAUDI
ARABIA

Persian Gulf
UNITED ARAB
EMIRATES

OMAN

Madeira Is.
(Portugal)

Marrakech
Bechar
Ouargla
Ghadamis

MOROCCO

TROPIC OF CANCER

Canary Is.
(Spain)
Las Palmas
El Aaiun
WESTERN
SAHARA
(adm. Morocco)

I-n-Salah

Ghat

Al Jawf

Aswan

Lake
Nasser

Red
Sea

YEMEN

Socotra
(Yemen)

Fderik

ALGERIA

LIBYA

EGYPT

Port Sudan

Bareeda

MAURITANIA

Tessalit

Bardai

ERITREA
Asmara

Gulf of Aden

Nouakchott
Dakar

Timbuktu
MALI

I-n-Gall
Agadez

Gao

Omdurman
Khartoum

DJIBOUTI
Djibouti

SENEGAL
GAMBIA
Banjul
GUINEA-
BISSAU
Bissau

Bamako

Niamey
NIGER
Zinder

CHAD

N'Djamena
Lake
Chad

Malakal

Addis
Ababa

Harer
Hargeysa

Conakry
Freetown
SIERRA
LEONE
Monrovia

GUINEA
Ouagadougou
BURKINA FASO

Kano
NIGERIA

Am Timan

SUDAN

White Nile
Waw

ETHIOPIA

Maji

Mega

SOMALIA

LIBERIA
CÔTE
D'IVOIRE
(IVORY
COAST)

GHANA

Abuja
Ibadan
Lagos

BENIN
TOGO

Porto-
Novo
Accra

Lomé
Cotonou

Port
Harcourt
CAMEROON
Douala
Malabo

Moundou
Sarh

CENTRAL AFRICAN
REPUBLIC

Bangui

Juba

Blue Nile

Lake
Turkana

Mogadishu

Abidjan

Gulf of
Guinea

EQUATORIAL GUINEA
SAO TOME &
PRINCIPE
Sao
Tome

Yaounde

Libreville

CONGO REPUBLIC

Congo

Ubangi R.

Kismaayo

Lake
Albert

UGANDA
Kampala

KENYA

Nairobi

EQUATOR

Annobon
(Eq. Guinea)

GABON

Mbandaka

Kisangani

RWANDA
Kigali

Lake
Victoria

Mombasa
Pemba I.

ATLANTIC

Ascension
(U.K.)

Brazzaville

Pointe-Noire
CABINDA
(Angola)
Kinshasa

CONGO
(ZAIRE)

Kasai
R.

Kananga

Bujumbura
BURUNDI
Kalemie

Mwanza

Dodoma
TANZANIA

Lake
Tanganyika

Zanzibar
Dar es Salaam

Victoria

SEYCHELLES

Luanda

Mbuji-Mayi

Lake
Mweru

Mbeya

OCEAN

St. Helena
(U.K.)

Lobito
Huambo
ANGOLA

Kolwezi
Lubumbashi
Kitwe

Lake
Bangweulu

COMOROS
Moroni

Agalega Is.
(Mauritius)

Lubango

ZAMBIA

Lilongwe
Lusaka

Lake
Nyasa

MALAWI

MOZAMBIQUE

Mayotte
(Fr.)

Cunene R.

Victoria
Falls

Kariba L.

Zambezi R.

Quelimane

MADAGASCAR

Antananarivo

MAURITIUS
Port-Louis

Etosha
Pan

Makgadikgadi
Pans

Harare
ZIMBABWE
Bulawayo

Beira

Mozambique Channel

Reunion
(Fr.)

NAMIBIA

Limpopo R.

Walvis Bay

BOTSWANA

Gaborone

Pretoria

Maputo
Mbabane SWAZILAND

TROPIC OF CAPRICORN

Windhoek

Johannesburg

Orange R.

SOUTH
Bloemfontein

Maseru
LESOTHO
Durban

INDIAN

AFRICA

Cape Town

Port Elizabeth

OCEAN

N

Prince Edward Is.
(South Africa)

Crozet Is.
(Fr.)

AFRICA
Political

BOUNDARIES

——————— International boundary

------------- Other boundary
(disputed or undefined)

CITIES

● Alexandria

● Durban

• Lubango

⊛ Algiers

A city's relative size is
shown by the size of
its symbol and lettering.

National capital

0   250   500   750   1000 Miles

0 250 500 750 1000 Kilometers

Complete legend on page 7

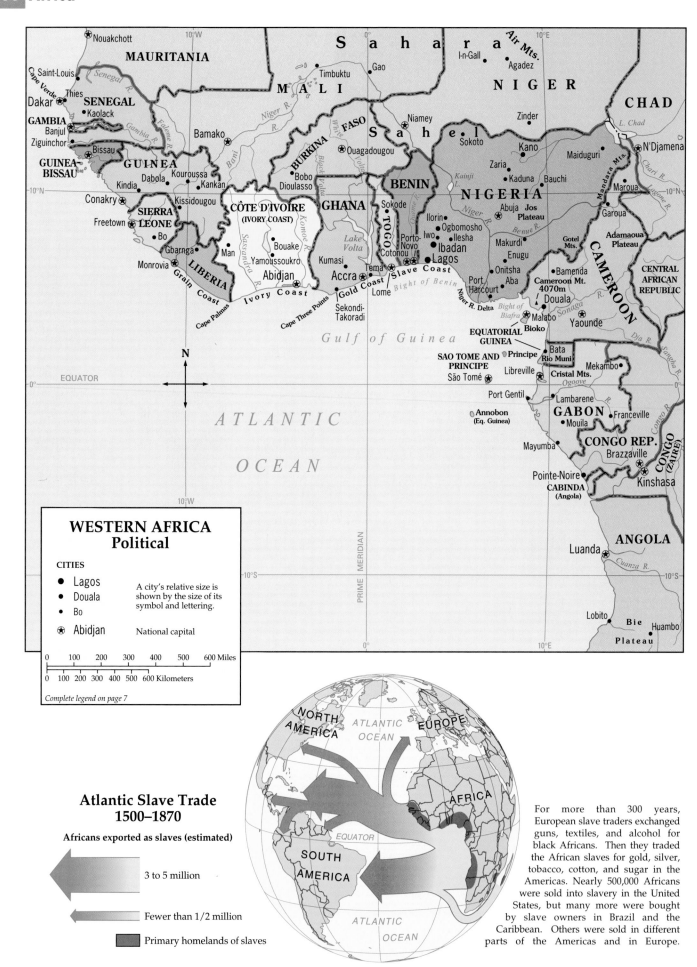

WESTERN AFRICA
Political

CITIES

● **Lagos**

● **Douala**

● Bo   A city's relative size is shown by the size of its symbol and lettering.

⊛ **Abidjan**   National capital

```
0    100   200   300   400   500   600 Miles
0  100 200 300 400 500 600 Kilometers
```

Complete legend on page 7

Atlantic Slave Trade
1500–1870

Africans exported as slaves (estimated)

3 to 5 million

Fewer than 1/2 million

Primary homelands of slaves

For more than 300 years, European slave traders exchanged guns, textiles, and alcohol for black Africans. Then they traded the African slaves for gold, silver, tobacco, cotton, and sugar in the Americas. Nearly 500,000 Africans were sold into slavery in the United States, but many more were bought by slave owners in Brazil and the Caribbean. Others were sold in different parts of the Americas and in Europe.

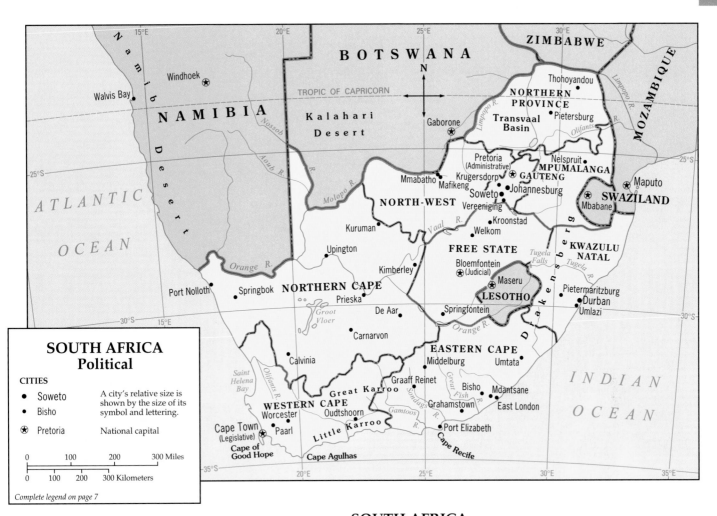

SOUTH AFRICA
Political

CITIES

●   Soweto   A city's relative size is shown by the size of its symbol and lettering.

•   Bisho

✪   Pretoria   National capital

| 0 | 100 | 200 | 300 Miles |
| 0 | 100 | 200 | 300 Kilometers |

Complete legend on page 7

SOUTH AFRICA
Balance of Trade

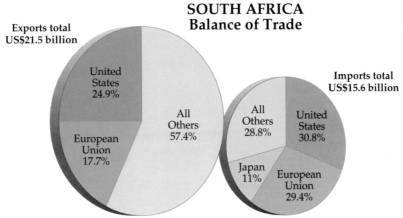

Exports total
US$21.5 billion

United States 24.9%

European Union 17.7%

All Others 57.4%

Imports total
US$15.6 billion

All Others 28.8%

United States 30.8%

Japan 11%

European Union 29.4%

Ethnic Composition of South Africa

Other African ethnic groups include Setswana, Shangaan, Siswati, and others.

Europeans are primarily Dutch and British.

Sotho 15.4%

Xhosa 18.1%

African 76.4%

Others 20.9%

Zulu 22%

European 12.6%

Mixed 8.5%

Asian 2.5%

South Africa's total population: 39.1 million

With the end of legal apartheid in 1994, a new future lies ahead for the children of South Africa.

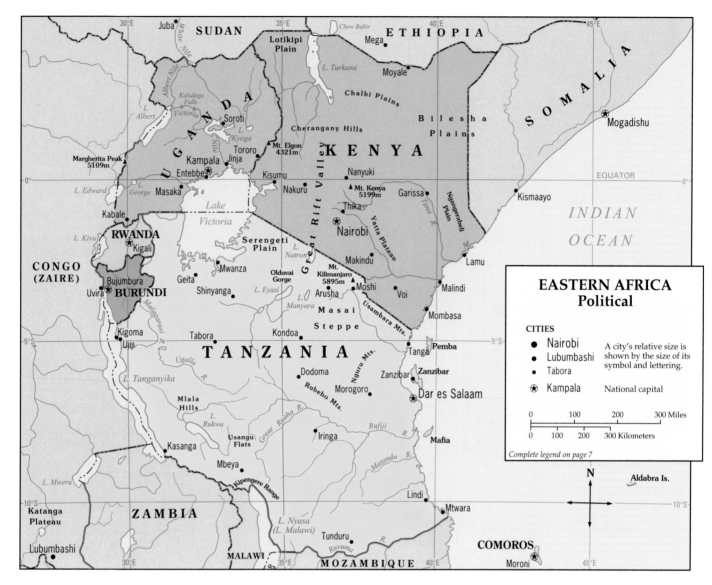

EASTERN AFRICA
Political

CITIES
● Nairobi   A city's relative size is shown by the size of its symbol and lettering.
● Lubumbashi
● Tabora
⊛ Kampala   National capital

0   100   200   300 Miles
0   100   200   300 Kilometers

Complete legend on page 7

N

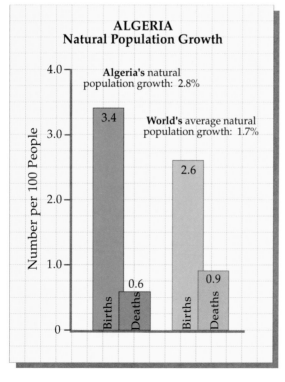

ALGERIA
Natural Population Growth

Algeria's natural population growth: 2.8%

World's average natural population growth: 1.7%

Number per 100 People

4.0
3.4 Births
3.0
2.6 Births
2.0
1.0
0.6 Deaths
0.9 Deaths
0

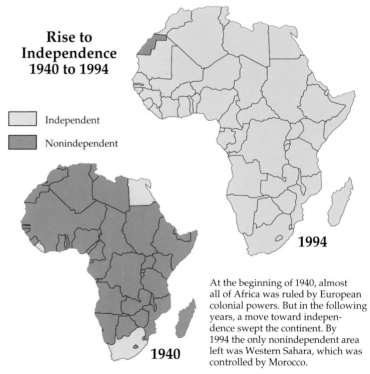

Rise to Independence 1940 to 1994

☐ Independent
■ Nonindependent

1994

1940

At the beginning of 1940, almost all of Africa was ruled by European colonial powers. But in the following years, a move toward independence swept the continent. By 1994 the only nonindependent area left was Western Sahara, which was controlled by Morocco.

Endangered Species

Present range of species

- Cheetah
- Black Rhinoceros
- Mountain Gorilla
- North African Ostrich

The cheetah, a hunter of incredible speed, is losing both its habitat and prey to human encroachment into its territory.

The black rhinoceros lives on grassland and brush vegetation. Its distinctive horn makes it a target for poachers.

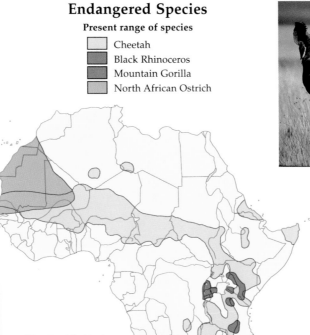

The cheetah, black rhino, ostrich, and gorilla are only four of the many endangered species that once freely roamed Africa.

The mountain gorilla leads a quiet life, living off forest vegetation. It has no real enemies except human beings.

The flightless ostrich can roam the plains for long periods without water. Demand for its skin and plumes threaten its survival in the wild.

Ivory Trade

Annual exports

Kilograms	Pounds
More than 20 000	More than 44,000
10 000 to 20 000	22,000 to 44,000
Less than 10 000	Less than 22,000
None exported	
Not reported	

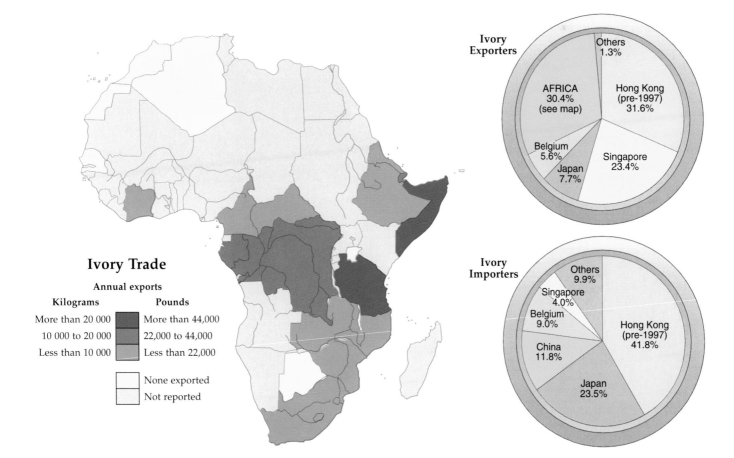

Ivory Exporters

- Others 1.3%
- Hong Kong (pre-1997) 31.6%
- AFRICA 30.4% (see map)
- Singapore 23.4%
- Belgium 5.6%
- Japan 7.7%

Ivory Importers

- Others 9.9%
- Singapore 4.0%
- Belgium 9.0%
- China 11.8%
- Japan 23.5%
- Hong Kong (pre-1997) 41.8%

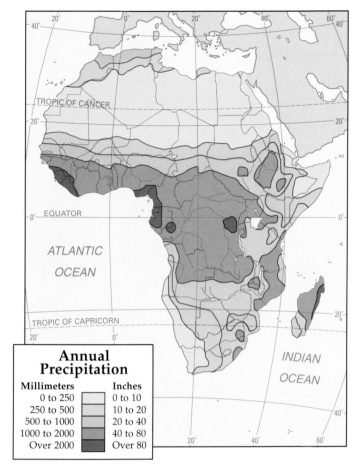

Annual Precipitation

Millimeters	Inches
0 to 250	0 to 10
250 to 500	10 to 20
500 to 1000	20 to 40
1000 to 2000	40 to 80
Over 2000	Over 80

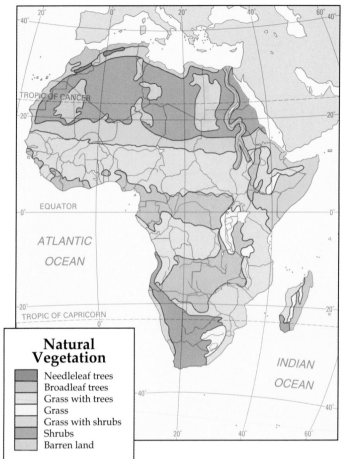

Natural Vegetation

- Needleleaf trees
- Broadleaf trees
- Grass with trees
- Grass
- Grass with shrubs
- Shrubs
- Barren land

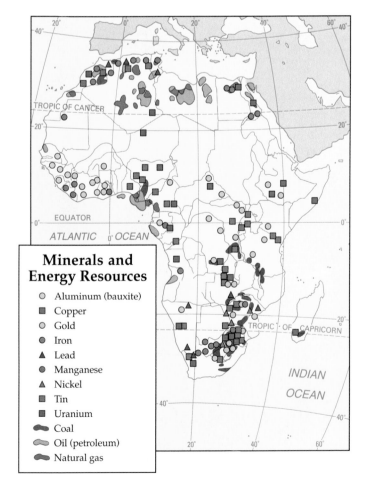

Minerals and Energy Resources

- Aluminum (bauxite)
- Copper
- Gold
- Iron
- Lead
- Manganese
- Nickel
- Tin
- Uranium
- Coal
- Oil (petroleum)
- Natural gas

A Moroccan market displays locally grown produce and handwoven carpets. Many Moroccans and other North Africans dress in traditional Islamic style.

The Changing Sahara

The Sahara stretches across a greater area than mainland Canada. During droughts it expands southward and in wet periods it shrinks back. Most recent years have been dry.

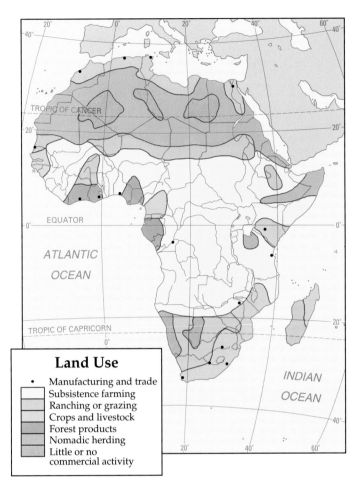

Land Use

- Manufacturing and trade
- Subsistence farming
- Ranching or grazing
- Crops and livestock
- Forest products
- Nomadic herding
- Little or no commercial activity

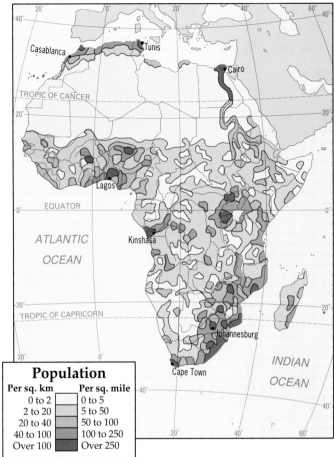

Population

Per sq. km	Per sq. mile
0 to 2	0 to 5
2 to 20	5 to 50
20 to 40	50 to 100
40 to 100	100 to 250
Over 100	Over 250

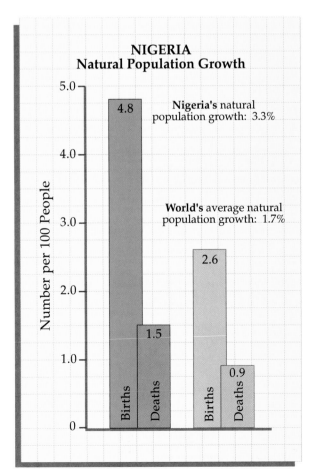

NIGERIA
Natural Population Growth

Number per 100 People

5.0

4.8 (Births)

Nigeria's natural population growth: 3.3%

4.0

World's average natural population growth: 1.7%

3.0

2.6 (Births)

2.0

1.5 (Deaths)

1.0

0.9 (Deaths)

0

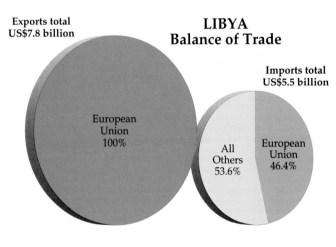

Exports total US$7.8 billion

LIBYA
Balance of Trade

Imports total US$5.5 billion

European Union 100%

All Others 53.6%

European Union 46.4%

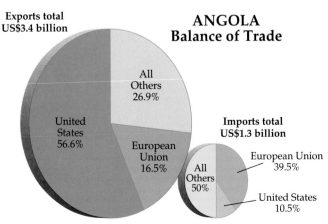

Exports total US$3.4 billion

ANGOLA
Balance of Trade

All Others 26.9%

United States 56.6%

European Union 16.5%

Imports total US$1.3 billion

European Union 39.5%

All Others 50%

United States 10.5%

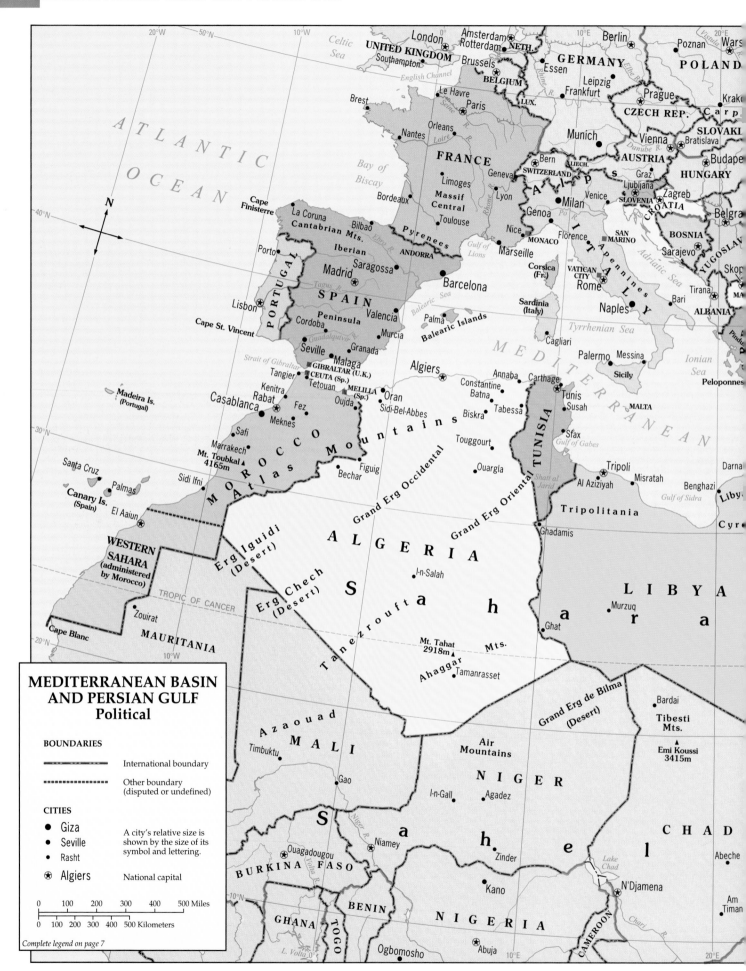

ATLANTIC OCEAN

Celtic Sea

London
UNITED KINGDOM
Southampton
Brest
English Channel
Amsterdam
Rotterdam NETH.
Brussels
BELGIUM
Le Havre
LUX.
Berlin
GERMANY
Essen
Leipzig
Frankfurt
Poznan
Wars
POLAND
Prague
CZECH REP.
Krako
Carp

Paris
Orleans
Nantes
Loire R.
Seine R.
Rhine R.

FRANCE
Limoges
Massif Central
Bordeaux
Toulouse
Rhône R.

Bay of Biscay

Cape Finisterre

N

40°N

La Coruna
Cantabrian Mts.
Bilbao
Iberian
Porto
PORTUGAL
Saragossa
Ebro R.
Madrid
Tagus R.
SPAIN
Peninsula
Lisbon
Cordoba
Guadalquivir R.
Cape St. Vincent
Seville
Granada
Malaga
Tangier
GIBRALTAR (U.K.)
CEUTA (Sp.)
Tetouan
MELILLA (Sp.)
Strait of Gibraltar

Pyrenees
ANDORRA
Valencia
Murcia
Palma
Balearic Islands
Balearic Sea

Gulf of Lions
Marseille
Nice
MONACO
Corsica (Fr.)
Sardinia (Italy)

Geneva
Bern
SWITZERLAND
Lyon
Genoa
Florence
VATICAN CITY
Rome
Naples

Munich
LIECH.
AUSTRIA
Graz
Ljubljana
SLOVENIA
Venice
Po R.
Milan
Apennines
SAN MARINO
Tyrrhenian Sea
Palermo
Sicily
Cagliari
Messina

Vienna
Bratislava
SLOVAKI
Budape
HUNGARY
Zagreb
CROATIA
Belgra
BOSNIA
Sarajevo
YUGOSLAV
Adriatic Sea
Tirana
ALBANIA
Bari
Skop
MA
Pindu
Ionian Sea
Peloponnes

Madeira Is. (Portugal)

Santa Cruz
Palmas
Canary Is. (Spain)
El Aaiun

30°N

Casablanca
Rabat
Kenitra
Fez
Meknes
Safi
Marrakech
Mt. Toubkal 4165m
MOROCCO
Oujda
Sidi-Bel-Abbes
Oran
Atlas Mountains

Sidi Ifni

WESTERN SAHARA (administered by Morocco)

Cape Blanc

MAURITANIA
10°W
20°N

Algiers
Annaba
Constantine
Batna
Tabessa
Biskra
Touggourt
Ouargla
Bechar
Figuig

Carthage
Tunis
Susah
TUNISIA
Sfax
Gulf of Gabes
Shatt al Jarid
Al Aziziyah
MALTA

MEDITERRANEAN

Tripoli
Misratah
Tripolitania
Benghazi
Gulf of Sidra
Darna
Liby
Cyr

ALGERIA
Grand Erg Occidental
Grand Erg Oriental
Ghadames

Erg Iguidi (Desert)
Erg Chech (Desert)
Tanezroufta
S
TROPIC OF CANCER
Zouirat

I-n-Salah
a
Mt. Tahat 2918m Mts.
Ahaggar
Tamanrasset
h
Ghat
a
Murzuq
r

LIBYA
Bardai
Tibesti Mts.
Emi Koussi 3415m

Azaouad
MALI
Timbuktu
Gao
Niger R.
S
Ouagadougou
BURKINA FASO
Niamey
a
BENIN
TOGO
GHANA
L. Volta
Ogbomosho
Abuja
NIGERIA

Air Mountains
I-n-Gall
Agadez
NIGER
Zinder
h
Kano
Lake Chad
e
N'Djamena
l
CHAD
Abeche
Am Timan
Chari R.
CAMEROON

Grand Erg de Bilma (Desert)

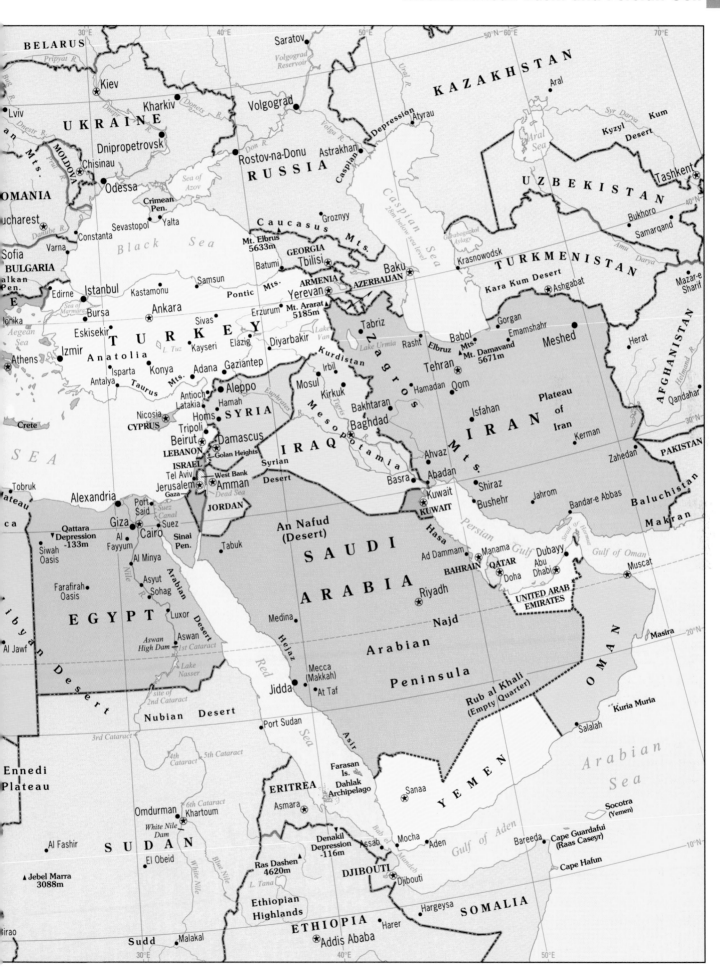

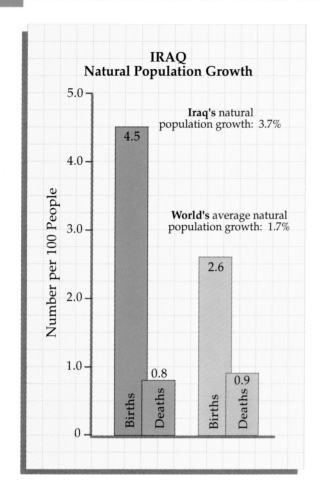

IRAQ
Natural Population Growth

Number per 100 People

Iraq's natural population growth: 3.7%

World's average natural population growth: 1.7%

4.5 Births
0.8 Deaths
2.6 Births
0.9 Deaths

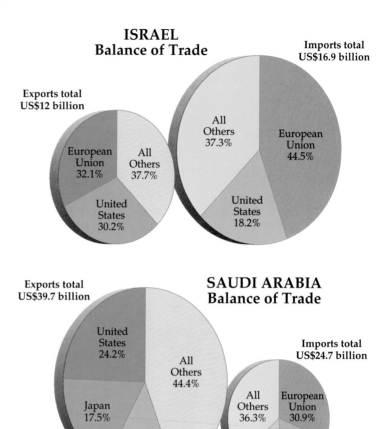

ISRAEL
Balance of Trade

Exports total US$12 billion

European Union 32.1%
All Others 37.7%
United States 30.2%

Imports total US$16.9 billion

All Others 37.3%
European Union 44.5%
United States 18.2%

SAUDI ARABIA
Balance of Trade

Exports total US$39.7 billion

United States 24.2%
All Others 44.4%
Japan 17.5%
European Union 13.9%

Imports total US$24.7 billion

All Others 36.3%
European Union 30.9%
United States 18.4%
Japan 14.4%

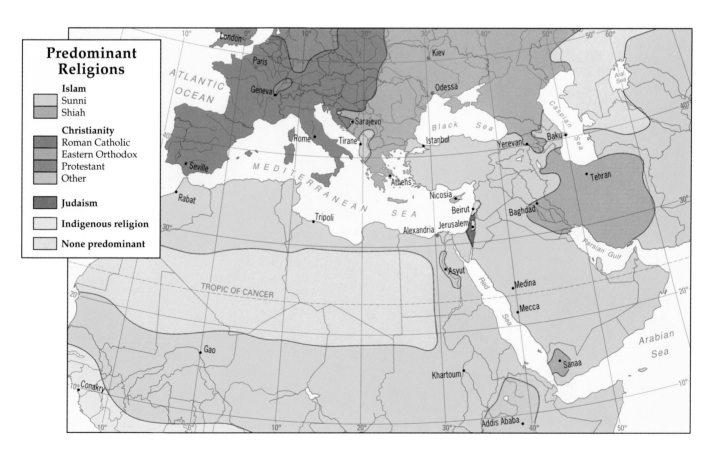

Predominant Religions

Islam
Sunni
Shiah

Christianity
Roman Catholic
Eastern Orthodox
Protestant
Other

Judaism

Indigenous religion

None predominant

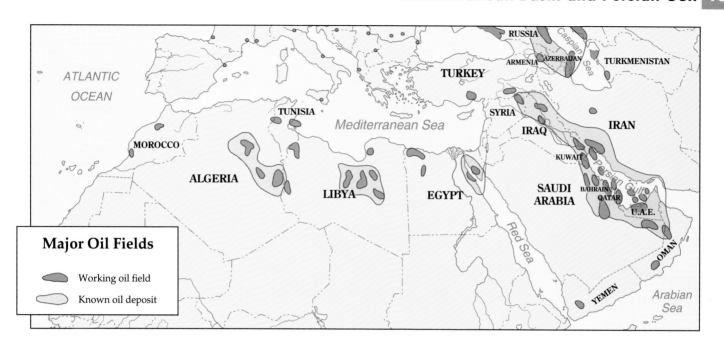

Major Oil Fields

- Working oil field
- Known oil deposit

Dependence on OPEC Oil

Canada both imports and exports petroleum. About 35% of its imports come from OPEC countries, accounting for about 1.1% of total OPEC exports.

Annual OPEC exports (number of barrels)

Number of barrels	Country	Percentage of total OPEC exports
2,778,500,000	All other countries	44.5%
271,000,000	Germany	4.3%
311,900,000	France	5.0%
427,800,000	Italy	6.8%
1,147,700,000	Japan	18.4%
1,309,800,000	United States	21.0%

OPEC: Organization of Petroleum Exporting Countries

Changing Boundaries

Israel occupied the area shown in dark orange until 1967. After the Six Day War of that year, it also controlled the parts of Egypt, Jordan, and Syria shown in light orange.

In stages during 1975, 1979, and 1982, Israel returned the Sinai Peninsula to Egypt. But Israel remained in control of the Gaza Strip, West Bank, and Golan Heights.

In 1993 Israeli and Palestinian leaders agreed on self-rule for Palestinians in Gaza and the city of Jericho. Jordan and Israel reached peace in 1994 and adjusted part of their boundary.

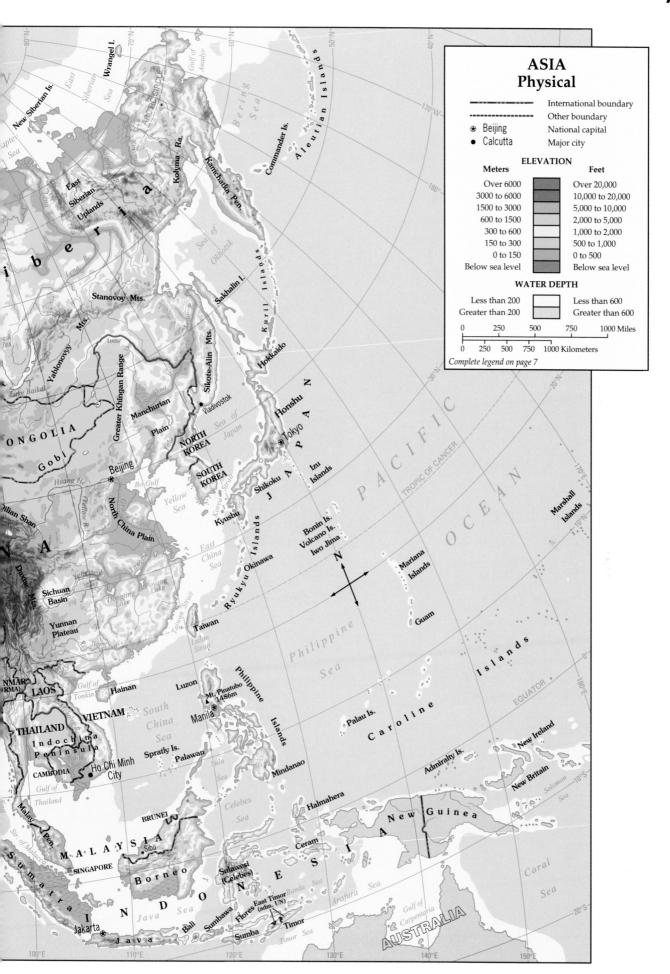

ASIA
Physical

—————————— International boundary
- - - - - - - - - - - Other boundary
⊛ Beijing   National capital
● Calcutta   Major city

ELEVATION

Meters		Feet
Over 6000		Over 20,000
3000 to 6000		10,000 to 20,000
1500 to 3000		5,000 to 10,000
600 to 1500		2,000 to 5,000
300 to 600		1,000 to 2,000
150 to 300		500 to 1,000
0 to 150		0 to 500
Below sea level		Below sea level

WATER DEPTH

Less than 200		Less than 600
Greater than 200		Greater than 600

0   250   500   750   1000 Miles

0   250   500   750   1000 Kilometers

Complete legend on page 7

Map labels

New Siberian Is.
Wrangel I.
East Siberian Sea
Laptev Sea
East Siberian Uplands
S i b e r i a
Gulf of Anadyr
ARCTIC CIRCLE
Kolyma Ra.
Kamchatka Pen.
Commander Is.
Aleutian Islands
Bering Sea
Stanovoy Mts.
Yablonovoy Mts.
Lena
Lake Baikal
Greater Khingan Range
Amur
Sikhote-Alin Mts.
Sakhalin I.
Sea of Okhotsk
Kuril Islands
Hokkaido
Manchurian Plain
Vladivostok
NORTH KOREA
Sea of Japan
Honshu
Tokyo
J A P A N
MONGOLIA
Gobi
Beijing
Bo Gulf
Huang He
Yellow R.
Yellow Sea
SOUTH KOREA
Korea Strait
Kyushu
Shikoku
Izu Islands
Qilian Shan
North China Plain
Grand Canal
East China Sea
Ryukyu Islands
Okinawa
Bonin Is.
Volcano Is.
Iwo Jima
PACIFIC OCEAN
TROPIC OF CANCER
Marshall Islands
N
Mariana Islands
Guam
Daxue Mts.
Sichuan Basin
Yunnan Plateau
Xi Jiang
Dongting Lake
Poyang Lake
Yangtze
Taiwan
Taiwan Strait
Luzon Strait
Philippine Sea
MYANMAR (BURMA)
LAOS
Gulf of Tonkin
Hainan
VIETNAM
South China Sea
Luzon
Mt. Pinatubo 1486m
Manila
Philippine Islands
Palau Is.
Caroline Islands
New Ireland
THAILAND
Indochina Peninsula
CAMBODIA
Ho Chi Minh City
Gulf of Thailand
Spratly Is.
Palawan
Sulu Sea
Mindanao
Admiralty Is.
New Britain
Solomon Sea
Malay Pen.
Str. of Malacca
MALAYSIA
SINGAPORE
Sibu
BRUNEI
Borneo
Celebes Sea
Halmahera
Ceram
New Guinea
AUSTRALIA
Coral Sea
Sulawesi (Celebes)
I N D O N E S I A
Banda Sea
Sumatra
Jakarta
Java
Java Sea
Bali
Sumbawa
Flores
East Timor (adm. UN)
Sumba
Timor
Timor Sea
Arafura Sea
Gulf of Carpentaria

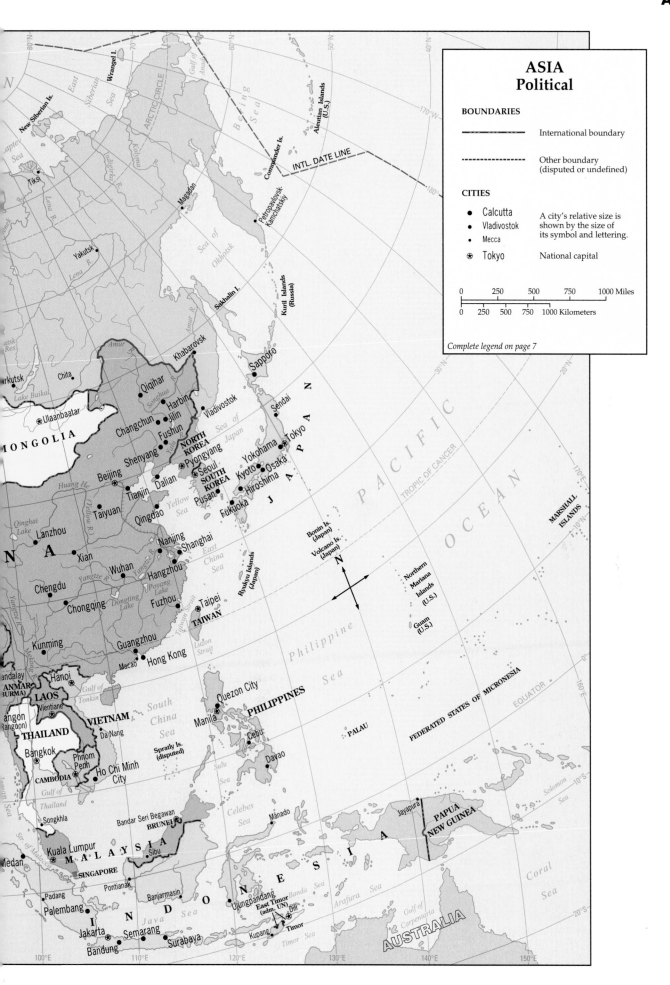

ASIA
Political

BOUNDARIES

— · — · — · — International boundary

– – – – – – – – Other boundary
(disputed or undefined)

CITIES

● Calcutta

● Vladivostok

· Mecca

A city's relative size is
shown by the size of
its symbol and lettering.

⊛ Tokyo   National capital

0   250   500   750   1000 Miles

0 250 500 750 1000 Kilometers

Complete legend on page 7

ARCTIC CIRCLE

New Siberian Is.

East
Siberian
Sea

Wrangel I.

Laptev
Sea

Gulf of
Anadyr

Chukchi
Sea

Bering
Sea

Aleutian Islands
(U.S.)

Commander Is.

INTL. DATE LINE

Tiksi

Indigirka R.

Kolyma R.

Magadan

Petropavlovsk-
Kamchatskiy

Lena R.

Yakutsk

Sea of
Okhotsk

Sakhalin I.

Kuril Islands
(Russia)

Irkutsk

Chita

Lake Baikal

Amur

Khabarovsk

Amur R.

Ussuri R.

Sapporo

Sendai

JAPAN

Ulaanbaatar

MONGOLIA

Qiqihar

Songhua

Harbin

Changchun

Jilin

Fushun

Vladivostok

Sea of
Japan

NORTH
KOREA

Pyongyang

Shenyang

Yalu

Yokohama
Tokyo

Beijing

Seoul
SOUTH
KOREA

Kyoto
Osaka
Hiroshima

Dalian

Pusan

Huang He
(Yellow R.)

Tianjin

Fukuoka

Qinghai
Lake

Lanzhou

Taiyuan

Qingdao

Yellow
Sea

PACIFIC

TROPIC OF CANCER

C H I N A

Xian

Nanjing

Shanghai

East
China
Sea

OCEAN

MARSHALL
ISLANDS

Chengdu

Wuhan

Yangtze R.

Hangzhou

Dongting
Lake

Poyang
Lake

Bonin Is.
(Japan)

Chongqing

Fuzhou

Ryukyu Islands (Japan)

Volcano Is.
(Japan)

Kunming

Yangtze R.

Guangzhou

Taipei

TAIWAN

N

Northern
Mariana
Islands
(U.S.)

Macao

Hong Kong

Luzon
Strait

Mandalay

Hanoi

Guam
(U.S.)

Gulf of
Tonkin

Philippine

Sea

MYANMAR
(BURMA)

LAOS

Vientiane

VIETNAM

Quezon City

Mekong

Da Nang

South
China
Sea

Manila

PHILIPPINES

FEDERATED STATES OF MICRONESIA

EQUATOR

Rangoon
(Yangon)

THAILAND

Bangkok

Phnom
Penh

Cebu

Spratly Is.
(disputed)

CAMBODIA

Ho Chi Minh
City

Davao

PALAU

Songkhla

Gulf of
Thailand

Sulu
Sea

Celebes
Sea

Manado

Solomon
Sea

Jayapura

PAPUA
NEW GUINEA

Str. of Malacca

Bandar Seri Begawan

BRUNEI

Medan

Kuala Lumpur

M A L A Y S I A

Sibu

I N D O N E S I A

SINGAPORE

Banda Sea

Arafura
Sea

Coral
Sea

Padang

Pontianak

Palembang

I N D

Banjarmasin

Java Sea

Ujungpandang

East Timor
(adm. UN)

Dili

Timor

Jakarta

Semarang

O N E S I A

Kupang

Gulf of
Carpentaria

Bandung

Surabaya

Timor Sea

AUSTRALIA

100°E   110°E   120°E   130°E   140°E   150°E

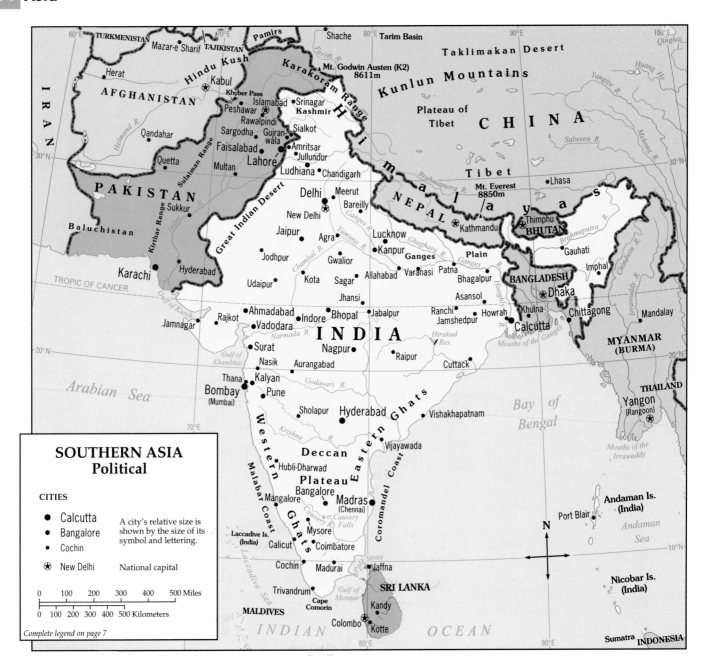

SOUTHERN ASIA
Political

CITIES

● Calcutta

● Bangalore

• Cochin

A city's relative size is shown by the size of its symbol and lettering.

⊛ New Delhi   National capital

```
0   100  200  300  400  500 Miles
0 100 200 300 400 500 Kilometers
```

Complete legend on page 7

India's Ganges River is considered sacred by Hindus, who bathe in its waters to purify themselves.

Dry Monsoon

The climate of Southeastern Asia and India is greatly influenced by large-scale seasonal wind systems called **monsoons.** In winter, dry winds generated over the cold surface of the land blow toward the warmer oceans and keep clouds away.

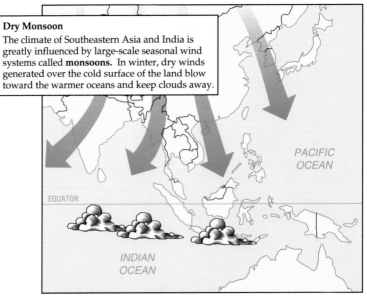

SOUTHEASTERN ASIA
Political

CITIES

● Calcutta

● Medan   A city's relative size is shown by the size of its symbol and lettering.

• Ipoh

☆ Bangkok   National capital

| 0 | 100 | 200 | 300 | 400 Miles |

| 0 | 100 | 200 | 300 | 400 Kilometers |

Complete legend on page 7

Himalayas
Thimphu
BHUTAN
INDIA
BANGLADESH
Dhaka
Calcutta
N
Bay
of
Bengal
Myitkyina
Namtu
Mandalay
MYANMAR
(BURMA)
Thayetmyo
Myanaung
Pegu
Bassein
Moulmein
Yangon
(Rangoon)
Mouths of
the Irrawaddy
Andaman Is.
(India)
Port Blair
Andaman
Sea
Mergui
Archipelago
Isthmus
of Kra
Surat Thani
Nicobar Is.
(India)
Songkhla
INDIAN
OCEAN
Malay
Peninsula
Pinang
(George Town)
Ipoh
Medan
Pematangsiantar
Simeulue
Kelang
Kuala Lumpur
Nias
Sumatra
Johor Baharu
SINGAPORE
Chongqing
Zunyi
Yunnan Plateau
Kunming
CHINA
Changsha
Wuzhou
Guangzhou
Macao
Hong Kong
TROPIC OF CANCER
Chiang Rai
Chiang Mai
Dien Bien Phu
Louangphrabang
LAOS
Vientiane
(Viangchan)
THAILAND
Khon Kaen
Savannakhet
Nakhon
Ratchasima
Thon Buri
Bangkok
Gulf
of
Thailand
CAMBODIA
Phnom Penh
Tonle
Sap
Kratie
Long
Xuyen
Can
Tho
Con Son Is.
Mouths
of the Mekong
Hanoi
Haiphong
Nam Dinh
Gulf of
Tonkin
Hainan
Haikou
Vinh
Hue
Da Nang
VIETNAM
Plateau
of
Kontum
Qui Nhon
Nha Trang
Bien Hoa
Ho Chi Minh City (Saigon)
Annamite Mts.
Khone
Falls
South
China
Sea
Paracel Is.
(disputed)
Spratly Is.
(disputed)
Mt. Pinatubo
1486m
Luzon
Strait
Luzon
Quezon
City
Manila
Mindoro
PHILIPPINES
Palawan
Sulu
Sea
Balabac Strait
Kota Kinabalu
Bandar Seri Begawan
BRUNEI
Sabah
Sandakan
Tarakan
Celebes
Sea
MALAYSIA
Sibu
Sarawak
Kuching
Borneo
Makassar
Strait
Sulawesi
Natuna I.
(Indonesia)
Serasun
Strait
Pontianak
INDONESIA
EQUATOR

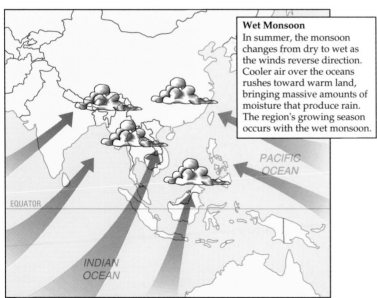

Wet Monsoon
In summer, the monsoon changes from dry to wet as the winds reverse direction. Cooler air over the oceans rushes toward warm land, bringing massive amounts of moisture that produce rain. The region's growing season occurs with the wet monsoon.

PACIFIC
OCEAN

INDIAN
OCEAN

EQUATOR

Terraces maximize the growing space for rice in hilly terrain. Rice is the most important food crop in southeastern Asia.

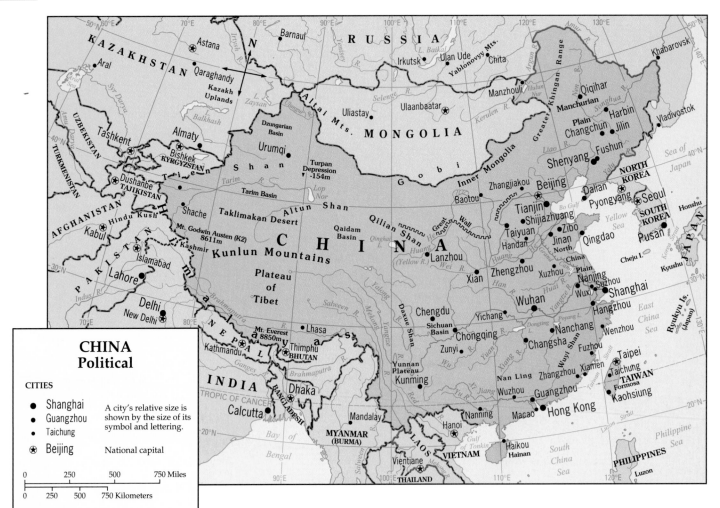

CHINA
Political

CITIES

● Shanghai   A city's relative size is
● Guangzhou shown by the size of its
• Taichung   symbol and lettering.

⊛ Beijing   National capital

0	250	500	750 Miles
0	250	500	750 Kilometers

Complete legend on page 7

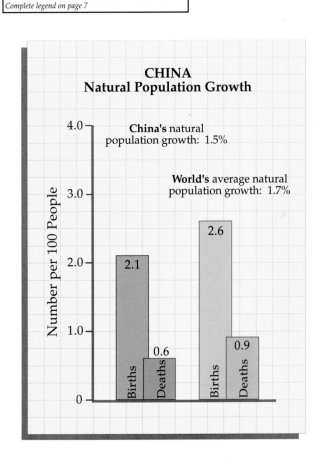

CHINA
Natural Population Growth

China's natural
population growth: 1.5%

World's average natural
population growth: 1.7%

Number per 100 People

4.0

3.0

2.0 — 2.1 (Births) / 2.6 (Births)

1.0 — 0.6 (Deaths) / 0.9 (Deaths)

0

Births Deaths Births Deaths

Bicycles in China

Number of bicycles in use: 369.2 million

Number of automobiles in use: 1.4 million

Nearly half of the people who work in
urban China commute by bicycle.

CHINA
Area Comparison

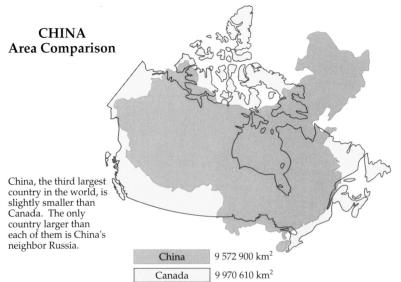

China, the third largest
country in the world, is
slightly smaller than
Canada. The only
country larger than
each of them is China's
neighbor Russia.

China	9 572 900 km²
Canada	9 970 610 km²

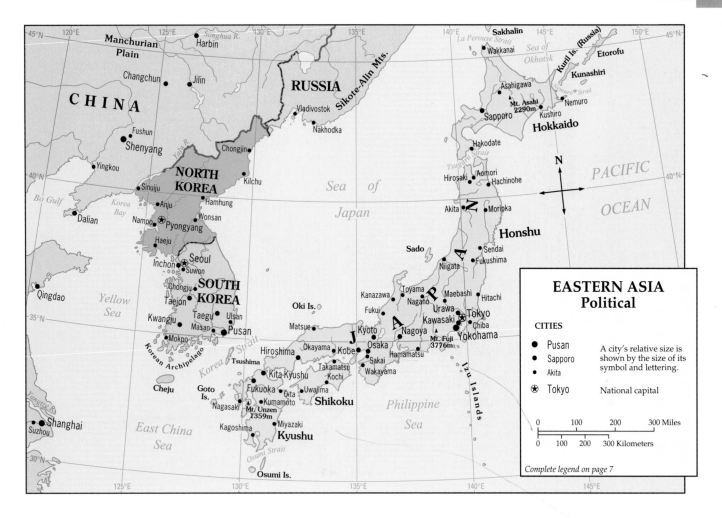

EASTERN ASIA
Political

CITIES

● Pusan

● Sapporo

● Akita   A city's relative size is shown by the size of its symbol and lettering.

✪ Tokyo   National capital

| 0 | 100 | 200 | 300 Miles |

| 0 | 100 | 200 | 300 Kilometers |

Complete legend on page 7

SOUTH KOREA
Balance of Trade

Exports total US$70.3 billion

United States 27.5%

Japan 18%

All Others 54.5%

Imports total US$74.9 billion

Japan 26%

United States 23.8%

All Others 50.2%

JAPAN
Balance of Trade

Exports total US$360.9 billion

United States 29.6%

European Union 9.8%

All Others 60.6%

Imports total US$269.7 billion

United States 22.4%

All Others 77.6%

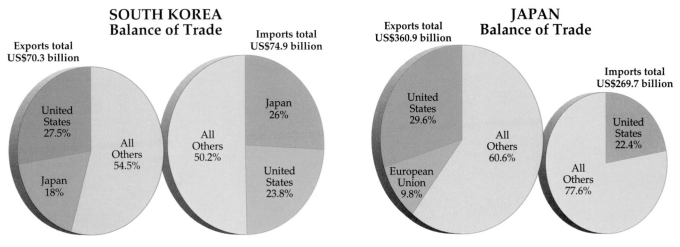

Leading Automobile Manufacturers

	Automobiles manufactured per year	Percentage of world production
Japan	9,693,000	27.7%
United States	5,726,000	16.4%
Germany	4,829,000	13.8%
France	3,271,000	9.4%
Canada	1,048,000	3.0%
Other countries	10,391,000	29.7%

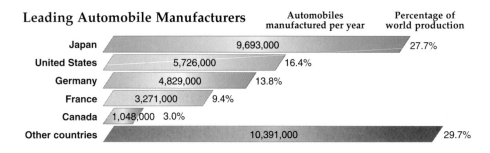

Japan's automakers have assembly plants in a number of locations in the United States.

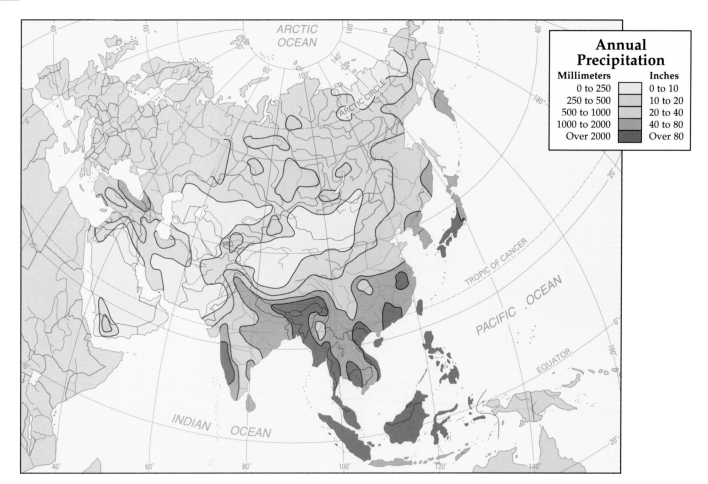

Annual Precipitation

Millimeters		Inches
0 to 250		0 to 10
250 to 500		10 to 20
500 to 1000		20 to 40
1000 to 2000		40 to 80
Over 2000		Over 80

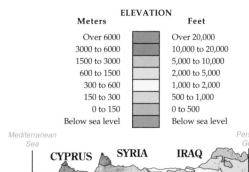

The Himalayas, located in southern Asia, are the world's highest mountain system.

INDONESIA
Area Comparison

The combined land area of Indonesia's 17,000 islands is about one-fifth the size of Canada. Three islands located partly or entirely in Indonesia—Sumatra, Borneo and New Guinea— are each larger than all five Great Lakes combined.

Indonesia	1 919 317 km²
Canada	9 970 610 km²

Cross Section of Asia

ELEVATION

Meters		Feet
Over 6000		Over 20,000
3000 to 6000		10,000 to 20,000
1500 to 3000		5,000 to 10,000
600 to 1500		2,000 to 5,000
300 to 600		1,000 to 2,000
150 to 300		500 to 1,000
0 to 150		0 to 500
Below sea level		Below sea level

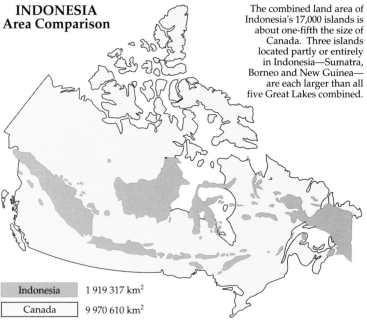

Plateau

Mediterranean Sea
CYPRUS SYRIA IRAQ
Persian Gulf
IRAN AFGHANISTAN
PAKISTAN INDIA

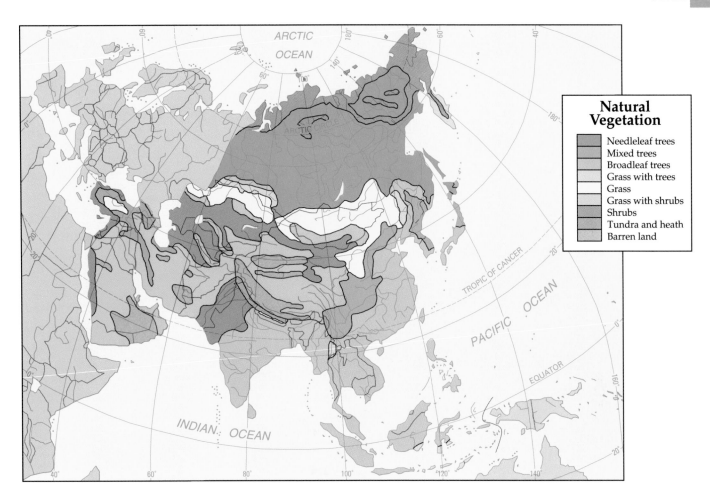

Natural Vegetation

- Needleleaf trees
- Mixed trees
- Broadleaf trees
- Grass with trees
- Grass
- Grass with shrubs
- Shrubs
- Tundra and heath
- Barren land

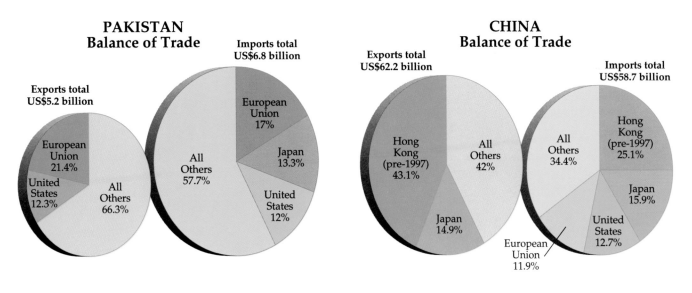

PAKISTAN
Balance of Trade

Exports total
US$5.2 billion

- European Union 21.4%
- United States 12.3%
- All Others 66.3%

Imports total
US$6.8 billion

- European Union 17%
- Japan 13.3%
- United States 12%
- All Others 57.7%

CHINA
Balance of Trade

Exports total
US$62.2 billion

- Hong Kong (pre-1997) 43.1%
- All Others 42%
- Japan 14.9%

Imports total
US$58.7 billion

- Hong Kong (pre-1997) 25.1%
- All Others 34.4%
- Japan 15.9%
- United States 12.7%
- European Union 11.9%

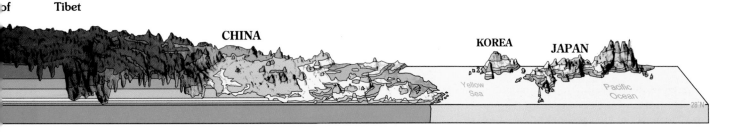

of Tibet   CHINA   KOREA   JAPAN

Yellow Sea   Pacific Ocean

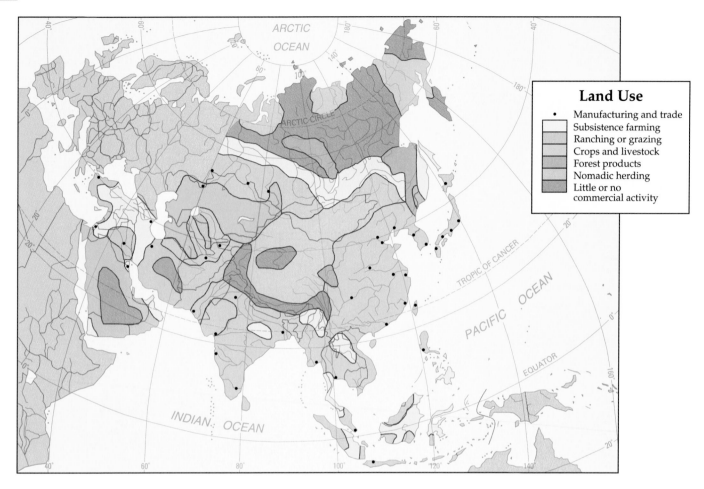

Land Use

- Manufacturing and trade
- Subsistence farming
- Ranching or grazing
- Crops and livestock
- Forest products
- Nomadic herding
- Little or no commercial activity

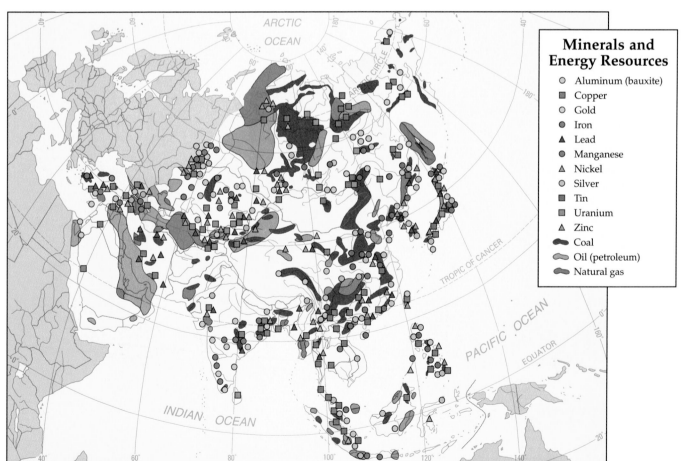

Minerals and Energy Resources

- ○ Aluminum (bauxite)
- ■ Copper
- ○ Gold
- ● Iron
- ▲ Lead
- ● Manganese
- △ Nickel
- ○ Silver
- ■ Tin
- ■ Uranium
- ▲ Zinc
- Coal
- Oil (petroleum)
- Natural gas

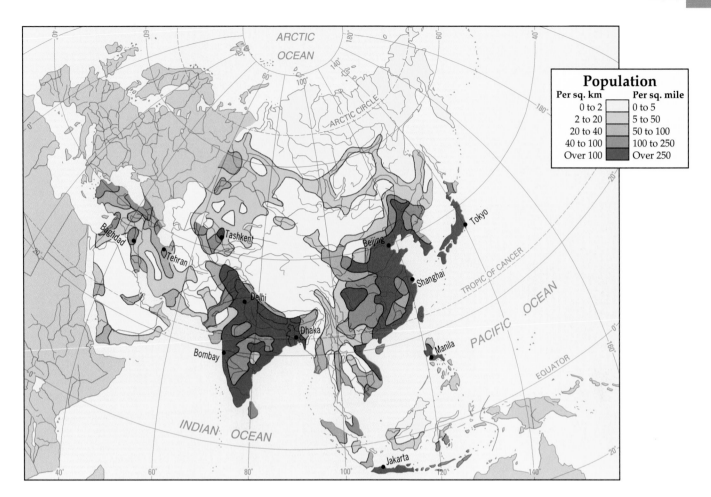

Population

Per sq. km	Per sq. mile
0 to 2	0 to 5
2 to 20	5 to 50
20 to 40	50 to 100
40 to 100	100 to 250
Over 100	Over 250

Six Asian Populations

Six Asian countries are home for nearly half of the world's population. But the 2,600,000,000 people living there occupy less than 12% of the world's land area.

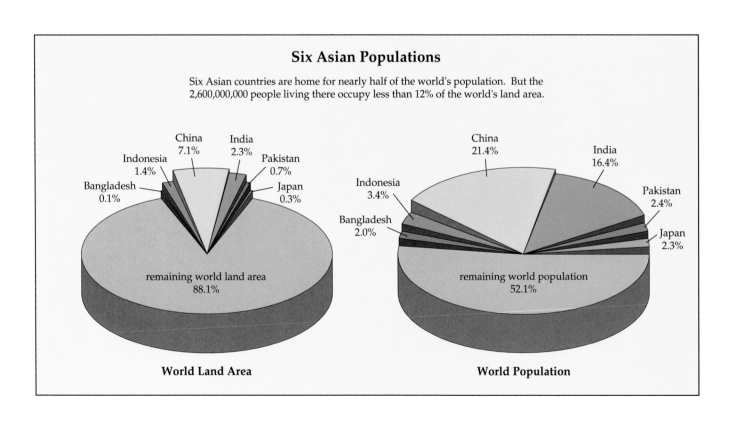

World Land Area

Indonesia 1.4%
China 7.1%
India 2.3%
Pakistan 0.7%
Bangladesh 0.1%
Japan 0.3%
remaining world land area 88.1%

World Population

China 21.4%
India 16.4%
Indonesia 3.4%
Bangladesh 2.0%
Pakistan 2.4%
Japan 2.3%
remaining world population 52.1%

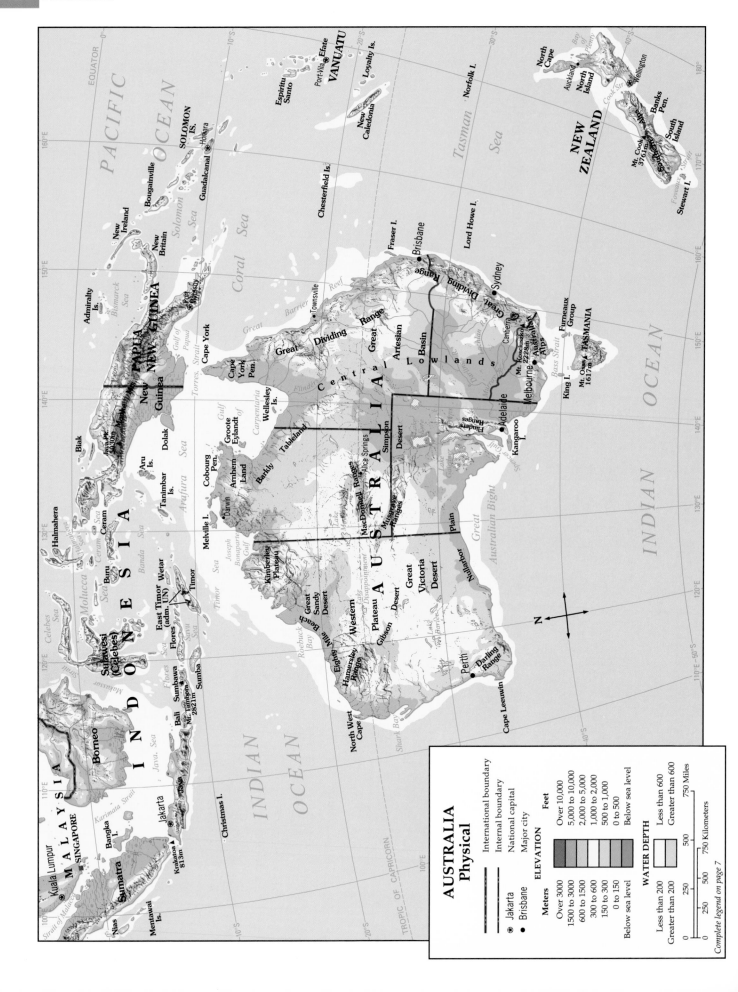

PACIFIC OCEAN

EQUATOR

SOLOMON IS.
Bougainville
Honiara
Guadalcanal

Espiritu Santo
Port-Vila · Efate
VANUATU
New Caledonia
Loyalty Is.

Norfolk I.

North Cape
Bay of Plenty
Auckland
North Island
Wellington
Cook Str.
Banks Pen.
South Island
NEW ZEALAND
Mt. Cook 3761m
Southern Alps
Foveaux Str.
Stewart I.

Tasman Sea

Chesterfield Is.

Coral Sea

Lord Howe I.

Fraser I.
Brisbane

Sydney
Great Dividing Range
Canberra
Mt. Kosciuszko 2228m
Australian Alps
Melbourne
Bass Strait
King I.
Furneaux Group
Mt. Ossa 1617m
TASMANIA

Admiralty Is.
New Ireland
New Britain
Bismarck Sea
Port Moresby
PAPUA NEW GUINEA
New Guinea
Java Pk. 4130m

Biak
Aru Is.
Tanimbar Is.
Dolak

Cape York
Townsville
Great Barrier Reef

Great Dividing Range
Central Lowlands
Great Artesian Basin

Cape York Pen.
Wellesley Is.
Flinders
Gulf of Carpentaria

Cobourg Pen.
Groote Eylandt
Barkly Tableland
MacDonnell Ranges
Alice Springs
Simpson Desert
Musgrave Ranges

Adelaide
Kangaroo I.
Flinders Ranges
Spencer Gulf

Arnhem Land
Darwin
Melville I.
Joseph Bonaparte Gulf

Kimberley Plateau
Great Sandy Desert
Gibson Desert
Western Plateau
Great Victoria Desert

Nullarbor Plain
Great Australian Bight

AUSTRALIA

Roebuck Bay
Eighty Mile Beach
Hamersley Range

North West Cape
Shark Bay

Perth
Darling Range

Cape Leeuwin

INDONESIA

Halmahera
Celebes Sea
Sulawesi (Celebes)
Molucca Sea
Buru
Ceram
Ceram Sea
Banda Sea

East Timor (adm. UN)
Wetar
Timor
Flores
Savu Sea
Flores Sea
Sumbawa
Sumba
Bali
Mt. Tambora 2821m

Timor Sea
Arafura Sea

MALAYSIA
Kuala Lumpur
SINGAPORE
Borneo
Bangka I.
Sumatra
Mentawai Is.
Nias
Krakatoa 813m
Java
Jakarta
Java Sea
Karimata Strait
Strait of Malacca
Makassar Strait

Christmas I.

INDIAN OCEAN

TROPIC OF CAPRICORN

N

PACIFIC OCEAN

EQUATOR

EQUATOR

SOLOMON IS.

VANUATU

Espiritu Santo

Port-Vila ★ Éfaté

Loyalty Is. (France)

New Caledonia (France)

Norfolk I. (Austr.)

North Cape

Bay of Plenty

Napier

Auckland

North Island

Wellington

Christchurch

NEW ZEALAND

Westport

South Island

Dunedin

Cook Str.

Foveaux Strait

Stewart I.

Bougainville

Guadalcanal ★ Honiara

New Ireland

New Britain

Bismarck Sea

Admiralty Is.

Solomon Sea

Coral Sea

Chesterfield Is. (France)

Fraser I.

Brisbane

Gold Coast

Lord Howe I. (Austr.)

Tasman Sea

Rockhampton

Great

Barrier

Reef

Newcastle

Sydney

Wollongong

AUSTRALIAN CAPITAL TERRITORY

Furneaux Group

NEW PAPUA GUINEA

New Guinea

Gulf of Papua

Port Moresby ★

Torres Strait

Cairns

Townsville

QUEENSLAND

NEW SOUTH WALES

Penrith

Darling R.

Lachlan R.

Canberra ★

Launceston

Hobart

Jayapura

West Papua (Irian Jaya)

Dolak

Flinders

Carpentaria

Wellesley Is.

Mt. Isa

Murray

Murrumbidgee

VICTORIA

Geelong • Melbourne

Bass Strait

King I.

TASMANIA

Biak

Manokwari

Fakfak

Aru Is.

Tanimbar Is.

Arafura Sea

Groote Eylandt

Gulf of Carpentaria

NORTHERN TERRITORY

Alice Springs

SOUTH AUSTRALIA

Lake Eyre

Lake Torrens

Lake Gairdner

Woomera

Salisbury

Adelaide

Whyalla

Kangaroo I.

Spencer Gulf

Manado

Halmahera

Ceram Sea

Buru

Ceram

Banda Sea

Melville I.

Darwin

Victoria R.

Daly R.

Roper R.

Lake Mackay

Lake Disappointment

A U S T R A L I A

Lake Gairdner

Lake Torrens

Spencer Gulf

Great Australian Bight

INDIAN OCEAN

Sulawesi (Celebes)

Ujungpandang

Celebes Sea

Molucca Sea

Makassar Strait

East Timor (adm. UN)

Wetar

Dili

Timor

Kupang

Savu Sea

Timor Sea

Joseph Bonaparte Gulf

Derby

Fitzroy R.

Roebuck Bay

Port Hedland

WESTERN AUSTRALIA

Lake Carnegie

Lake Barlee

Kalgoorlie

Geraldton

Perth

Fremantle

Cape Leeuwin

I N D O N E S I A

Borneo

Banjarmasin

Pontianak

Bangka I.

Palembang

Sumatra

Mentawai Is.

Nias

Java Sea

Semarang

Surabaya

Malang

Bali

Java

Bandung

Jakarta

Flores Sea

Sumbawa

Sumba

Flores

Christmas I. (Austr.)

INDIAN OCEAN

North West Cape

Shark Bay

MALAYSIA

Kuala Lumpur

SINGAPORE

Strait of Malacca

Karimata Strait

TROPIC OF CAPRICORN

INDIAN OCEAN

N

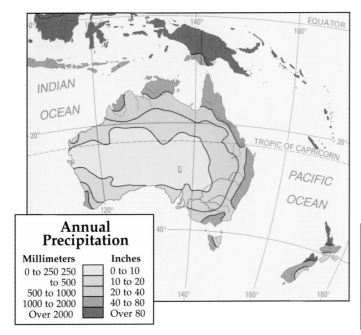

Annual Precipitation

Millimeters		Inches
0 to 250	250	0 to 10
to 500		10 to 20
500 to 1000		20 to 40
1000 to 2000		40 to 80
Over 2000		Over 80

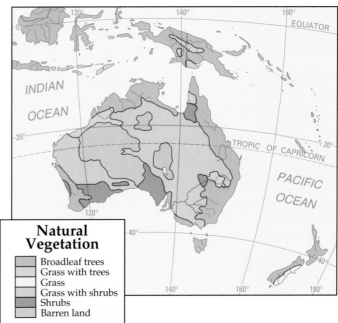

Natural Vegetation

- Broadleaf trees
- Grass with trees
- Grass
- Grass with shrubs
- Shrubs
- Barren land

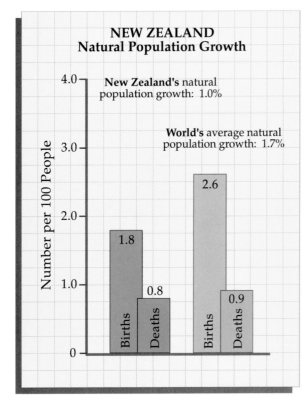

NEW ZEALAND Natural Population Growth

New Zealand's natural population growth: 1.0%

World's average natural population growth: 1.7%

Number per 100 People

- Births 1.8
- Deaths 0.8
- Births 2.6
- Deaths 0.9

Sydney is Australia's largest city. Its Opera House and Harbour Bridge are internationally recognized landmarks.

Isolated Australia is home to many unique animals, including marsupials such as the kangaroo.

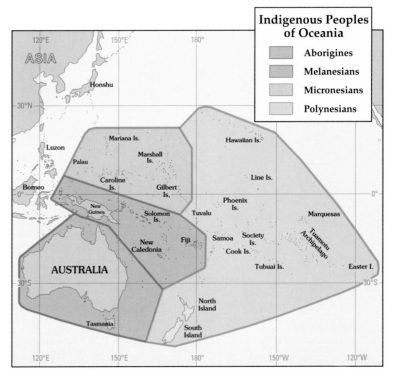

Indigenous Peoples of Oceania

- Aborigines
- Melanesians
- Micronesians
- Polynesians

ASIA

Honshu
Luzon
Borneo
Mariana Is.
Palau
Marshall Is.
Caroline Is.
Gilbert Is.
New Guinea
Solomon Is.
New Caledonia
Fiji
Tuvalu
Samoa
Cook Is.
Society Is.
Phoenix Is.
Hawaiian Is.
Line Is.
Marquesas
Tuamotu Archipelago
Tubuai Is.
Easter I.

AUSTRALIA

Tasmania
North Island
South Island

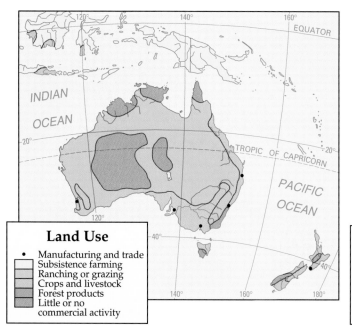

Land Use

- Manufacturing and trade
- Subsistence farming
- Ranching or grazing
- Crops and livestock
- Forest products
- Little or no commercial activity

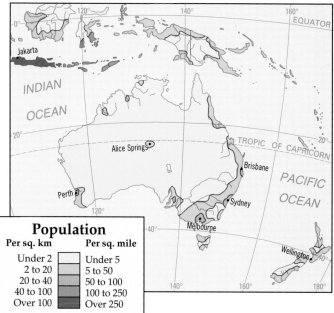

Population

Per sq. km	Per sq. mile
Under 2	Under 5
2 to 20	5 to 50
20 to 40	50 to 100
40 to 100	100 to 250
Over 100	Over 250

Australia's Isolation

Tokyo

5,000 miles
8100 kilometers

Honolulu

Singapore

3,900 miles
6300 kilometers

5,100 miles
8200 kilometers

Sydney

7,200 miles
11 600 kilometers

to Buenos Aires

EQUATOR

INDIAN OCEAN

PACIFIC OCEAN

Distances and time zone differences kept Australia isolated for many years.

AUSTRALIA
Balance of Trade

Exports total
US$37.4 billion

- Japan 26.7%
- United States 10.4%
- All Others 62.9%

Imports total
US$36.4 billion

- United States 26.5%
- Japan 18.5%
- European Union 18%
- All Others 37%

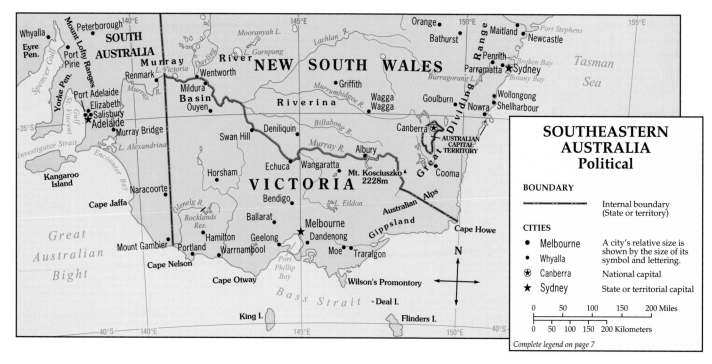

Whyalla
Eyre Pen.
Mount Lofty Ranges
Peterborough
Port Pirie

SOUTH
AUSTRALIA

Murray
Darling
River
L. Garnpung
Mooranyah L.

NEW SOUTH WALES

Orange
Bathurst
Maitland
Newcastle
Port Stephens

Renmark
L. Victoria
Wentworth
Mildura
Basin
Ouyen

Murrumbidgee R.
Griffith

Penrith
Parramatta
Sydney
Broken Bay
Botany Bay
Burragorang L.

Tasman Sea

Port Adelaide
Elizabeth
Salisbury
Adelaide
Murray Bridge

Riverina
Wagga Wagga

Goulburn
Nowra
Wollongong
Shellharbour

Yorke Pen.
St. Vincent
Spencer Gulf
Gulf

Swan Hill
Deniliquin
Billabong R.
Murray R.
Albury

Canberra
AUSTRALIAN CAPITAL TERRITORY

Great Dividing Range

Kangaroo Island

Naracoorte

Horsham

Echuca
Wangaratta
Mt. Kosciuszko
2228m

Cooma

Investigator Strait
L. Alexandrina

Encounter Bay

VICTORIA

Bendigo
L. Eildon

Australian Alps

Gippsland

Cape Jaffa

Glenelg R.
Rocklands Res.

Ballarat

Melbourne
Dandenong

Hamilton
Geelong
Moe
Traralgon

Cape Howe

Mount Gambier
Portland
Warrnambool

Port Phillip Bay

Cape Nelson

Great
Australian
Bight

Cape Otway

Wilson's Promontory

Bass Strait

King I.

Deal I.

Flinders I.

N

SOUTHEASTERN AUSTRALIA
Political

BOUNDARY

———— Internal boundary (State or territory)

CITIES

- Melbourne — A city's relative size is shown by the size of its symbol and lettering.
- Whyalla
- ⊛ Canberra — National capital
- ★ Sydney — State or territorial capital

0   50   100   150   200 Miles
0 50 100 150 200 Kilometers

Complete legend on page 7

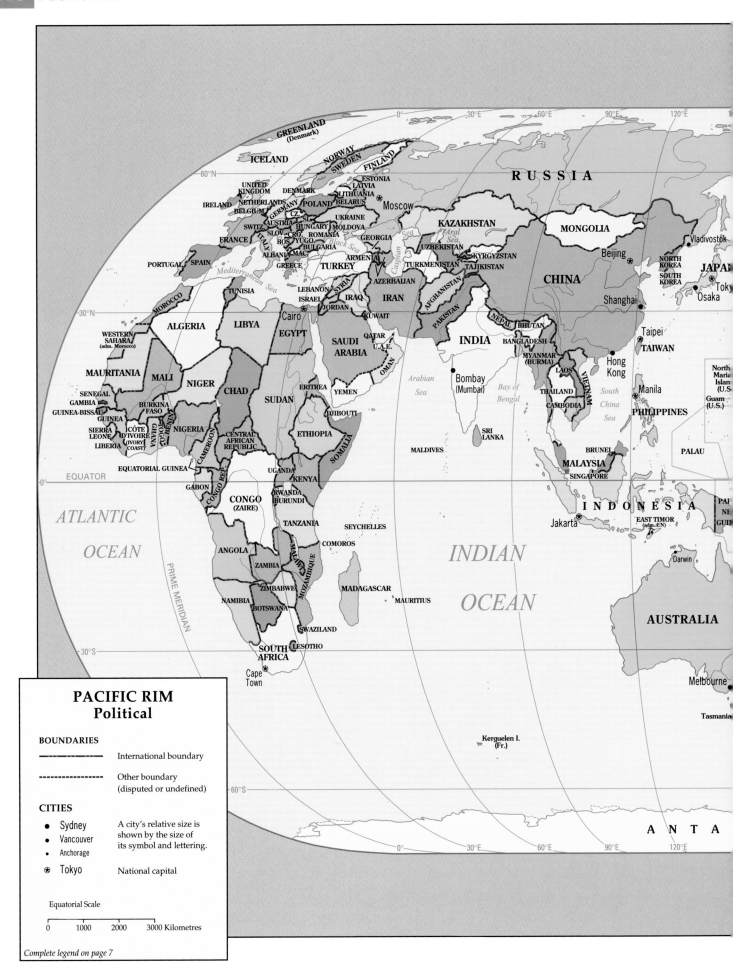

GREENLAND
(Denmark)

ICELAND

NORWAY
SWEDEN
FINLAND

R U S S I A

UNITED
KINGDOM
DENMARK
ESTONIA
LATVIA
LITHUANIA
BELARUS
IRELAND
NETHERLANDS
BELGIUM
GERMANY
POLAND
⊛ Moscow

SWITZ.
AUSTRIA
CZ.
SLK.
HUNGARY
UKRAINE
KAZAKHSTAN
MONGOLIA
FRANCE
ITALY
SLOV.
CRO.
BOS.
YUGO.
ROMANIA
MOLDOVA
GEORGIA
UZBEKISTAN
Vladivostok

PORTUGAL
SPAIN
ALBANIA
MAC.
BULGARIA
Black Sea
Aral Sea
KYRGYZSTAN
Beijing ⊛
NORTH
KOREA

GREECE
TURKEY
ARMENIA
AZERBAIJAN
TURKMENISTAN
TAJIKISTAN
CHINA
SOUTH
KOREA
JAPAN

Mediterranean Sea
LEBANON
SYRIA
Caspian Sea
AFGHANISTAN
Shanghai
Osaka
Toky

MOROCCO
TUNISIA
ISRAEL
IRAQ
IRAN
PAKISTAN
NEPAL
BHUTAN
Taipei

WESTERN
SAHARA
(adm. Morocco)
ALGERIA
LIBYA
Cairo ⊛
EGYPT
JORDAN
KUWAIT
QATAR
U.A.E.
INDIA
BANGLADESH
TAIWAN
Hong
Kong

MAURITANIA
MALI
NIGER
CHAD
SAUDI
ARABIA
OMAN
MYANMAR
(BURMA)
LAOS
Manila

SENEGAL
BURKINA
FASO
ERITREA
YEMEN
Arabian
Sea
Bombay
(Mumbai)
THAILAND
VIETNAM
CAMBODIA
PHILIPPINES

GAMBIA
GUINEA-BISSAU
GUINEA
SIERRA
LEONE
CÔTE
D'IVOIRE
(IVORY
COAST)
GHANA
TOGO
BENIN
NIGERIA
SUDAN
DJIBOUTI
ETHIOPIA
Bay of
Bengal
South
China
Sea

LIBERIA
CENTRAL
AFRICAN
REPUBLIC
SOMALIA
SRI
LANKA
BRUNEI
MALAYSIA
SINGAPORE

EQUATORIAL GUINEA
CAMEROON
UGANDA
KENYA
MALDIVES
PALAU

GABON
CONGO REP.
CONGO
(ZAIRE)
RWANDA
BURUNDI
EQUATOR

ATLANTIC
OCEAN
TANZANIA
SEYCHELLES
INDIAN
INDONESIA
EAST TIMOR
(adm. UN)
Jakarta

ANGOLA
MALAWI
MOZAMBIQUE
COMOROS

ZAMBIA
ZIMBABWE
MADAGASCAR
MAURITIUS
OCEAN
Darwin

NAMIBIA
BOTSWANA
PRIME MERIDIAN
SWAZILAND
AUSTRALIA

SOUTH
AFRICA
LESOTHO

Cape
Town ⊛
Melbourne

Tasmania

Kerguelen I.
(Fr.)

NORTH
KOREA

NORTH
Mariana
Island
(U.S.)
Guam
(U.S.)

PA
NE
GUI

ANTA

RCTIC OCEAN

GREENLAND
(KALAALLIT NUNAAT)
(Denmark)

ALASKA
(U.S.)

Bering
Sea

Anchorage

60°N

Hudson
Bay

C A N A D A

Vancouver

Montreal
Toronto

Chicago

New York

UNITED STATES

San Francisco

ATLANTIC

Los Angeles

30°N

Gulf of
Mexico

MEXICO

OCEAN

Honolulu

Hawaii
(U.S.)

CUBA

HAITI DOM.
REP.

Mexico
City

BELIZE

Caribbean Sea

MARSHALL
ISLANDS

GUATEMALA HONDURAS
EL SALVADOR
NICARAGUA

ERATED
ATES OF
RONESIA

PACIFIC

COSTA RICA PANAMA

VENEZUELA

GUYANA
SURINAME
French
Guiana
(Fr.)

QUATOR

N

COLOMBIA

EQUATOR 0°

NAURU

OCEAN

Galapagos Is.
(Ecuador)

ECUADOR

INTERNATIONAL DATE LINE

KIRIBATI

SOLOMON
IS.

TUVALU

Tokelau
(N.Z.)

PERU

BRAZIL

Wallis and
Futuna
(France)

SAMOA
Am.
Samoa
(U.S.)

Lima

VANUATU

New
Caledonia
(Fr.)

FIJI

Niue
(N.Z.)

Cook
Islands
(N.Z.)

French
Polynesia
(France)

BOLIVIA

PARAGUAY

TONGA

Sao Paulo

Pitcairn
Islands
(U.K.)

Easter I.
(Chile)

30°S

Jney

Auckland

Santiago

URUGUAY

NEW
ZEALAND

ARGENTINA

CHILE

Falkland Is.
(U.K.)

60°S

T I C A

180° 150°W 120°W 90°W 60°W

180° 150°W 120°W 90°W 60°W

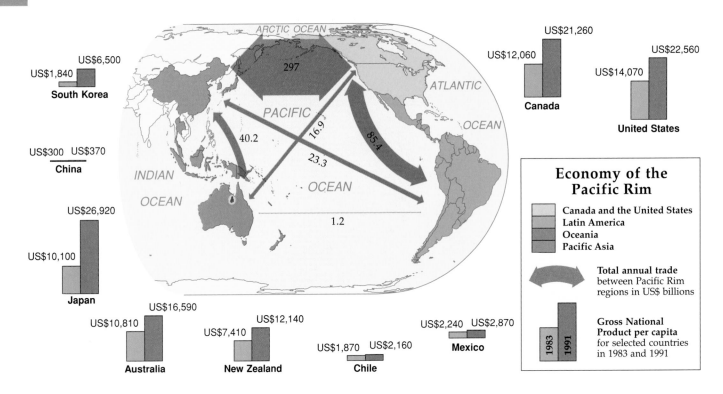

US$1,840 US$6,500
South Korea

US$300 US$370
China

US$26,920
US$10,100
Japan

US$10,810 US$16,590
Australia

US$7,410 US$12,140
New Zealand

US$1,870 US$2,160
Chile

US$2,240 US$2,870
Mexico

US$12,060 US$21,260
Canada

US$14,070 US$22,560
United States

297

PACIFIC

40.2   16.9   85.4

23.3

OCEAN

1.2

INDIAN

OCEAN

ARCTIC OCEAN

ATLANTIC

OCEAN

Economy of the Pacific Rim

Canada and the United States
Latin America
Oceania
Pacific Asia

Total annual trade between Pacific Rim regions in US$ billions

1983 1991

Gross National Product per capita for selected countries in 1983 and 1991

Container ships loaded with trans-Pacific cargo are a common sight in Hong Kong and in other Asian and North American ports.

JAPAN
Area Comparison

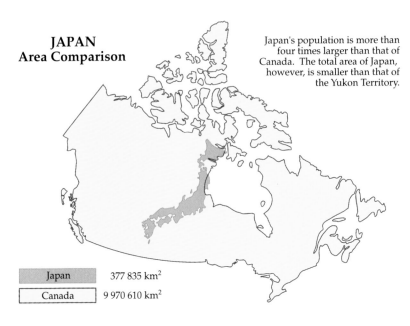

Japan's population is more than four times larger than that of Canada. The total area of Japan, however, is smaller than that of the Yukon Territory.

| Japan | 377 835 km^2 |
| Canada | 9 970 610 km^2 |

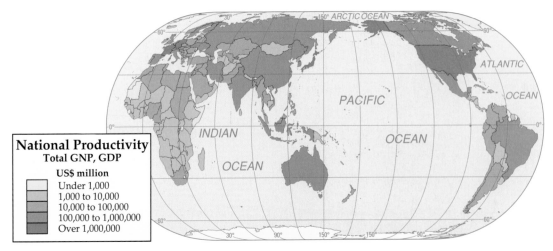

National Productivity
Total GNP, GDP
US$ million
Under 1,000
1,000 to 10,000
10,000 to 100,000
100,000 to 1,000,000
Over 1,000,000

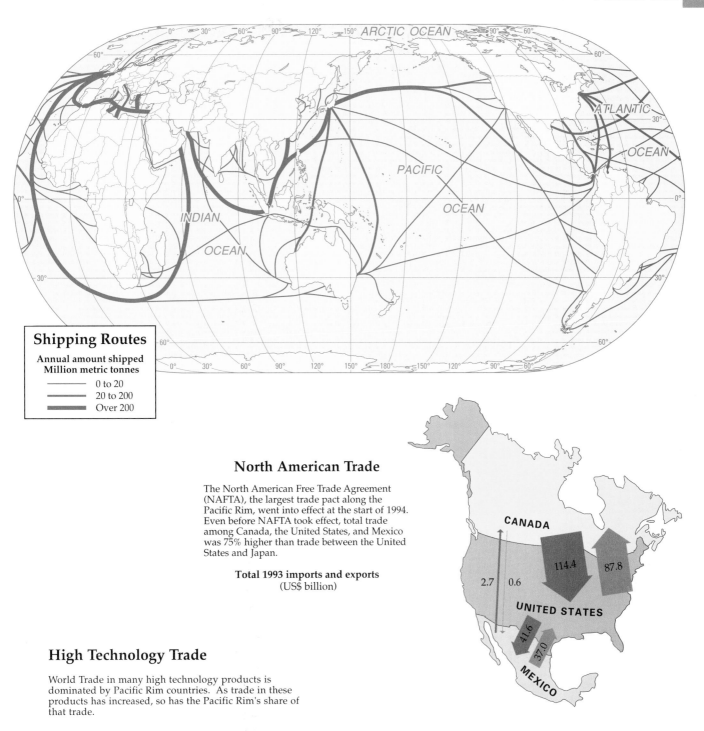

Shipping Routes

**Annual amount shipped
Million metric tonnes**

——	0 to 20
——	20 to 200
——	Over 200

North American Trade

The North American Free Trade Agreement
(NAFTA), the largest trade pact along the
Pacific Rim, went into effect at the start of 1994.
Even before NAFTA took effect, total trade
among Canada, the United States, and Mexico
was 75% higher than trade between the United
States and Japan.

Total 1993 imports and exports
(US$ billion)

CANADA

114.4 87.8

2.7 0.6

UNITED STATES

41.6 37.0

MEXICO

High Technology Trade

World Trade in many high technology products is
dominated by Pacific Rim countries. As trade in these
products has increased, so has the Pacific Rim's share of
that trade.

Telecommunications Equipment

1992

Total exports:
US$67.9 billion

26.0% **Japan**

15.3% **United States**

6.3% **Hong Kong**
4.3% **Singapore**
3.4% **South Korea**

44.7% **Other countries**

1987

Total exports:
US$40.7 billion

Japan 30.6%
United States 11.6%
Hong Kong 4.1%
South Korea 3.4%
Canada 3.2%

Other countries 47.1%

Percentage of total exports

Computers and Microchips

1992

Total exports:
US$65.9 billion

24.7% **United States**

18.8% **Japan**

9.9% **South Korea**

9.0% **Singapore**

6.3% **Malaysia**

31.3% **Other countries**

1987

Total exports:
US$26.2 billion

Japan 18.9%
United States 17.7%
South Korea 7.5%
Malaysia 7.5%
Singapore 6.6%
Other countries 41.8%

Percentage of total exports

JAPAN
CHINA
120°E
90°E
60°E
45°N
TURKEY

KAZAKHSTAN

R U S S I A

150°E

Amur R.

Sea of
Okhotsk

Verkhoyansk Ra.

Norilsk

Lena R.

Ob R.

Ural
Mountains

Volga R.

Moscow
⊛

30°E

Black Sea

UKRAINE

MOL.

ROMANIA

Kuril Is.

Magadan

ARCTIC CIRCLE

75°N

Kara Sea

Novaya Zemlya

Barents
Sea

Murmansk

BELARUS

LAT. LITH.

EST.

HUNGARY

POLAND

AUSTRIA

CZECH REP.

Kamchatka Pen.

New Siberian Is.

Severnaya
Zemlya

A R C T I C   O C E A N

FINLAND

Helsinki
⊛

Baltic Sea

SWEDEN

GERMANY

DENMARK

NORWAY

LUXEMBOURG

FRANCE

Aleutian

NORTH POLE

PRIME MERIDIAN

North Sea

NETHERLANDS
BELGIUM

London ⊛

Islands

180°

Bering
Sea

Chukchi
Sea

Greenland Sea

Jan
Mayen

UNITED
KINGDOM

Bering Strait

ICELAND

IRELAND

PACIFIC

Brooks Range

ALASKA
(U.S.)

Beaufort
Sea

Queen
Elizabeth Is

Ellesmere I.

GREENLAND
(KALAALLIT NUNAAT)
(Denmark)

30°W

Alaska

Anchorage

Yukon R.

Ra.

Baffin
Bay

OCEAN

Gulf of
Alaska

Mackenzie R.

75°N

Baffin I.

Davis Strait

Godthab
(Nuuk)

150°W

Rocky Mountains

C A N A D A

ARCTIC CIRCLE

45°N

Hudson
Bay

60°N

120°W

Edmonton

90°W

60°W

ASIA

90°E

60°N

ARCTIC CIRCLE

75°N

Moscow

EUROPE

180°

7000 Kilometers

7550 Kilometers

ARCTIC OCEAN

NORTH POLE

75°N

Anchorage

NORTH
AMERICA

60°N

Winnipeg

90°W

Arctic
Distances

The shortest distance
between some cities of
the Northern Hemi-
sphere is a great circle
route across the Arctic.

Polar bears live near salt water throughout the Arctic.
These hunters can smell prey up to 15 km away.

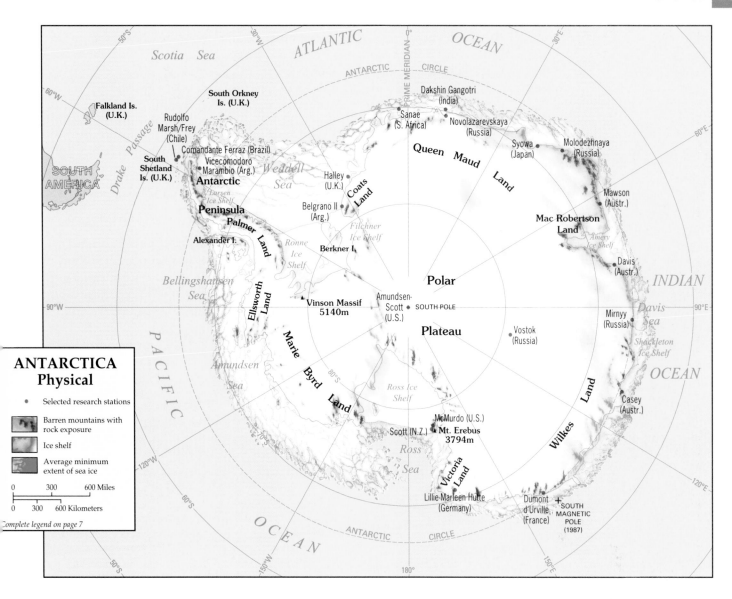

ANTARCTICA
Physical

- Selected research stations
- Barren mountains with rock exposure
- Ice shelf
- Average minimum extent of sea ice

0   300   600 Miles
0   300   600 Kilometers

Complete legend on page 7

Antarctica's Ice Cap

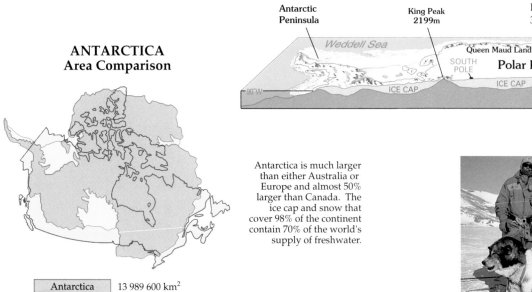

Antarctic Peninsula

King Peak 2199m

Ice cap on plateau is 3000 to 4000 meters thick.

Weddell Sea   Queen Maud Land   INDIAN OCEAN
SOUTH POLE   Polar Plateau
ICE CAP

ANTARCTICA
Area Comparison

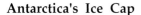

Antarctica is much larger than either Australia or Europe and almost 50% larger than Canada. The ice cap and snow that cover 98% of the continent contain 70% of the world's supply of freshwater.

| Antarctica | 13 989 600 km² |
| Canada | 9 970 610 km² |

Expeditions to the interior of Antarctica provide scientists with information about the earth's coldest region.

MAP PROJECTIONS

Map projections are the means by which the curved surface of a globe is transferred to the flat surface of a map. Because the earth is a sphere, a globe is its only perfect model. Even though there are an infinite number of map projections, none can be as accurate as a globe. A globe simultaneously shows accurate shapes, sizes, distances, and directions. No single world map can show all four of these properties accurately. Every world map distorts one or more of them. For example, a world map that shows correct shapes cannot show correct sizes, and vice versa.

The projections illustrated here can be classified according to their map properties. *Conformal* projections show true shapes, but distort sizes. (You can remember this term's meaning by associating *shape* with the word *form* in *conformal*.) *Equal-area* projections show all areas in their true relative sizes, but distort shapes. *Compromise* projections allow some size distortions in order to portray shapes more accurately. For all types of world map projections, distortion is generally least near the center of the map and greatest at its edges.

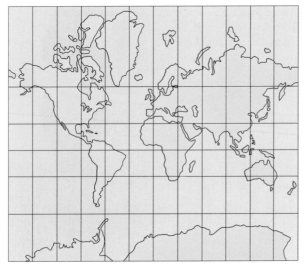

Mercator: First published in 1569, the Mercator is a conformal projection. North and South Poles are shown not as points, but as lines the same length as the Equator. The result is extreme size distortion in the higher latitudes. The Mercator map was designed for navigation, and the true compass direction between any two points can be determined by a straight line.

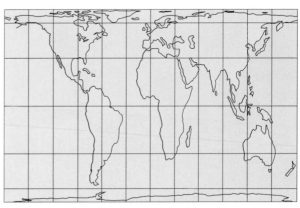

Gall-Peters: An equal-area projection first produced in the 1850s, the Gall-Peters greatly distorts shapes near the Equator as well as near the poles. Features near the Equator are stretched vertically, while features near the poles are flattened horizontally. The resulting shapes are quite different from those on the globe.

Armadillo: The Armadillo is a compromise projection that is intended to give young students the impression of a map being peeled from a globe. Because its unique appearance results in severe distortions, especially at the map's outer edges, it has seldom been used outside the classroom.

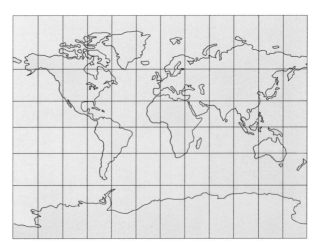

Miller Cylindrical: The Miller is a compromise projection based on the Mercator. Its shapes are not as accurate as those on the Mercator map, but it has much less size distortion in the higher latitiudes. The Miller cylindrical projection is frequently used when mapping world time zones.

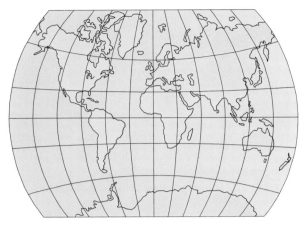

Van der Grinten: The Van der Grinten is a compromise between the Mercator and the Mollweide. The full projection is shaped like a circle, but the polar areas are normally not shown. Shapes, sizes, and directions are reasonably accurate between 60°N and 60°S, where most of the world's people live. The Van der Grinten has long been used for general reference maps.

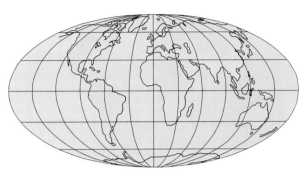

Mollweide: An equal-area projection, the Mollweide has an oval shape that reminds the viewer of a globe. The Mollweide projection is frequently used for world distribution maps. (A distribution map shows the relative location and extent of something—such as crops, livestock, or people—across the face of the earth.)

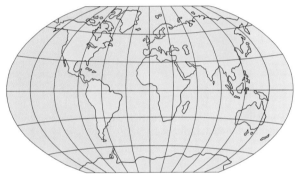

Winkel "Tripel": The Winkel "Tripel" is a compromise projection. Its oval shape and curving parallels result in a map with realistic shapes and minor size distortions at all latitudes. The Winkel has less size distortion than the Van der Grinten (above) and less shape distortion than the Robinson (below).

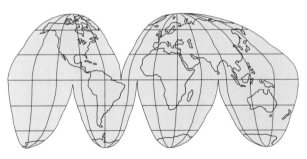

Goode's Homolosine: Goode's is an equal-area map that also shows shapes extremely well. Shapes can be shown more accurately than on most equal-area maps because the grid is *interrupted* or split in the ocean areas. The interruptions allow land areas to be shown with less stretch or distortion.

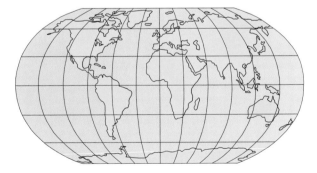

Robinson: First used in 1963, the Robinson is a compromise projection. Because it presents a reasonable overall picture of the world, it is often used for maps in educational materials. It looks similar to the Eckert IV (at right), but the Robinson is easily distinguished by its size distortion in the polar areas.

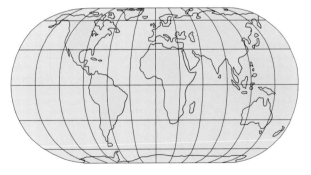

Eckert IV: An equal-area projection, the Eckert IV has relatively minor shape distortions near the Equator and the poles. The result is a map that is well-suited either for general reference or for showing world distributions. It has been used in several atlases to show world climates and other themes.

WORLD FACTS

Age and Dimensions of Earth

Age	4.6 billion years (4.6 x 10^9)
Mass	6 sextillion metric tonnes (6 x 10^{21})
Diameter	12 756.32 kilometres
Equatorial Circumference	40 075.16 kilometres
Polar Circumference	40 008.00 kilometres

Land Areas and Populations

Continent	Land Area km²	Percentage of World Land Area	Population	Percentage of World Population
Africa	30 225 400	20.2	669 752 000	12.2
Antarctica	13 989 600	9.3	0	0.0
Asia	45 024 300	30.0	3 353 432 000	60.8
Europe	9 856 900	6.6	710 237 000	12.9
North America	24 396 400	16.3	442 115 000	8.0
Oceania*	8 505 000	5.7	27 641 000	0.5
South America	17 821 200	11.9	308 770 000	5.6

Australia, New Zealand, and Pacific Islands

Largest Urban Areas

City and Country	Population Actual in 1992	Projected for 2010
Tokyo, Japan	25 800 000	28 900 000
Sao Paulo, Brazil	19 200 000	25 000 000
New York, United States	16 200 000	17 200 000
Mexico City, Mexico	15 300 000	18 000 000
Shanghai, China	14 100 000	21 700 000
Bombay, India	13 300 000	24 400 000
Los Angeles, United States	11 900 000	13 900 000
Buenos Aires, Argentina	11 800 000	13 700 000
Seoul, South Korea	11 600 000	13 800 000
Beijing, China	11 400 000	18 000 000
Rio de Janeiro, Brazil	11 300 000	13 300 000
Calcutta, India	11 100 000	15 700 000
Osaka, Japan	10 500 000	10 600 000
Jakarta, Indonesia	10 000 000	17 200 000
Tianjin, China	9 800 000	15 700 000
Manila, Philippines	9 600 000	16 100 000
Paris, France	9 400 000	9 600 000
Moscow, Russia	9 200 000	10 400 000
Cairo, Egypt	9 000 000	13 400 000
Delhi, India	8 800 000	15 600 000
Lagos, Nigeria	8 700 000	21 100 000
Karachi, Pakistan	8 600 000	17 000 000
Bangkok, Thailand	7 600 000	12 700 000
Dhaka, Bangladesh	7 400 000	17 600 000
London, United Kingdom	7 300 000	7 300 000
Istanbul, Turkey	7 000 000	11 800 000
Teheran, Iran	7 000 000	11 900 000

Extremes of Climate

Record Temperatures

Highest	57.7° C		
	Al Aziziyah, Libya	September 13, 1922
Lowest	−89.2° C		
	Vostok, Antarctica	July 21, 1983

Average Annual Precipitation

Highest	11 684.0 mm	
	Mt. Waialeale, Hawaii, U.S.	
Lowest	0.5 mm	
	Arica, Chile	

Maximum Precipitation

In 24 hours	1870.0 mm	
	Cilaos, Reunion Is.	March 16, 1952
In 1 hour	305.0 mm	
	Holt, Mo., U.S.	June 22, 1907

Ocean Areas and Average Depths

Ocean	Area km²	Average Depth m
Pacific Ocean	165 250 000	4280
Atlantic Ocean	82 440 000	3930
Indian Ocean	73 440 000	3060
Arctic Ocean	14 090 000	1205

Highest and Lowest Elevations

Continent	Highest Elevation	m above sea level	Lowest Elevation	m below sea level
Africa	Mt. Kilimanjaro, Tanzania	5895	Lake Assal, Djibouti	156
Antarctica	Vinson Massif	5140	unknown	
Asia	Mt. Everest, Nepal-China	8850	Dead Sea, Israel-Jordan	400
Europe	Mt. Elbrus, Russia	5642	Caspian Sea, Russia	29
North America	Mt. McKinley, U.S.	6194	Death Valley, U.S.	86
Oceania*	Jaya Peak, Indonesia	5030	Lake Eyre, Australia	15
South America	Mt. Aconcagua, Argentina	6959	Peninsula Valdez, Argentina	40

Australia, New Zealand, and Pacific Islands

Largest Lakes

Lake and Continent	Area km²
Caspian Sea, Asia	372 000
Superior, North America	82 103
Victoria, Africa	69 484
Huron, North America	59 699
Michigan, North America	57 757
Aral Sea, Asia	40 000
Tanganyika, Africa	32 893
Baikal, Asia	31 499
Great Bear, North America	31 153
Nyasa (Malawi), Africa	28 749
Great Slave, North America	28 570
Erie, North America	25 667
Winnipeg, North America	24 390
Ontario, North America	19 010
Chad, Africa	17 800
Ladoga, Europe	17 678
Balkhash, Asia	17 250
Maracaibo, South America	13 300
Bangweulu, Africa	9 800
Onega, Europe	9 720

Highest Waterfalls

Waterfall and Country	Total Height m
Angel (Churun Meru), Venezuela	979
Tugela, South Africa	948
Mtarazi, Zimbabwe	762
Yosemite, United States	739
Cuquenian, Venezuela	610
Sutherland, New Zealand	580
Kile, Norway	561
Kahiwa, United States	533
Mardal (Eastern), Norway	517
Ribbon, United States	491

Longest Rivers

River and Continent	Length km
Nile, Africa	6650
Amazon, South America	6437
Yangtze, Asia	6300
Mississippi-Missouri system, North America	6020
Yenisey, Asia	5540
Huang, Asia	5464
Ob, Asia	5409
Parana, South America	4880
Congo, Africa	4700
Amur, Asia	4444
Lena, Asia	4400
Mekong, Asia	4350
Mackenzie, North America	4241
Niger, Africa	4200
Zambezi, Africa	3540
Volga, Europe	3530
Madeira, South America	3350
Jurua, South America	3283
Purus, South America	3211

COUNTRY TABLES

COUNTRY	CAPITAL(S)	PRINCIPAL LANGUAGE(S)	POPULATION	AREA KM²	POP. DENSITY PER KM²	NATURAL POP. GROWTH PER 100 PEOPLE BIRTHS	– DEATHS	= % GAIN
Africa								
ALGERIA	Algiers	Arabic, French, Berber	26 401 000	2 381 741	11.1	3.4	0.6	2.8
ANGOLA	Luanda	Ovimbundu, Portuguese, Mbundu, Kongo	10 609 000	1 246 700	8.5	4.7	2.0	2.7
BENIN	Porto-Novo, Cotonou	Fon, French, Yoruba, Adja	4 928 000	112 600	43.8	4.9	1.8	3.1
BOTSWANA	Gaborone	Tswana, English, Shona	1 359 000	581 730	2.3	4.6	1.1	3.5
BURKINA FASO	Ouagadougou	Voltaic, Mande, Fulani, French	9 515 000	274 400	34.7	4.7	1.8	2.9
BURUNDI	Bujumbura	Rundi, French	5 657 000	27 816	203.4	4.7	1.5	3.2
CAMEROON	Yaounde	Fang, Bamileke, French, Duala, Fulani, Tikar, English	12 622 000	465 458	27.2	4.5	1.5	3.0
CAPE VERDE	Praia	Crioulo, Portuguese	346 000	4 033	85.8	3.2	0.8	2.4
CENTRAL AFRICAN REPUBLIC	Bangui	Banda, Baya, Sango, French, Ngbandi, Mbaka	2 930 000	622 436	4.7	4.5	1.8	2.7
CHAD	N'Djamena	Sara, Bagirmi, Kraish, Arabic, French	5 961 000	1 284 000	4.6	4.4	1.9	2.5
COMOROS	Moroni	Comorian, French, Arabic	497 000	1 862	266.9	4.7	1.3	3.4
CONGO (ZAIRE)	Kinshasa	Lingala, Swahili, Luba, Mongo, French	41 151 000	2 345 095	17.5	4.6	1.4	3.2
CONGO REPUBLIC	Brazzaville	Monokutuba, Kongo, French, Teke	2 692 000	342 000	7.9	4.5	1.5	3.0
CÔTE D'IVOIRE (IVORY COAST)	Abidjan	Akan, French, Kru, Gur Hindi	12 951 000	320 763	40.4	4.7	1.3	3.4
DJIBOUTI	Djibouti	Somali, Afar, French, Arabic	557 000	23 200	24.0	4.6	1.7	2.9
EGYPT	Cairo	Arabic	55 979 000	997 739	56.1	3.9	0.9	3.0
EQUATORIAL GUINEA	Malabo	Fana, Bubi, Spanish	367 000	28 051	13.1	4.3	1.8	2.5
ERITREA	Asmara	Tigrinya, Tigre	3 670 000	117 400	31.3	4.3	1.6	2.7
ETHIOPIA	Addis Ababa	Amharic, Oromo, Tigrinya	51 831 000	1 133 882	45.7	4.8	1.8	3.0
GABON	Libreville	Fang, French, Puna/Sira/Nzebi	1 253 000	267 667	4.7	4.0	1.6	2.4
GAMBIA	Banjul	Malinke, Fulani, English	921 000	10 689	86.2	4.6	2.1	2.5
GHANA	Accra	Hausa, Akan, Mole-Dagbani, English	15 237 000	238 533	63.9	4.4	1.3	3.1
GUINEA	Conakry	Fulani, Malinke, Susu, French	7 232 000	245 857	29.4	4.8	2.2	2.6
GUINEA-BISSAU	Bissau	Crioulo, Fulani, Balante, Portuguese	1 015 000	36 125	28.1	4.2	2.0	2.2
KENYA	Nairobi	Swahili, Kikuyu, Luhya, Luo, Kamba, Kalenjin	26 985 000	582 646	46.3	4.9	1.1	3.8
LESOTHO	Maseru	Sotho, Zulu, English	1 854 000	30 355	61.1	4.1	1.2	2.9
LIBERIA	Monrovia	Krio, English, Kepelle, Bassa, Grebo	2 780 000	99 067	28.1	4.6	1.4	3.2
LIBYA	Tripoli	Arabic, Berber	4 447 000	1 757 000	2.5	4.5	0.8	3.7

Country: all independent countries, as well as selected dependencies. **Principal Language(s):** all official languages, as well as other primary languages spoken by a substantial proportion of the population. **Pop. Density:** population density, computed as population divided by area. **Natural Pop. Growth:** annual population increase per 100 people; does not include population change due to immigration or emigration.

COUNTRY	CAPITAL(S)	PRINCIPAL LANGUAGE(S)	POPULATION	AREA KM²	POP. DENSITY PER KM²	NATURAL POP. GROWTH PER 100 PEOPLE BIRTHS – DEATHS = % GAIN		
MADAGASCAR	Antananarivo	Malagasy, French	12 803 000	587 041	21.8	4.6	1.4	3.2
MALAWI	Lilongwe, Zomba	Chewa, English, Lomwe, Yao, Ngoni	9 484 000	118 484	80.0	5.5	2.0	3.5
MALI	Bamako	Bambara, Fulani, Sehufo, Soninke, French	8 464 000	1 248 574	6.8	5.0	2.0	3.0
MAURITANIA	Nouakchott	Arabic, Wolof, French, Tukulor	2 108 000	1 030 700	2.0	4.7	1.9	2.8
MAURITIUS	Port-Louis	French Creole, Bhojpuri, Hindi, French, Tamil, Urdu, Telugu, English	1 081 000	2 040	529.9	2.0	0.6	1.4
MOROCCO	Rabat	Arabic, Berber	26 239 000	458 730	57.2	3.5	0.9	2.6
MOZAMBIQUE	Maputo	Makua, Tsonga, Senoc, Lomwe, Portuguese	14 842 000	812 379	18.3	4.5	1.8	2.7
NAMIBIA	Windhoek	Ovambo, Kavango, English	1 431 000	823 144	1.7	4.3	1.2	3.1
NIGER	Niamey	Hausa, Songhai/Zerma, French	8 281 000	1 186 408	7.0	5.1	2.0	3.1
NIGERIA	Abuja	English, Hausa, Yoruba, Igbo, Fulani	89 666 000	923 768	97.1	4.8	1.5	3.3
RWANDA	Kigali	Kwanda, French	7 347 000	26 338	279.0	5.1	1.7	3.4
SAO TOME AND PRINCIPE	Sao Tome	Crioulo, Portuguese	126 000	1 001	125.9	3.8	0.8	3.0
SENEGAL	Dakar	Wolof, Fulani, Serer Dyola, French, Malinke	7 691 000	196 712	39.1	4.5	1.8	2.7
SEYCHELLES	Victoria	Seselwa	71 000	453	156.7	2.4	0.8	1.6
SIERRA LEONE	Freetown	Mende, Temne, English, Krio	4 373 000	71 740	61.0	4.8	2.3	2.5
SOMALIA	Mogadishu	Somali, Arabic, English	7 872 000	637 000	12.4	4.9	1.9	3.0
SOUTH AFRICA	Cape Town, Pretoria, Bloemfontein	Zulu, Xhosa, Afrikaans, Sotho, English	39 085 000	1 225 815	31.9	3.3	0.9	2.4
SUDAN	Khartoum	Arabic, Dinka, Nubian, Beja, Nuer, Azande	29 971 000	2 503 890	12.0	4.5	1.5	3.0
SWAZILAND	Mbabane	Swazi, Zulu, English	826 000	17 364	47.6	4.7	1.2	3.5
TANZANIA	Dar es Salaam	Swahili, English, Nyamwezi	25 809 000	942 799	27.4	5.0	1.4	3.6
TOGO	Lome	Ewe-Adja, French, Tem-Kabre, Gurma	3 701 000	56 785	65.2	4.7	1.4	3.3
TUNISIA	Tunis	Arabic, French	8 413 000	154 530	54.4	2.6	0.5	2.1
UGANDA	Kampala	Swahili, Ganda, Teso, Soga, Nkole	17 194 000	241 040	71.3	5.1	1.5	3.6
WESTERN SAHARA (adm. Morocco)	El Aaiun	Arabic	209 000	252 120	0.8	4.8	2.3	2.5
ZAMBIA	Lusaka	Bemba, Tonga, Lozi, English, Chewa, Nyamja	8 303 000	752 614	11.0	5.1	1.3	3.8
ZIMBABWE	Harare	Shona, Ndebele, Nyanja, English	9 871 000	390 759	25.3	4.0	1.0	3.0

Country: all independent countries, as well as selected dependencies. **Principal Language(s):** all official languages, as well as other primary languages spoken by a substantial proportion of the population. **Pop. Density:** population density, computed as population divided by area. **Natural Pop. Growth:** annual population increase per 100 people; does not include population change due to immigration or emigration.

COUNTRY	CAPITAL(S)	PRINCIPAL LANGUAGE(S)	POPULATION	AREA KM^2	POP. DENSITY PER KM^2	NATURAL POP. GROWTH PER 100 PEOPLE BIRTHS – DEATHS = % GAIN		

Asia

COUNTRY	CAPITAL(S)	PRINCIPAL LANGUAGE(S)	POPULATION	AREA KM^2	POP. DENSITY PER KM^2	BIRTHS	DEATHS	% GAIN
AFGHANISTAN	Kabul	Pashto, Dari, Uzbek, Turkmen	18 052 000	652 225	27.7	4.4	2.0	2.4
ARMENIA	Yerevan	Armenian	3 426 000	29 800	115.0	2.2	0.7	1.5
AZERBAIJAN	Baku	Azerbaijani, Russian, Armenian	7 237 000	86 600	83.6	2.7	0.6	2.1
BAHRAIN	Manama	Arabic	531 000	692	767.3	3.0	0.4	2.6
BANGLADESH	Dhaka	Bengali	110 602 000	143 998	768.1	3.6	1.2	2.4
BHUTAN	Thimphu, Paro	Dzongkha, Assamese	1 511 000	47 000	32.1	3.8	1.6	2.2
BRUNEI	Bandar Seri Begawan	Malay, Chinese, English	268 000	5 765	46.5	2.8	0.3	2.5
CAMBODIA (KAMPUCHEA)	Phnom Penh	Khmer	8 974 000	181 916	49.3	4.2	1.7	2.5
CHINA	Beijing	Han: Mandarin; Han: other; Zhuang	1 165 888 000	9 572 900	121.8	2.1	0.6	1.5
CYPRUS	Nicosia	Greek, Turkish	756 000	9 251	81.7	1.9	0.9	1.0
GEORGIA	Tbilisi	Georgian, Armenian, Russian, Azerbaijani	5 482 000	69 700	78.7	1.7	0.8	0.9
INDIA	New Delhi	Hindi, Telugu, Bengali, Maratha, Tamil	889 700 000	3 165 596	281.1	3.1	1.0	2.1
INDONESIA	Jakarta	Sundanese, Bahasa Indonesia	184 796 000	1 919 317	96.3	2.9	1.1	1.8
IRAN	Tehran	Farsi, Azerbaijani, Kurdish, Gilaki	59 570 000	1 638 057	36.4	4.4	1.0	3.4
IRAQ	Baghdad	Arabic, Kurdish	18 838 000	435 052	43.3	4.5	0.8	3.7
ISRAEL	Jerusalem	Hebrew, Arabic, Yiddish, Russian	5 237 000	20 700	253.1	2.2	0.6	1.6
JAPAN	Tokyo	Japanese	124 330 000	377 835	329.1	1.0	0.7	0.3
JORDAN	Amman	Arabic	3 636 000	88 946	40.9	3.9	0.6	3.3
KAZAKHSTAN	Astana	Kazakh, Russian, German, Ukrainian	17 008 000	2 717 300	6.3	2.1	0.8	1.3
KUWAIT	Kuwait	Arabic	1 190 000	17 818	66.8	2.7	0.2	2.5
KYRGYZSTAN	Bishkek	Kyrgyz, Russian, Uzbek	4 533 000	198 500	22.8	2.9	0.7	2.2
LAOS	Vientiane	Lao, Mon-Khmer, Miao and Munt	4 409 000	236 800	18.6	4.0	1.6	2.4
LEBANON	Beirut	Arabic, French, Armenian	2 803 000	10 230	274.0	2.9	0.7	2.2
MALAYSIA	Kuala Lumpur	Malay, English, Chinese, Tamil	18 630 000	330 442	56.4	2.9	0.5	2.4
MALDIVES	Male	Divehi	230 000	298	771.8	4.2	0.9	3.3
MONGOLIA	Ulaanbaatar	Khalkar, Kazakh	2 182 000	1 566 500	1.4	3.7	0.9	2.8
MYANMAR (BURMA)	Yangon (Rangoon)	Burmese, Shan, Karen	43 446 000	676 577	64.2	3.2	1.2	2.0

Country: all independent countries, as well as selected dependencies. **Principal Language(s):** all official languages, as well as other primary languages spoken by a substantial proportion of the population. **Pop. Density:** population density, computed as population divided by area. **Natural Pop. Growth:** annual population increase per 100 people; does not include population change due to immigration or emigration.

COUNTRY	CAPITAL(S)	PRINCIPAL LANGUAGE(S)	POPULATION	AREA KM²	POP. DENSITY PER KM²	NATURAL POP. GROWTH PER 100 PEOPLE BIRTHS – DEATHS = % GAIN		
NEPAL	Kathmandu	Nepali, Maithili, Bhojpuri	19 795 000	147 181	134.5	3.9	1.5	2.4
NORTH KOREA	Pyongyang	Korean	22 227 000	122 762	181.1	2.5	0.6	1.9
OMAN	Muscat	Arabic, Baluchi	1 640 000	306 000	5.4	4.4	0.9	3.5
PAKISTAN	Islamabad	Panjabi, Pashto, Sindhi, Urdu	130 129 000	879 811	147.9	4.2	1.0	3.2
PHILIPPINES	Manila	Tagalog, English, Cebuanco	63 609 000	300 000	212.0	3.4	0.8	2.6
QATAR	Doha	Arabic	520 000	11 427	45.5	3.1	0.2	2.9
SAUDI ARABIA	Riyadh	Arabic	15 267 000	2 240 000	6.8	3.7	1.1	2.6
SINGAPORE	Singapore	Mandarin, English, Bahasa, Malaysian, Tamil	2 792 000	622	4 488.7	1.9	0.5	1.4
SOUTH KOREA	Seoul	Korean	43 663 000	99 263	439.9	1.7	0.6	1.1
SRI LANKA	Colombo, Kotte	Sinhalese, Tamil, English	17 464 000	65 610	266.2	2.2	0.6	1.6
SYRIA	Damascus	Arabic, Kurdish, Armenian	12 958 000	185 180	70.0	4.4	0.7	3.7
TAIWAN	Taipei	Min, Mandarin, Hakka	20 727 000	36 179	572.9	1.6	0.5	1.1
TAJIKISTAN	Dushanbe	Tajik, Uzbek, Russian	5 568 000	143 100	38.9	3.9	0.6	3.3
THAILAND	Bangkok	Thai, Lao, Chinese, Mon-Khmer	56 801 000	513 115	110.7	2.1	0.7	1.4
TURKEY	Ankara	Turkish, Kurdish, Arabic	58 584 000	779 452	75.2	2.8	0.7	2.1
TURKMENISTAN	Ashgabat	Turkmenian, Russian, Uzbek	3 859 000	488 100	7.9	3.3	0.7	2.6
UNITED ARAB EMIRATES	Abu Dhabi	Arabic	1 989 000	77 700	25.6	3.2	0.4	2.8
UZBEKISTAN	Tashkent	Uzbek, Russian	21 363 000	447 400	47.7	3.4	0.6	2.8
VIETNAM	Hanoi	Vietnamese, Tay, Tai	69 052 000	329 566	209.5	3.1	0.9	2.2
YEMEN	Sanaa	Arabic	12 147 000	531 869	22.8	5.1	1.9	3.2

Australia and Oceania

COUNTRY	CAPITAL(S)	PRINCIPAL LANGUAGE(S)	POPULATION	AREA KM²	POP. DENSITY PER KM²	BIRTHS	DEATHS	% GAIN
AUSTRALIA	Canberra	English	17 562 000	7 682 300	2.3	1.5	0.7	0.8
FIJI	Suva	Fijian, Hindi, English	748 000	18 274	40.9	2.5	0.5	2.0
FRENCH POLYNESIA (Fr.)	Papeete	Polynesian, French, Chinese	206 000	4 000	51.5	2.7	0.5	2.2
KIRIBATI	Tarawa (Bairiki)	Kiribati, English	75 000	811	92.1	3.2	0.9	2.3

Country: all independent countries, as well as selected dependencies. **Principal Language(s):** all official languages, as well as other primary languages spoken by a substantial proportion of the population. **Pop. Density:** population density, computed as population divided by area. **Natural Pop. Growth:** annual population increase per 100 people; does not include population change due to immigration or emigration.

COUNTRY	CAPITAL(S)	PRINCIPAL LANGUAGE(S)	POPULATION	AREA KM²	POP. DENSITY PER KM²	NATURAL POP. GROWTH PER 100 PEOPLE BIRTHS – DEATHS = % GAIN		
MARSHALL ISLANDS	Majuro	Marshallese, English	50 000	181	276.2	4.2	0.6	3.6
MICRONESIA	Palikir	Chuukese, Pohnpeian, English	114 000	701	162.6	3.4	0.5	2.9
NAURU	Yaren	Nauruan, Kiribati	10 000	21.2	452.8	2.1	0.5	1.6
NEW CALEDONIA (Fr.)	Noumea	English, Maori, Melanesian, Polynesian	174 000	18 576	9.4	2.1	0.7	1.4
NEW ZEALAND	Wellington	English, Maori	3 481 000	270 534	12.9	1.7	0.8	0.9
PALAU	Koror	Palauan, English	16 000	488	32.2	2.5	0.6	1.9
PAPUA NEW GUINEA	Port Moresby	Papuan, English, Melanesian	3 834 000	462 840	8.3	3.5	1.2	2.3
SAMOA	Apia	Samoan, English	160 000	2 831	56.5	3.3	0.7	2.6
SOLOMON ISLANDS	Honiara	Melanesian, Papuan, English	339 000	28 370	11.9	4.4	1.0	3.4
TONGA	Nukualofa	Tongan, English	97 000	780	124.7	3.0	0.7	2.3
TUVALU	Funafuti	Tuvaluan, English, Kiribati	10 000	24.0	395.8	2.9	1.0	1.9
VANUATU	Port-Vila	Melanesian, English	154 000	12 190	12.6	4.1	0.8	3.3

Europe

COUNTRY	CAPITAL(S)	PRINCIPAL LANGUAGE(S)	POPULATION	AREA KM²	POP. DENSITY PER KM²	BIRTHS	DEATHS	% GAIN
ALBANIA	Tirana	Albanian	3 357 000	28 748	116.8	2.5	0.5	2.0
ANDORRA	Andorra la Vella	Spanish, Catalan, French, Portuguese	57 000	468	122.0	1.4	0.4	1.0
AUSTRIA	Vienna	German, Serbo-Croatian	7 857 000	83 859	93.7	1.2	1.1	0.1
BELARUS	Minsk	Belorussian, Russian	10 321 000	207 600	49.7	1.3	1.1	0.2
BELGIUM	Brussels	Dutch, French	10 021 000	30 528	328.3	1.2	1.1	0.1
BOSNIA AND HERZEGOVINA	Sarajevo	Serbo-Croatian	4 397 000	51 129	86.0	1.4	0.6	0.8
BULGARIA	Sofia	Bulgarian, Turkish	8 985 000	110 994	81.0	1.2	1.2	0.0
CROATIA	Zagreb	Serbo-Croatian	4 808 000	56 538	85.0	1.2	1.1	0.1
CZECH REPUBLIC	Prague	Czech, Moravian	10 323 000	78 864	130.9	1.2	1.2	0.0
DENMARK	Copenhagen	Danish	5 167 000	43 093	119.9	1.2	1.2	0.0
ESTONIA	Tallinn	Estonian, Russian	1 536 000	45 226	33.9	1.2	1.3	−0.1
FINLAND	Helsinki	Finnish, Swedish	5 033 000	338 145	14.9	1.3	1.0	0.3
FRANCE	Paris	French, Arabic	57 289 000	543 965	105.3	1.4	0.9	0.5
GERMANY	Berlin	German, Turkish	79 122 000	356 733	221.8	1.0	1.1	−0.1
GREECE	Athens	Greek	10 288 000	131 957	78.0	1.0	0.9	0.1
HUNGARY	Budapest	Hungarian, Romany	10 318 000	93 033	110.9	1.2	1.4	−0.2
ICELAND	Reykjavik	Icelandic	261 000	102 819	2.5	1.9	0.7	1.2
IRELAND	Dublin	English, Irish	3 519 000	70 285	50.1	1.5	0.9	0.6

Country: all independent countries, as well as selected dependencies. **Principal Language(s):** all official languages, as well as other primary languages spoken by a substantial proportion of the population. **Pop. Density:** population density, computed as population divided by area. **Natural Pop. Growth:** annual population increase per 100 people; does not include population change due to immigration or emigration.

COUNTRY	CAPITAL(S)	PRINCIPAL LANGUAGE(S)	POPULATION	AREA KM^2	POP. DENSITY PER KM^2	NATURAL POP. GROWTH PER 100 PEOPLE BIRTHS – DEATHS = % GAIN		
ITALY	Rome	Italian, Sardinian	57 158 000	301 277	189.7	1.0	0.9	0.1
LATVIA	Riga	Latvian, Russian	2 685 000	64 610	41.6	1.2	1.4	–0.2
LIECHTENSTEIN	Vaduz	German	30 000	160	185.0	1.3	0.6	0.7
LITHUANIA	Vilnius	Lithuanian, Russian, Polish	3 801 000	65 301	58.2	1.4	1.1	0.3
LUXEMBOURG	Luxembourg	Luxemburgian, Portuguese, Italian, French, German	387 000	2 586	149.7	1.2	1.0	0.2
MACEDONIA	Skopje	Macedonian, Albanian	2 050 000	25 713	79.7	1.7	0.7	1.0
MALTA	Valletta	Maltese, English	360 000	316	1 139.2	1.5	0.8	0.7
MOLDOVA	Chisinau	Romanian, Russian, Ukrainian, Gagauz	4 394 000	33 700	130.4	1.7	1.1	0.6
MONACO	Monaco	French, Italian, Monegasque, English	30 000	1.95	15 538.5	2.2	1.8	0.4
NETHERLANDS	Amsterdam, The Hague	Dutch, Frisian, Turkish, Arabic	15 163 000	41 863	362.2	1.3	0.9	0.4
NORWAY	Oslo	Norwegian	4 283 000	323 878	13.2	1.4	1.1	0.3
POLAND	Warsaw	Polish	38 429 000	312 683	122.9	1.5	1.0	0.5
PORTUGAL	Lisbon	Portuguese	10 429 000	92 389	112.9	1.2	0.9	0.3
ROMANIA	Bucharest	Romanian	23 332 000	237 500	98.2	1.5	1.1	0.4
RUSSIA	Moscow	Russian	149 469 000	17 075 400	8.8	1.2	1.1	0.1
SAN MARINO	San Marino	Italian	24 000	61	386.9	1.0	0.7	0.3
SLOVAKIA	Bratislava	Slovak, Hungarian	5 282 000	49 036	107.7	1.4	1.0	0.4
SLOVENIA	Ljubljana	Slovene	1 985 000	20 256	98.0	1.1	1.0	0.1
SPAIN	Madrid	Castilian Spanish, Catalan, Galician, Basque	39 085 000	504 783	77.4	1.1	0.8	0.3
SWEDEN	Stockholm	Swedish	8 673 000	449 964	19.3	1.4	1.1	0.3
SWITZERLAND	Bern	German, French, Italian, Romansch	6 911 000	41 293	167.4	1.2	0.9	0.3
UKRAINE	Kiev	Ukrainian, Russian	52 135 000	603 700	86.4	1.2	1.3	–0.1
UNITED KINGDOM	London	English, Welsh, Scots-Gaelic	57 730 000	244 110	236.5	1.4	1.1	0.3
VATICAN CITY	Vatican City	Italian, Latin	1 000	0.44	1 768.2	0.0	0.0	0.0
YUGOSLAVIA	Belgrade	Serbo-Croatian, Albanian	10 394 000	102 173	101.7	1.4	0.9	0.5

Country: all independent countries, as well as selected dependencies. **Principal Language(s):** all official languages, as well as other primary languages spoken by a substantial proportion of the population. **Pop. Density:** population density, computed as population divided by area. **Natural Pop. Growth:** annual population increase per 100 people; does not include population change due to immigration or emigration.

COUNTRY	CAPITAL(S)	PRINCIPAL LANGUAGE(S)	POPULATION	AREA KM^2	POP. DENSITY PER KM^2	NATURAL POP. GROWTH PER 100 PEOPLE BIRTHS – DEATHS = % GAIN		
North America								
ANTIGUA AND BARBUDA	St. John's	English	64 000	442	144.8	1.4	0.5	0.9
ARUBA (Neth.)	Oranjestad	Dutch, Papiamento	69 000	193	358.0	1.7	0.6	1.1
BAHAMAS	Nassau	English, French	264 000	13 939	18.9	1.9	0.5	1.4
BARBADOS	Bridgetown	English	259 000	430	602.3	1.6	0.9	0.7
BELIZE	Belmopan	English, Spanish, Mayan, Garifuna	196 000	22 965	8.5	3.8	0.5	3.3
CANADA	Ottawa	English, French	28 398 000	9 970 610	2.8	1.5	0.7	0.8
COSTA RICA	San Jose	Spanish	3 161 000	51 100	61.9	2.8	0.4	2.4
CUBA	Havana	Spanish	10 848 000	110 861	97.9	1.8	0.6	1.2
DOMINICA	Roseau	English, French	72 000	750	96.0	2.2	0.7	1.5
DOMINICAN REPUBLIC	Santo Domingo	Spanish	7 471 000	48 443	154.2	2.7	0.7	2.0
EL SALVADOR	San Salvador	Spanish	5 460 000	21 041	259.5	3.4	0.8	2.6
GREENLAND (KALAALLIT NUNAAT) (Den.)	Godthab (Nuuk)	Greenlandic, Danish	57 000	2 175 600	0.0	2.2	0.8	1.4
GRENADA	St. George's	English	91 000	348	261.2	3.2	0.8	2.4
GUADELOUPE (Fr.)	Basse-Terre	French	400 000	1 780	224.7	2.0	0.6	1.4
GUATEMALA	Guatemala City	Spanish, Mayan, Black Carib	9 442 000	108 889	86.7	3.9	0.7	3.2
HAITI	Port-au-Prince	French	6 764 000	27 700	244.2	3.5	1.3	2.2
HONDURAS	Tegucigalpa	Spanish	4 996 000	112 088	44.6	3.8	0.7	3.1
JAMAICA	Kingston	English	2 445 000	10 991	222.5	2.5	0.6	1.9
MARTINIQUE (Fr.)	Fort-de-France	French	369 000	1 128	327.1	1.9	0.6	1.3
MEXICO	Mexico City	Spanish	84 439 000	1 958 201	43.1	3.3	0.5	2.8
NETHERLANDS ANTILLES (Neth.)	Willemstad	Dutch, Papiamento, English	191 000	800	238.8	1.8	0.6	1.2
NICARAGUA	Managua	Spanish, Miskito	4 131 000	130 700	31.6	3.9	0.7	3.2
PANAMA	Panama City	Spanish, English, Chibchan	2 515 000	75 517	33.3	2.5	0.5	2.0
PUERTO RICO (U.S.)	San Juan	Spanish, English	3 581 000	9 104	393.3	1.9	0.7	1.2
ST. KITTS AND NEVIS	Basseterre	English	43 000	269	160.2	2.2	1.1	1.1
ST. LUCIA	Castries	English, French	135 000	617	218.8	2.5	0.6	1.9
ST. VINCENT AND THE GRENADINES	Kingstown	English	109 000	389	280.2	2.6	0.6	2.0
TRINIDAD AND TOBAGO	Port-of-Spain	English	1 261 000	5 128	245.9	2.2	0.7	1.5
UNITED STATES OF AMERICA	Washington, D.C.	English, Spanish	257 908 000	9 529 063	27.1	1.6	0.9	0.7

Country: all independent countries, as well as selected dependencies. **Principal Language(s):** all official languages, as well as other primary languages spoken by a substantial proportion of the population. **Pop. Density:** population density, computed as population divided by area. **Natural Pop. Growth:** annual population increase per 100 people; does not include population change due to immigration or emigration.

COUNTRY	CAPITAL(S)	PRINCIPAL LANGUAGE(S)	POPULATION	AREA KM^2	POP. DENSITY PER KM^2	NATURAL POP. GROWTH PER 100 PEOPLE BIRTHS – DEATHS = % GAIN		
South America								
ARGENTINA	Buenos Aires	Spanish	33 070 000	2 780 400	11.9	2.0	0.9	1.1
BOLIVIA	La Paz, Sucre	Spanish, Quechua, Aymara	7 739 000	1 098 581	7.0	4.3	1.4	2.9
BRAZIL	Brasilia	Portuguese	151 381 000	8 511 996	17.8	2.8	0.8	2.0
CHILE	Santiago, Valparaiso	Spanish, Mapuche	13 599 000	756 626	18.0	2.3	0.6	1.7
COLOMBIA	Bogota	Spanish	34 252 000	1 141 748	30.0	2.7	0.7	2.0
ECUADOR	Quito	Spanish, Quechua	10 607 000	270 667	39.2	3.5	0.8	2.7
FRENCH GUIANA (Fr.)	Cayenne	French	123 000	86 504	1.4	3.0	0.5	2.5
GUYANA	Georgetown	English, Hindi	748 000	215 083	3.5	2.4	0.6	1.8
PARAGUAY	Asuncion	Guarani, Spanish, Portuguese	4 519 000	406 752	11.1	3.4	0.7	2.7
PERU	Lima	Spanish, Quechua, Aymara	22 454 000	1 285 216	17.5	3.3	0.8	2.5
SURINAME	Paramaribo	Sranantonga, Dutch	404 000	163 820	2.5	2.6	0.6	2.0
URUGUAY	Montevideo	Spanish	3 130 000	176 215	17.8	1.8	1.0	0.8
VENEZUELA	Caracas	Spanish	20 184 000	912 050	22.1	2.8	0.4	2.4

Country: all independent countries, as well as selected dependencies. **Principal Language(s):** all official languages, as well as other primary languages spoken by a substantial proportion of the population. **Pop. Density:** population density, computed as population divided by area. **Natural Pop. Growth:** annual population increase per 100 people; does not include population change due to immigration or emigration.

GLOSSARY

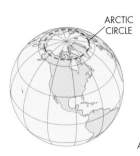 

acid rain Rain or snow that carries acids formed from chemical pollutants in the atmosphere.

Antarctic Circle An imaginary line of latitude located at 66½°S, approximately 1,630 miles (2620 kilometers) from the South Pole.

Arctic Circle An imaginary line of latitude located at 66½°N, approximately 1,630 miles (2620 kilometers) from the North Pole.

balance of trade The difference between how much a country exports and how much it imports, commonly measured in U.S. dollars. A country that exports more than it imports has a positive balance of trade, or *trade surplus*. A country that imports more than it exports has a negative balance of trade, or *trade deficit*.

Census Metropolitan Area (CMA) One or more cities with more than 100 000 residents, as well as the adjacent municipalities and parts of townships, as recognized for purposes of the census.

climate The usual weather conditions for a large area over a long period of time and through all seasons. Climate is affected by latitude, elevation, topography, ocean currents, and wind.

climograph Graph showing annual patterns of temperature and precipitation.

commodity One of the goods sold on the world market. Commodities may be agricultural products, manufactured items, or such natural resources as minerals.

deforestation Massive removal of trees from a forest.

elevation Height above sea level.

emigration Movement of people away from their native country or region to a new home elsewhere. The people moving away are called *emigrants*.

Equator An imaginary line that divides the earth into the Northern and Southern Hemispheres. All points along the Equator have a latitude of 0°.

European Union (EU) A group of 15 European nations whose main goal is to establish themselves for trading purposes as a single market. The EU grew out of the European Economic Community.

export The sale of goods to a foreign country.

fossil fuels Natural fuels that were formed from the remains of plants and animals over millions of years. Principal fossil fuels are petroleum, natural gas, and coal.

gross domestic product (GDP) Annual value of all goods and services produced within a country's borders. GDP includes production by foreign-owned facilities.

gross national product (GNP) Annual value of all goods and services produced by companies that are owned by a country's citizens. GNP includes production in facilities operated by the nation's citizens in other countries.

immigration Movement of people into a new country of residence. The people moving in are called *immigrants*.

imperialism Action taken by one country to control or influence another country or territory in order to gain economic or political advantage.

import The purchase of goods produced in a foreign country.

indigenous Native to a particular region. Indigenous peoples are related to the earliest inhabitants of a region.

land use How people use the earth's surface and natural resources for economic purposes. Regions are identified by the dominant form of economy, such as farming, herding, or manufacturing.

latitude Distance from the Equator measured in degrees. Lines of latitude, or *parallels*, are numbered north and south from the Equator and appear on maps as east-west lines.

life expectancy The average number of years that a group of people may expect to live based on the prevailing death rates for that population. Life expectancy reflects the group's general health and welfare.

literacy The ability to both read and write. The percentage of literate people is a good indicator of a country's educational level, although literacy standards vary by country.

longitude Distance from the Prime Meridian measured in degrees. Lines of longitude, or *meridians*, are numbered east and west from the Prime Meridian and appear on maps as north-south lines.

map projection Any system for drawing lines of latitude and longitude onto a map. Projections are never completely accurate, distorting either sizes or shapes of the earth's land and water features.

natural population growth Annual population increase for a region or country. It is the difference between the number of births and the number of deaths and does not include change due to population movement.

natural vegetation The type of vegetation that can grow in a specific region's climate and soil without benefit of human intervention or cultivation.

Oceania Collective name for islands of the central and southern Pacific Ocean, usually including New Zealand and sometimes also including Australia.

Organization of Petroleum Exporting Countries (OPEC) Association of 11 nations that control most of the world's known oil reserves. OPEC members are Algeria, Indonesia, Iran, Iraq, Kuwait, Libya, Nigeria, Qatar, Saudi Arabia, United Arab Emirates, and Venezuela.

ozone A form of oxygen that occurs naturally in the atmosphere in small amounts. The layer of ozone in the upper atmosphere blocks most of the sun's harmful ultraviolet rays.

permafrost Permanently frozen soil. In some areas an *active layer* at the surface melts during the short summer, then freezes again in the autumn.

precipitation Water from the atmosphere that accumulates on the earth's surface as dew, rain, hail, sleet, or snow. For annual measures, ten millimetres of snow, sleet, or hail are counted as one millimetre of rain.

Prime Meridian The 0° meridian, which passes through Greenwich, England.

Sahel The drought-ridden area south of Africa's Sahara and extending east-west between Somalia and Senegal.

staple food A foodstuff that constitutes a major part of the diet for a region's population.

taiga A cold, mostly coniferous forest located just south of the tundra in North America, Europe, or Asia.

Tropic of Cancer An imaginary line of latitude located at 23½°N. It marks the northern boundary of the earth's tropical zone.

Tropic of Capricorn An imaginary line of latitude located at 23½°S. It marks the southern boundary of the earth's tropical zone.

tundra A treeless Arctic region of North America, Europe, or Asia; also, the short, frost-resistant vegetation or the cold, dry climate of this region.

wetlands A transition zone between land and water where the water level remains near or above the ground's surface for most of the year. Wetlands include swamps, marshes, and bogs.

PRIME MERIDIAN
TROPIC OF CANCER (23½°N)
EQUATOR
TROPIC OF CAPRICORN (23½°S)

Abbreviations

adm.	administered by	L., l.	Lake, Lac	Pen., pen.	Peninsula
Alb.	Albania	Lat.	Latvia	Pk., pk.	Peak
Alta.	Alberta	lat.	latitude	Port.	Portugal
Am. Samoa	American Samoa	Liech.	Liechtenstein	poss.	possession
Ang.	Angola	Lith.	Lithuania	Prov., prov.	Province
Arg.	Argentina	long.	longitude	Pt.	Point
Aus.	Austria	Lux.	Luxembourg	Que.	Quebec
Austr.	Australia	m	metres	R., r.	River, Riviere
Azer.	Azerbaijan	Mac.	Macedonia	Ra.	Range
B.C.	British Columbia	Man.	Manitoba	Res., res.	Reservoir
Bos.	Bosnia and Herzegovina	Mex.	Mexico	S. Afr.	South Africa
		mi.	miles	Sask.	Saskatchewan
C.	Cape	Mont.	Montana	Sl., Slovak.	Slovakia
C. Afr. Rep.	Central African Republic	Mt., Mts.	Mount, Mont, Mountain, Mountains	Slov.	Slovenia
				Sp.	Spain
Congo Rep.	Congo Republic	N.B.	New Brunswick	sq.	square
Cro.	Croatia	Neth.	Netherlands	St., Ste.	Saint, Sainte
Cz., Cz. Rep.	Czech Republic	Nfld.	Newfoundland	Str.	Strait
D.C.	District of Columbia	Nor.	Norway	Switz.	Switzerland
Den.	Denmark	Nun.	Nunavut	Terr., terr.	Territory
Dom. Rep.	Dominican Republic	N.P.	National Park	U.A.E.	United Arab Emirates
Eq. Guinea	Equatorial Guinea	N.S.	Nova Scotia	U.K.	United Kingdom
Est.	Estonia	N.W.T.	Northwest Territories	U.S.	United States
Fk.	Fork	N.Z.	New Zealand	US$	United States dollars
Fr.	France, French	O.	Ocean	U.S.S.R.	Union of Soviet Socialist Republics
ft.	feet	Ont.	Ontario		
I., Is.	Island, Islands	P.E.I.	Prince Edward Island	Yugo.	Yugoslavia
Intl.	International	P.P.	Provincial Park	Yukon	Yukon Territory
It.	Italy	P.W.P.	Provincial Wilderness Park		
km	kilometres				

The index lists all the place names that appear in the book. Each entry includes a brief description of what or where it is, its latitude and longitude, and its main page reference. Many of the entries also include phonetic pronunciations. The key to the system of phonetic respelling is given on page 168, facing the inside back cover.

The entry for a physical feature is alphabetized by the proper part of its name, not by the descriptive part. For example, Lake Superior is listed as *Superior, L.,* and Mount Etna is listed as *Etna, Mt.* The entry for a city, however, is alphabetized by the first word in its name, no matter what it is, so that the city of Lake Charles, Louisiana, is listed as *Lake Charles.* Similarly, foreign names such as Rio Grande are alphabetized by the first word in the name.

Names beginning with *St.* are spelled *Saint* in the index. Abbreviations that are used in the index and in other parts of the book are listed on page 145.

L